ELEMENTS OF BANKRUPTCY

SIXTH EDITION

by

DOUGLAS G. BAIRD
Harry A. Bigelow Distinguished Service Professor
The University of Chicago

CONCEPTS AND INSIGHTS SERIES®

FOUNDATION
PRESS

Concepts and Insights Series is a trademark registered in the U.S. Patent and Trademark Office.

© 1992, 1993, 2001 FOUNDATION PRESS
© 2006 THOMSON REUTERS/FOUNDATION PRESS
© 2010 By THOMSON REUTERS/FOUNDATION PRESS
© 2014 LEG, Inc. d/b/a West Academic
   444 Cedar Street, Suite 700
   St. Paul, MN 55101
   1-877-888-1330
Printed in the United States of America

ISBN: 978-1-60930-354-9
Mat #41435946

For Walter J. Blum

Contents

INTRODUCTION

Modern bankruptcy law is a domain with identifiable and coherent boundaries. In *The Elements of Bankruptcy*, I offer an introduction to this world for lawyers and others who want to understand bankruptcy's fundamental rules and principles. My ambition is to show that modern bankruptcy law is at once rich, interesting, and accessible. This edition reflects the state of the law as of June 2014.

The first three chapters chart the landscape. Chapter 1 explores both the substantive provisions of the Bankruptcy Code and the procedural rules that govern bankruptcy cases. Chapter 2 looks at the rights of the individual debtor in bankruptcy. Bankruptcy law gives the individual a fresh start: the "honest but unfortunate" debtor overwhelmed by debt can file a bankruptcy petition and walk away with the right to enjoy future income free from past debt. Ensuring that such individuals enjoy a fresh start while preventing those able to repay their debts from abusing the system introduces considerable complexity into the law.

Chapter 3 examines the absolute priority rule, the basic principle of corporate reorganizations. Corporations enter into bankruptcy for reasons different from those of individuals. Corporations already have limited liability under state law: when a corporation fails, its shareholders are not liable to the corporation or its creditors. By reorganizing under Chapter 11 of the Bankruptcy Code, an ailing but otherwise strong business replaces its existing capital structure with a sensible one that better reflects the condition in which it finds itself. The corporation, like the individual, discharges old debts through bankruptcy, but the reasons for doing so have nothing to do with protecting flesh-and-blood human beings from their creditors.

The different legal problems of financially troubled individuals and corporations are adjudicated in the same place—bankruptcy court—not only for historical reasons but also because they present similar administrative difficulties. In both situations, one needs to hold creditors at bay while sorting through the debtor's affairs, gathering the assets, ascertaining the liabilities, determining wrongdoing (if any), and authoritatively establishing who gets what. The remaining chapters in this book focus on the way in which this process works.

Chapter 4 examines how rights originating outside of bankruptcy are treated inside of bankruptcy. For the most part, a creditor's claim in bankruptcy turns on what the creditor had outside bankruptcy. Chapter 5 shows how the Bankruptcy Code ensures that the debtor's assets available to creditors outside of bankruptcy are available to them inside of bankruptcy as well. Chapter 6 completes our examination of the basic rights and obligations of the debtor and those with whom it has dealt by examining *executory contracts*. An executory contract is one in which each party owes obligations to the other. Hence, it is at once a liability and an asset.

A debtor may not transfer assets while insolvent unless it receives reasonably equivalent value in return, nor may it engage in other activities whose principal effect is to thwart creditors' ability to be repaid. This basic principle of fraudulent conveyance law, thus stated, is uncontroversial, but its effects are far reaching. Fraudulent conveyance law and the related issues of equitable subordination and substantive consolidation are the subject of chapter 7. Chapter 8 examines the law of voidable preferences. When bankruptcy is on the horizon, a debtor is no longer free to choose which creditors to pay. Existing preference law implements this idea through a complicated mixture of rules and standards.

When a bankruptcy petition is filed, creditors must cease their efforts to collect payment, but the debtor must continue to deal with the rest of the world as before. The Bankruptcy Code tries to achieve both ends through the automatic stay, which is the subject of chapter 9. Chapter 10 explores the dynamics of small and large Chapter 11 cases. Most Chapter 11 petitions are filed by small corporations; the challenge in these cases is not to preserve an ongoing business but to facilitate an entrepreneur's transition from one business to another. The corporation is the entity that formally files the petition, but the entrepreneur who owns it is the central focus. Large Chapter 11 cases, in contrast, are few in number but contain the vast bulk of the total assets in bankruptcy. In these cases, the business has an identity distinct from those who run it, and Chapter 11 allows the financially distressed company to obtain a new capital structure in a process akin to a merger or acquisition outside of bankruptcy. The book's final two chapters look at the process of creating and confirming a plan of reorganization.

This idea for this book grew out of my fruitful collaboration with Thomas Jackson, who introduced me to bankruptcy law when I was a student. The first edition took shape while I was giving a series of seminars at the law firm of Sonnenschein, Nath, and Rosenthal in the early 1990s. I have continued to learn from long conversations with many splendid judges and lawyers, including Tom Ambro, Frank Easterbrook, Robert Gerber, Barbara Hauser, Richard Levin, Harvey Miller, Sally Neely, Chris Sontchi, Ronald Trost, and Eugene Wedoff. Work with a number of colleagues, especially Barry Adler, Donald Bernstein, Tony Casey, Edward Morrison, and Robert Rasmussen, has helped me with this, the sixth edition. Jessica Arett, Justin Mecurio, and Michael Turkel provided fine research assistance, and Ashlee Garcia proved a most able copyeditor. Finally, I am grateful for the research support of the John M. Olin Fund.

CHAPTER ONE

A Road Map to Bankruptcy Law

The Structure of the Bankruptcy Code

The word *bankruptcy* derives from the medieval Italian custom of breaking the benches of a banker or merchant who absconded and left creditors unpaid. As the roots of the word suggest, the first English bankruptcy statutes were directed at merchant debtors, and they were viciously punitive. Indeed, their harsh character prompted one delegate to the Constitutional Convention in Philadelphia in 1787 to oppose granting Congress the power to enact uniform bankruptcy laws. Under English law, uncooperative bankrupts were at risk of being hanged, and the Convention delegate feared that Congress might follow suit. For modern lawyers, the very incongruity of bankruptcy and the death penalty suggests, correctly, that bankruptcy law not be linked too closely with its seventeenth- and eighteenth-century English counterparts. We will do better by focusing on the law as it is today and turning to the history of bankruptcy law when appropriate.

The Bankruptcy Code is embodied in Title 11 of the United States Code. Although easily located, bankruptcy law remains a common law discipline in which a lawyer must reason by analogy and constantly be aware of general principles. Bankruptcy law is neither mechanical in its application nor narrow in the range of problems it confronts. A client in bankruptcy can face every legal problem that a person can face outside of bankruptcy.

Bankruptcy law is built on nonbankruptcy law; as a result, the bankruptcy lawyer must understand both the applicable nonbankruptcy law and the ways in which bankruptcy law may change it. An example will help to illustrate this point. Suppose you represent a computer hardware manufacturer that has a patented process for making computer chips. Your client discovers that a competitor is using its process and that the competitor has also filed a bankruptcy petition. You need to know how the patent would be enforced outside of bankruptcy, and then look at how bankruptcy changes both the underlying right and the manner in which it can be vindicated.

This task is not as formidable as it might seem. Bankruptcy law changes nonbankruptcy law only when the purposes of bankruptcy require it. Ensuring flesh-and-blood individuals a fresh start requires such a change, but surprisingly little else does. In the absence of a specific bankruptcy provision to the contrary, bankruptcy takes non-bankruptcy rights as it finds them. Only the procedures change, and these change only to solve the particular problems bankruptcy is designed to address. The Bankruptcy Code thus works against the background of nonbankruptcy law. A general mandate, reinforced by 28 U.S.C. §959, requires that the trustee act in accordance with applicable nonbankruptcy law. A trustee enjoys the right to use property under §363, but the trustee must act consistently with applicable nonbankruptcy law. The trustee cannot use the debtor's chemistry laboratory to manufacture cocaine, nor may the trustee dump toxic waste on the debtor's property, not because of anything in the Bankruptcy Code, but simply because these activities are illegal outside of bankruptcy.

The Supreme Court set forth this principle in *Butner v. United States*:

> Congress has generally left the determination of property rights in the assets of a bankrupt's estate to state law. Property interests are created and defined by state law. Unless some federal interest requires a different result, there is no reason why such interests should be analyzed differently simply because an interested party is involved in a bankruptcy proceeding.[1]

Butner thus allows us to draw from a complicated statute a single organizing principle. Knowing the outcome under nonbankruptcy law can go a long way toward understanding the problem in bankruptcy. When a litigant seeks an outcome different from the one that would hold outside of bankruptcy, the bankruptcy judge will likely ask the litigant to identify the part of the Bankruptcy Code that compels the departure.

We can begin with a sketch of the basic structure of the Bankruptcy Code. The 1978 Bankruptcy Reform Act restructured the bankruptcy courts and bankruptcy procedure. The substantive provisions of the 1978 Act put in place the Bankruptcy Code, which constitutes Title 11 of the United States Code. It has been amended periodically. The most sweeping change, enacted in 2005, added considerable complexity to the Bankruptcy Code, but its basic structure and principles re-

[1] Butner v. United States, 440 U.S. 48, 55 (1979).

main intact. Like other titles of the United States Code, Title 11 is divided into chapters. Chapters 1, 3, and 5 contain provisions that generally apply to all bankruptcy cases. The remaining chapters set out different procedures for distinct kinds of bankruptcy cases. Chapter 15 sets out the principles needed to facilitate cross-border insolvencies, the rules needed when a debtor in the United States has assets in another country, or when a foreign debtor has assets here.

The United States Trustee is responsible for overseeing the administration of bankruptcy cases. The United States Trustee should ensure that cases do not languish in bankruptcy court, a fate not uncommon when the stakes are small and no single creditor has the incentive to investigate the debtor. This job is important not only to protect the general creditors but also to ferret out fraud, which often contributes to business failure. In large Chapter 11 cases, the United States Trustee casts a long shadow as well. The United States Trustee appoints the creditors' committee and often appears as a party in interest.

Chapter 1 provides definitions (§101), tells us which parts of the Code apply to which kinds of cases (§103), and sets out eligibility requirements for each kind of bankruptcy case (§109). Chapter 1 also contains what appears to be a broad grant of power to the bankruptcy judge. Bankruptcy was originally in the province of the Chancellor, and §105 reflects these equitable origins. It grants the bankruptcy judge the power to "issue any order, process or judgment that is necessary or appropriate to carry out the provisions" of the Bankruptcy Code. But the section confers no independent powers on the judge. The power that a judge enjoys under §105 must derive ultimately from some other provision of the Bankruptcy Code.[2] Lawyers who advance an argument that relies solely on §105 should expect to lose. The Bankruptcy Code does not "constitute a roving commission to do equity."[3]

The heart of any code lies in its definitional section, and the definitions in §101 are the focal point of many disputes. The definitions of *creditor* and *claim*, for example, will play a central role in the bankruptcy of a business that faces mass tort liability. Suppose a

---

[2] See, e.g., Law v. Siegel, 134 S. Ct. 1188 (2014). (In rejecting an argument based on §105, the Court observed, "We have long held that whatever equitable powers remain in the bankruptcy courts must and can only be exercised within the confines of the Bankruptcy Code.") (internal quotation marks omitted).

[3] United States v. Sutton, 786 F.2d 1305 (5th Cir. 1986).

business sells a product that causes harm many years later. Whether the business can deal with its tort liability in bankruptcy turns on whether these future victims are considered creditors and whether they have "claims" within the meaning of §101.

Section 101 also introduces us to the language of modern bankruptcy practice. It tells us, for instance, that the person whom a bankruptcy case concerns is a *debtor*. A person or a corporation in bankruptcy is no longer called a *bankrupt*. Although that word retains some currency among lay people, among bankruptcy lawyers it sounds old-fashioned and precious. Section 101 defines most of the terms that apply throughout the Bankruptcy Code, but not all. One of the most important definitions in the Bankruptcy Code, that of *notice and a hearing*, is found in §102, which nominally deals with rules of construction.

Many provisions in the Bankruptcy Code allow actions to take place after notice and a hearing. One should not, however, assume that everyone must receive actual notice or that a hearing is required in every instance. Section 102 tells us that we need to give only "such notice as is appropriate in the particular circumstances." Moreover, if no party requests a hearing or if a court finds there is insufficient time to have one, an actual hearing is not necessary. Over the years, a body of learning has developed around who needs to be notified at each stage and the consequences that follow if they are not.[4] As in many other contexts, the basic principles in bankruptcy track those outside. Most analyses begin with the observation of the Supreme Court in *Mullane v. Central Hanover Bank & Trust Company*:[5]

> An elementary and fundamental requirement of due process in any proceeding which is to be accorded finality is notice reasonably calculated, under all the circumstances, to apprise interested parties of the pendency of the action and afford them an opportunity to present their objections.

One section that is easy to miss is §104, which provides for indexing of many of the dollar thresholds elsewhere in the Bankruptcy Code. These thresholds are changed every three years through administrative regulation to reflect the consumer price index. Under §109, for instance, individuals wishing to file under Chapter 13 can have no more than a specified amount in unsecured claims. Section 109 also

---

[4] See, e.g., Fogel v. Zell, 221 F.3d 955 (7th Cir. 2000).
[5] 339 U.S. 306, 314 (1950).

sets out who can take advantage of various chapters of the Bankruptcy Code.

Section 109 is as good a place as any to see how the Bankruptcy Code works. To know whether a limited liability company may be a debtor under Chapter 11, one looks first to §109(d). It states that to be a debtor under Chapter 11, one must qualify as a debtor under Chapter 7. Section 109(b) excludes some "persons" from Chapter 7, but does not mention limited liability companies. This brings us to §109(a). It tells us that a debtor can enjoy the benefits of bankruptcy only if it is a "person." Section 101 tells us that "person" as used in the Bankruptcy Code includes a corporation. Section 101 goes on to define a corporation. It extends considerably beyond entities that are called corporations under state law, and its language is broad enough to include a limited liability company. Hence, a limited liability company can file for bankruptcy. It is a "corporation," and a corporation is a "person," and persons, unless specifically excluded, can file bankruptcy petitions.

There is no explicit requirement that an individual or business be in financial distress or insolvent before filing for bankruptcy. Section 101 of the Bankruptcy Code defines insolvency as the condition that exists when a debtor's liabilities fairly discounted exceed its assets, but insolvency itself is not a prerequisite for bankruptcy for individuals or for corporations. Indeed, there is a negative inference that can be drawn from §109(c). It specifies that a municipality must be insolvent to file a Chapter 9 petition. The absence of any mention of insolvency in other parts of §109 creates the negative inference that other debtors need not be insolvent to be eligible for bankruptcy.

The absence of such an explicit requirement makes sense. Suppose a corporation has assets of $100, ordinary debt of $49, and a 50–50 chance of losing a lawsuit that would expose it to an additional $100 of liability. It is technically solvent: it has liabilities, fairly discounted, of $99 and assets of $100. Nevertheless, its ordinary creditors may recognize that there is a 50–50 chance they will not be paid. Hence, they will be restless and may trigger the kind of destructive race to assets that a bankruptcy proceeding can prevent.[6]

Moreover, insolvency may not be easy to measure at the outset of the case. When confronting the question whether a debtor can be put into bankruptcy involuntarily, the Bankruptcy Code uses a different

---

[6] See In re Johns-Manville, 36 Bankr. 727 (Bankr. S.D.N.Y. 1984).

measure of financial distress. Creditors can put a debtor in bankruptcy involuntarily only if the debtor is unable to pay debts as they become due. This benchmark is much easier to apply than an insolvency measure, and it overlaps with it substantially. Most loans include terms that accelerate a debtor's obligations under circumstances when it is likely that the debtor's liabilities exceed its assets. When the second condition exists, the first tends to follow. At one time, we distinguished between these two benchmarks of financial distress by calling the first (excess of liabilities over assets) "insolvency in the bankruptcy sense" and the second (inability to pay debts as they become due) "insolvency in the equity sense."

None of this, however, should suggest that those in good financial health make use of bankruptcy law. Bankruptcy law tracks nonbankruptcy law, and a solvent debtor must pay all its creditors 100 cents on the dollar. When an opportunity for abuse exists (when, for example, bankruptcy's procedures offer a way to force a favorable settlement of an irritating antitrust suit or allow a solvent debtor to cap liabilities to its landlord), courts are likely to dismiss the case on the ground that it was filed in bad faith.[7] The *Butner* principle—the idea that bankruptcy law should respect nonbankruptcy entitlements unless a particular bankruptcy policy is being vindicated—limits the number of such cases.

Chapter 3 of the Bankruptcy Code deals with case administration. Sections 301 through 307 tell us how a bankruptcy case begins. Sections 321 through 331 set out the rules governing those who administer the bankruptcy estate. The court must issue an order before the debtor can hire lawyers or other professionals. Under §329 attorneys must file a statement with the court showing how much they will be compensated and the source of the compensation, even if they do not ask the debtor for payment. In addition, Rule 2014 requires that lawyers disclose all their connections with the debtor, creditors, any other parties in interest, and their accountants. Such disclosure is needed to satisfy §327(a), which requires that the debtor's attorneys be disinterested.

The disinterestedness requirement complicates the job of any lawyer who wants to continue representing a corporate client after it files a bankruptcy petition. If a business owes its lawyer anything for services

---

[7] See In re Integrated Telecom Express, Inc., 384 F.3d 108 (3d Cir. 2004); In re SGL Carbon Corp., 200 F.3d 154 (3d Cir. 1999).

provided before the petition, the lawyer may not be able to represent the business in the bankruptcy proceeding. By virtue of being owed money, the lawyer is a creditor within the meaning of §101, and hence may no longer be disinterested. Similarly, a lawyer who is paid for services already rendered outside the ordinary course of business within 90 days before the filing of the petition may be subject to a voidable preference attack, and this may also keep the lawyer from being disinterested. A lawyer who represents any of the corporation's directors or shareholders personally may not be able to represent the corporation in bankruptcy. A lawyer who sits on the corporation's board, or who has partners who sit on the board, may also fail to meet this requirement.

Even if a lawyer herself has had no previous relationship with the debtor or creditors, she must ensure that none of her associates or partners has worked for them, either. Although a lawyer is not disqualified solely because of past representation of a creditor, see §327(c), determining when a lawyer is disqualified is not always easy. Here, as elsewhere in bankruptcy, it is often useful to begin with the nonbankruptcy baseline. In this instance, however, even identifying that baseline is difficult. Nonbankruptcy conflicts rules turn on whether one is representing a client in a transaction or in ongoing litigation. In bankruptcy, much of what goes on is negotiation, but litigation with almost any party is possible.

In all events, disclosure must be full. When a court finds that a lawyer is not disinterested or has failed to make proper disclosure, it can disqualify the lawyer, disallow fees, and force the lawyer to bear the expenses of any investigation triggered by the failure to disclose. One court imposed a $1 million sanction for nondisclosure notwithstanding a finding that the firm had done its work well. Indeed, in the same opinion the court found the firm's work so crucial to the reorganization that it wanted the firm to continue working on the case.[8] Nondisclosure can, in the extreme case, trigger the criminal sanctions imposed by 18 U.S.C. §152(3) for knowingly and fraudulently making a false declaration in a bankruptcy case.[9]

---

[8] See In re Leslie Fay Companies, 175 Bankr. 525 (Bankr. S.D.N.Y. 1994). For a general discussion of the law, see In re Gluth Bros. Constr., 459 Bankr. 351 (Bankr. N.D. Ill. 2011).

[9] United States v. Gellene, 182 F.3d 578 (7th Cir. 1999) (lawyer at prominent New York firm sentenced to 15 months in prison for failing to disclose his firm's representation of a major secured creditor in another matter).

The duty to disclose is an ongoing one. Suppose you discover while representing a debtor that some of its directors have perpetrated a fraud. You now must investigate all the directors, including ones that are independent. At this point, you have to find out whether any of your partners or associates has done work for the principal employers of these directors. You have a potential conflict if you must lead an investigation of someone who is a senior officer of a major client. Sensitivity to such issues varies across different judicial districts and even among judges within the same district. This is an area in which all lawyers, but particularly young lawyers, need to be especially vigilant.

In a Chapter 7 case, the provisions of §321 through §331 must be read in conjunction with §701 through §705. The principal officer in a Chapter 7 case is the bankruptcy trustee. The trustee acts as the representative of the bankruptcy estate and is charged with managing the assets of the debtor and protecting the rights of creditors and others. The trustee, for example, has the power to bring actions the debtor could have brought outside of bankruptcy. Similarly, in a Chapter 11 case, the provisions of §321 through §331 must be read in conjunction with §1101 through §1109. For example, in Chapter 11 cases there is usually no trustee; instead, under §1107 the debtor in possession takes on the duties and responsibilities of the trustee. Bankruptcy Code provisions authorizing the trustee to take certain actions apply with equal force to the debtor in possession. In the case of a corporation, the old managers of the debtor corporation act as debtor in possession. Thus, when §363 authorizes the trustee to use, lease, or sell assets of the estate in the ordinary course of business without first obtaining court approval, it is also authorizing the debtor in possession to do the same. Sometimes the creditors' committee or other party asks to take actions nominally reserved to the trustee when no trustee in appointed. The debtor in possession may lack the incentive to pursue such actions, especially if they are against an insider. The Bankruptcy Code does not address this question explicitly, but most courts have concluded that the bankruptcy court has the power to authorize such actions in appropriate cases.[10]

Sections 341 through 350 set out a number of basic procedures. One of the crucial moments in the life of a bankruptcy case is the initial meeting of creditors that §341 requires. In a Chapter 7 case, for

---

[10] See, e.g., In re Cybergenics, 330 F.3d 548 (3d Cir. 2003) (en banc). But see In re Fox, 305 Bankr. 912 (Bankr. App. 10th Cir. 2004).

example, the creditors elect a trustee during the §341 meeting. They also decide, under §705(a), whether to form a creditors' committee to monitor the course of the case. The bankruptcy judge is forbidden from attending the §341 meeting. Under the 1898 Bankruptcy Act, bankruptcy judges became closely involved in the administration of the bankruptcy case. Many thought that this involvement prevented them from having the degree of detachment needed to decide disputes between the parties. Since 1978, however, increasing concerns about the length of many bankruptcy cases have led to a number of changes, principally in §105, to expedite cases. Bankruptcy judges must, for example, hold such status conferences as are necessary to further the expeditious and economical resolution of the case. Bankruptcy judges, however, are not reverting to their earlier roles as much as they are adopting the case management practices that have become commonplace in federal district courts.

Because even the simplest bankruptcy cases take time, rules are necessary to allow the trustee (and the debtor in possession) to act and to keep the creditors from taking matters into their own hands. These rules are largely the province of §361 through §366. By far the most important of these sections is §362, which imposes an automatic stay on all creditors. It requires creditors to cease all debt collection efforts the moment a petition is filed. The automatic stay looms so large that it is easy to forget that the stay is simply a presumption. The court can lift the stay whenever a creditor shows that there is cause or that its interest is inadequately protected. Moreover, a court has the power under §105 to stay actions that do not come within the scope of §362 as long as a policy embraced in some other part of the Bankruptcy Code justifies it. Sections 363 and 364 authorize the trustee (and hence the debtor in possession in Chapter 11 cases) to sell, use, and lease property and to borrow money. When these transactions fall outside the ordinary course of business, however, the Bankruptcy Code requires notice and a hearing and may impose other requirements as well.

A crucial step in any bankruptcy case is to identify the claims against the debtor and the assets owned by the debtor. Chapter 5 of the Bankruptcy Code tells us how to go about doing this. Sections 501 through 510 focus on claims against the estate. Among other things, this part of the Bankruptcy Code embraces the idea that the general creditors must bear the costs the debtor incurs during the course of the bankruptcy case. Under §507(a)(1), these costs are paid off first, and the remainder is divided among the general creditors. These costs, called *administrative expense claims,* include the expenses of the bankruptcy proceeding proper and those of running the business in the meantime.

This assumption underlying administrative expenses—that bankruptcy is run for the benefit of general creditors—is at times out of step with current practice. Many large businesses enter Chapter 11 with insufficient resources to pay secured creditors in full. The costs of administering the case must necessarily come from the secured creditors. The trustee enjoys a limited ability to charge the assets under §506(c), but it is more common for the secured creditor to allow the expenses of administration to be "carved out" of its collateral. The exact shape of the carve out in each case is negotiated at the start of the case as part of the cash collateral order or the debtor-in-possession financing agreement.[11]

Section 506 addresses the rights of a creditor who has properly perfected a security interest in collateral. (*Perfection* has a singular meaning in bankruptcy. To have a perfected interest a creditor must ordinarily give the world notice of the property claim. A mortgagee must typically record its interest in the local real estate records. A creditor with a security interest in personal property must typically file a financing statement in the secretary of state's office.) Outside of bankruptcy, a creditor with a properly perfected security interest in collateral is entitled to be paid to the extent of the value of the collateral before other creditors. As a general matter, properly perfected secured creditors beat (or, to use the words lawyers commonly employ, *prime* or *trump*) the rights of general creditors in bankruptcy as well. The secured creditor, however, has a right to priority only to the extent of the *value* of its collateral. It may not be able to take possession of the collateral itself. If the collateral is worth more than the amount of the debt (that is, if the creditor is oversecured), the creditor has a secured claim equal to the amount of the debt. In addition, §506(b) allows the creditor to enjoy interest on its claim during bankruptcy and also to be paid any reasonable expenses it incurs. The oversecured creditor, however, must have obliged the debtor to pay for the expenses in the security agreement.[12]

---

[11] Richard B. Levin, Almost All You Ever Wanted to Know About Carve Out, 76 Am. Bankr. L.J. 445, 458 (2002).

[12] See United States v. Ron Pair Enterprises, 489 U.S. 235 (1989).

If the collateral is worth less than the amount of the debt (that is, if the claim is undersecured), the claim is bifurcated under §506(a). The creditor has a secured claim equal to the value of the collateral and an unsecured claim for the difference. It also has rights against particular assets by virtue of its security interest in those assets. In a simple Chapter 7 liquidation, the security interest—the lien—may simply pass through bankruptcy.

Suppose a bank lends a debtor $100 and takes a security interest in a piece of real property that the debtor owns. A subsequent recession causes the property value to drop to $25, and the debtor files a Chapter 7 petition. Because the debt exceeds the value of the land, the trustee cannot possibly benefit the general creditors by keeping the property. The trustee may therefore give the property back (or *abandon* it, to use the language of §554) to the debtor. The Bankruptcy Code provides that the debtor's personal liability to the bank and all other creditors is discharged. The bank, however, remains free to foreclose on the land once it is in the debtor's hands because the lien survives (or passes through) bankruptcy. The doctrine of lien pass-through was first set out in *Long v. Bullard*.[13] The scope of this principle of lien pass-through, however, is more limited than it might appear because of special treatment provided for liens in Chapters 11 and 13.

Sections 541 through 560 establish what assets the estate has. These provisions are built on the central idea that one must begin with the set of rights and obligations that exist outside of bankruptcy and then identify specific bankruptcy policies that require departing from the nonbankruptcy baseline. Section 541 defines the central concept of the *property of the estate*. The trustee (or the debtor in possession) is charged with assembling the assets that are available to meet the creditors' claims and then distributing them. These assets, called the property of the estate, form the bankruptcy estate. Section 541 draws a sharp distinction between individuals and corporations. The future income of individuals does not become property of the estate, while the future income of a corporation does. Drawing this distinction is a crucial feature of bankruptcy's fresh start for individual debtors, and it is the focus of the next chapter of this book.

In many cases, property to which the creditors of a debtor are entitled is property to which a third party lays claim. In these cases, the trustee may have to bring an action to vindicate the creditors' right to

---

[13] 117 U.S. 617 (1886).

the property. If the debtor itself could have brought the cause of action, the property is deemed property of the estate under §541. In other cases, the trustee must exercise one of the so-called avoiding powers. Section 544(a) is the "strong arm" power of the trustee. Using it the trustee may, for example, set aside unperfected security interests. A creditor who takes collateral may not be able to take the collateral in bankruptcy if it has failed to record its interest through a public filing.

The avoiding powers also allow the trustee to set aside fraudulent conveyances, a power creditors generally enjoy outside of bankruptcy. These include transfers made and obligations incurred for less than reasonably equivalent value while the debtor was insolvent and those done with the intent to hinder, delay, or defraud creditors. §548. Such transactions include not only instances of outright fraud but also those that bear "badges of fraud," indicia suggesting that the transactions had no legitimate business purpose and were aimed instead at thwarting the creditors' ability to be repaid. Another provision allows the trustee to set aside transfers that were made to a creditor on the eve of bankruptcy. §547. This policy against preferential transfers prevents creditors from racing to the assets when they know bankruptcy is on the horizon.

The general provisions of the Bankruptcy Code in Chapters 1, 3, and 5 are not perfectly organized. A number of provisions could well have been placed elsewhere. Section 108, for example, gives the trustee a grace period for taking certain actions. Because the consequences of failing to take action often turn on whether the automatic stay is implicated, this provision is best read in conjunction with §362. Section 365, which deals with executory contracts, is perhaps the provision most conspicuously out of place. Executory contracts inherently involve mutual rights and obligations between a debtor and a third party. They are best seen as combinations of claims and assets. Executory contracts are claims against the estate because they give a third party rights against the debtor. They are simultaneously assets of the estate because they give the debtor rights against a third party. Because both claims and assets fall within the ambit of Chapter 5 of the Bankruptcy Code, the section on executory contracts belongs there. The failure to put §365 in the correct place should not, in principle, affect how it is interpreted, but its faulty positioning may have compounded the difficulties lawyers and judges have faced in applying it consistently.

The remaining chapters in Title 11 set out the different kinds of bankruptcy cases. Chapter 9 is reserved for municipalities. Under §101, *municipality* means "any political subdivision or public agency or instrumentality of a State." In addition to cities and towns, debtors in Chapter 9 may include water and power districts. Chapter 9 has not been widely used since the Great Depression, but the bankruptcy filing by the city of Detroit in 2013 may be the harbinger of a new era as municipalities confront the enormous pension burdens and other obligations owed to their workers.

Municipal bankruptcies have a dynamic entirely different from other types. The substantive provisions of Chapter 9 are largely the same, but the rights of creditors against a municipality depart strikingly from their rights against ordinary creditors. Outside of bankruptcy, the law typically provides that the assets that might have value, such as the town hall or the fire trucks, are not owned by the city itself, but rather held in trust by the city for the benefit of its citizens. Creditors cannot look to these assets for payment, but must instead look to the tax revenues of the city. Reaching these is notoriously hard. As Justice Frankfurter famously observed:

> The principal asset of a municipality is its taxing power and that, unlike an asset of a private corporation, cannot be available for distribution. An unsecured municipal security is therefore merely a draft on the good faith of a municipality in exercising its taxing power.[14]

Even apart from the willingness of a municipality to exercise it, the taxing power is itself limited. If taxes rise too much relative to those elsewhere, citizens will simply leave. There is a natural ceiling on the amount that can be raised to pay debts in addition to what is needed to provide basic municipal services. This ceiling is likely to be especially low in a city such as Detroit where the population has declined precipitously. It is not obvious how it can support its existing infrastructure, quite apart from its debt burden. Such constraints provide the backdrop against which Chapter 9 operates.

To confirm a Chapter 9 plan, the court must find that the plan complies with many of the same standards as a plan under Chapter 11, but because of the different rights creditors have against the municipality under nonbankruptcy law, they have acquired a different gloss. The requirement that the plan be "fair and equitable" requires complying with the absolute priority rule in Chapter 11, but in the context of municipal bankruptcy, it requires instead that "the payments provided

---

[14] Faitoute Iron & Steel Co. v. City of Asbury Park, 316 U.S. 502, 509 (1942).

for in the plan of composition are all that the [municipality] is reasonably able to pay in the circumstances."[15]

The provisions of Chapter 9 are neither long nor complicated. Section 901 identifies the general provisions of the Bankruptcy Code that apply. Most significantly, §1113 does not apply in Chapter 9 cases. Hence, a municipality in Chapter 9 has correspondingly more freedom to reject collective bargaining agreements than a corporation in Chapter 11.[16] The interaction between federal bankruptcy law and non-bankruptcy state law, such as the state's laws governing a municipality's pension obligations, remains largely unexplored.

Chapter 15 provides firms whose business is centered in another jurisdiction with a way to sort out their rights in this country in conjunction with an insolvency proceeding in another jurisdiction. It is based on the Model Law on Cross Border Insolvency. It allows a foreign proceeding to extend its reach and take advantage of the automatic stay and gain control of assets located in the United States. The provisions are largely procedural, and many of the substantive consequences of cross-border insolvencies remain largely unchartered.[17] The bankruptcy court has the power to grant "appropriate relief" at the request of the foreign representative, taking into account the general principles of comity. §1507. Bankruptcy judges are willing to defer to the substantive insolvency law of other jurisdictions.[18] There are, however, limits. In a recent case, for example, the court refused to respect a plan that was confirmed under Mexican law under dubious circumstances. Among other things, it released third party non-debtors from liability in a way that inured to the benefit of the insiders promoting the plan. Such a plan would emphatically not be allowed under domestic law.[19]

Individuals and corporations can usually choose to file under one of several different chapters. An individual debtor will most often choose Chapter 7 or Chapter 13. An ordinary corporation can file either a Chapter 7 petition or a Chapter 11 petition. The kind of bankruptcy petition that is brought depends on the goals of the person filing the

[15] Lorber v. Vista Irrigation, 127 F.2d 628, 639 (9th Cir. 1942).

[16] See In re City of Vallejo, 403 Bankr. 72 (Bankr. E.D. Cal. 2009).

[17] See, e.g., In re Bear Stearns High-Grade Structured Credit Strategies Master Fund, LTD, 389 Bankr. 325 (S.D.N.Y. 2008).

[18] See, e.g., In re Sino-Forest Corporation, 501 Bankr. 655 (Bankr. S.D.N.Y. 2013); In re Metcalfe & Mansfield Alternative Investments, 421 Bankr. 685 (Bankr. S.D.N.Y. 2010).

[19] See, e.g., In re Vitro S.A.B. de C.V., 701 F.3d 1031 (5th Cir. 2012).

petition. The court, however, enjoys a broad power to convert a case brought under one chapter into a case brought under another. Moreover, under §706(a) the debtor can convert a case that creditors file under Chapter 7 to one under Chapter 11.

As we shall discover below in chapter 2, Chapter 7 tries to distinguish the honest but unfortunate flesh-and-blood debtors from those who can repay their debts or whose use of Chapter 7 would be abusive. An individual who is hopelessly in debt with only a modest income needs a fresh start. She should be able to file a Chapter 7 bankruptcy petition, give up nonexempt assets, and walk away from prebankruptcy obligations. Someone who makes enough to repay creditors a substantial sum should not be able to use bankruptcy to escape her obligations. Section 707(b) implements a "means test" that attempts to distinguish the two types of debtors from one another. Section 727 gives the honest but unfortunate debtor a *discharge*. Because future income of an individual does not become property of the estate under §541, the effect of §727 is to give the individual debtor the right to enjoy future income free of creditors' claims.

Section 726 sets out how the debtor's property is divided among the creditors, but this section and others dealing with the administration of the estate in Chapter 7 often have little relevance in the case of the individual debtor. Individuals who file for bankruptcy typically have few unencumbered hard assets. Their largest asset is their human capital, their ability to earn money in the future. The principal policy choice is deciding which debtors should be able to enjoy their future earnings free of the claims of creditors.

Chapter 13 also provides individuals with a substantive fresh start, but it takes a different shape. It is useful for debtors who are not eligible for Chapter 7 or who have substantial assets. Chapter 13 allows an individual to keep all assets, but in return the debtor must create a plan under which creditors receive as much out of the debtor's future income as they would have received had the debtor filed under Chapter 7.

Like individuals, corporations may file under Chapter 7. In many cases, a corporation finds itself in Chapter 7 only after first having tried unsuccessfully to reorganize under Chapter 11. See §1112(b). These cases have nothing to do with giving an individual a fresh start. Chapter 7 offers no discharge to a corporation. In a typical corporate Chapter 7 case, the business has ceased its operations or will cease them in short order. Any assets remaining after the secured creditors take their collateral usually go to the tax collector, who enjoys a special priority under §507(a)(8). The purpose of allowing corporations to file Chapter 7 petitions is not to give ordinary general creditors assets but to assure creditors that there is nothing worth pursuing. A Chapter 7 petition is the easiest way for corporate managers, who are being constantly harassed, to convince a corporation's creditors that the corporation has no assets and lawsuits are pointless. The bankruptcy process can offer scrutiny of the debtor's overall health not otherwise available to individual creditors.

Liquidation under Chapter 7 does not require that all the assets be broken up and sold piecemeal. To the contrary, the trustee is obliged to sell the assets for as much as possible, and sometimes this means selling the assets together as a going concern. In practice, however, operating businesses rarely file Chapter 7 petitions. Those in control of the corporation outside of bankruptcy usually want to retain that control in bankruptcy. Chapter 11 allows the retention of control, while Chapter 7 requires the appointment of a trustee to manage the affairs of the business.

It is worth noting that the creditors of large corporations exercise considerable control outside of bankruptcy when the business becomes financially distressed, and they retain much of this control inside of bankruptcy. Indeed, the existing managers are often sufficiently beholden to them that major creditors typically do not demand the appointment of a trustee in Chapter 11 even when the presence of fraud, such as we saw in Enron or WorldCom, gives them an unequivocal right to do so.

Chapter 11 is the vehicle designed to straighten out the affairs of corporations in financial distress. When the corporation cannot continue as a going concern, Chapter 11 provides a mechanism for shutting it down and sorting out its financial affairs in a coherent way. Chapter 11 is better suited than Chapter 7 for corporations that are dissolving when there are problems beyond the simple sale of assets. Consider the following case. Apart from a secured creditor that has repossessed its collateral, the only other creditor is the Internal Revenue Service, which is owed Federal Insurance Contributions Act (FICA) and withholding taxes. The owner-managers of the business are personally (and potentially criminally) liable for these taxes, and they have filed Chapter 11 petitions as well. (Individuals are eligible for Chapter 11 relief, but apart from cases in which the debtor's affairs are tied up with those of a business, Chapter 13 or Chapter 7 is a more attractive place to resolve their financial problems.) We need to sort out who is going to pay what and on what schedule. In such situations,

Chapter 11 is often the forum of choice for both the debtors and the IRS. If no one asks for the case to be dismissed or converted, the court is unlikely to do so.

In many large bankruptcy cases, the petition is filed because the bankruptcy forum provides a straightforward way to sell the business as a going concern. Chapter 11 allows such sales and gives buyers confidence that they will acquire clean title. Finally, Chapter 11 provides a forum for a business that will be kept in intact but needs a new capital structure. Past misfortunes may have left it unable to meet its obligations, but its assets are being put to their best use. By scaling back the business's fixed obligations the creditors as a group are left better off.

Chapter 11 replaced Chapters X, XI, and XII of the old Bankruptcy Act. (The convention is to use Roman numerals for chapters of the 1898 Act and Arabic numerals for those of the 1978 Code.) In Chapter 11, the debtor in possession rather than the trustee ordinarily continues to run the business. When the debtor is a substantial operating company with a decent chance of surviving as a going concern, enough may be at stake so that the general creditors play an active role. In many Chapter 11 cases, however, the capital structure consists of two or more layers of secured debt. In the absence of any unencumbered assets (such as avoidance actions), the general creditors are likely to play only a small role, if any.

In theory, the United States Trustee chooses a committee of creditors at the start of every Chapter 11 case, but the committee is active only in cases in which enough is at stake. Section 1102(b) suggests that the creditors' committee consist of creditors who hold the seven largest claims and are willing to serve. In practice, however, the United States Trustee often attempts to find a "representative" creditors' committee, and §1102(a)(4) allows a small business to insist on becoming a member if its claim against the debtor is large enough to put its own survival at risk. The creditors' committee in Chapter 11 may also consist of the members of a committee organized by creditors before the case begins, if that committee is fairly chosen and represents the different kinds of claims that exist. The United States Trustee thus often looks well beyond the seven largest creditors because they may look more like each other than the class of general creditors as a whole. In the largest cases, there may be multiple committees of creditors as well as a committee of the equityholders.

Serving on a creditors' committee can be a mixed blessing. Doing so ensures that one is close to the action and knows what is going on.

But one may receive information that the debtor considers confidential, and this may interfere with a creditor's ability to act (such as its ability to sell its claim or buy additional ones). Moreover, service on the committee is time consuming. Creditors' committees in Chapter 11 cases (unlike committees in Chapter 7) can retain professionals such as lawyers and accountants, and the cost of hiring them is an administrative expense entitled to priority under §507. The creditors themselves, however, are not compensated for their efforts. Moreover, as a member of the committee, a creditor is charged with looking out not only for its own interests but also for those of the other general creditors. Creditors who actively participate in the case may be subject to disclosure obligations even if they are not members of an official committee.[20]

Section 1104 allows the court to appoint an examiner, who may be given the powers of the trustee; the United States Trustee chooses the examiner, subject to court approval. An examiner may be retained simply to mediate between the various factions. Examiners are sometimes appointed to investigate whether the debtor should bring a cause of action (such as a fraudulent conveyance action against shareholders) that the debtor in possession might not pursue as vigorously because of its conflict of interest. Such investigations can be enormously expensive and risk duplicating work already done or that will be done subsequently when the action is brought. But they can also lead to substantial recoveries for creditors. In the bankruptcy of Enron, for example, the examiner's investigation cost nearly $100 million and occupied dozens of lawyers and professionals for nearly two years, but the ensuing settlements exceeded $1 billion.

One of the debtor's most important rights in Chapter 11 is its exclusive right to propose a plan of reorganization for the first 120 days after the filing of the petition. The court may extend this period for up to 18 months. If the debtor does propose a plan, it has another 60 days to secure its acceptance under §1121(c)(3). When exclusivity expires, any party in interest can file a plan. If more than one plan meets all the rules of Chapter 11, then §1129(c) directs the bankruptcy judge to consider the "preferences of creditors and equity security holders in determining which plan to confirm." Terminating the exclusivity peri-

---

[20] See In re Northwest Airlines Corp., 363 Bankr. 704 (Bankr. S.D.N.Y. 2007). Recent changes to Bankruptcy Rule 2019 set out disclosure obligations of unofficial committees, but this rule does not limit the disclosures that the bankruptcy judge may require.

od can lead to the proposal and eventual confirmation of a liquidating plan of reorganization. From the perspective of a secured creditor, terminating exclusivity in such a case has the same effect as lifting the automatic stay.

Recognizing that they lack the ability to gather detailed information about a business's operations, bankruptcy judges try to ensure that sensible decisions are made about the debtor's assets by establishing clear benchmarks and taking decisive action when the debtor fails to meet them. At the start of the case, the principal lender may ask that the stay be lifted so it can foreclose on the collateral. The debtor's managers might argue that the stay should continue because the business can be sold as a going concern to another company. The bankruptcy judge might turn down the secured creditor's lift-stay motion but rule that the motion will be granted six weeks hence if no buyer appears in the interim.

The Chapter 11 debtor spends much of its time negotiating with its postbankruptcy suppliers of goods, services, and capital equipment. Chapter 11 provides a forum for the renegotiation of leases, contracts, and labor agreements. Sometimes, the negotiations are indistinguishable from those that take place outside of bankruptcy. Rules ensure that the third party possesses rights that correspond as closely as possible to the rights it would have enjoyed outside of bankruptcy. The rules in §1110 governing aircraft leases are a good example. In other situations, Chapter 11 provides rules that enhance the debtor's bargaining position dramatically relative to the nonbankruptcy baseline. Under such rules, creditors benefit at the expense of third parties relative to the nonbankruptcy baseline. The treatment of collective bargaining agreements under §1113 is a telling example. Negotiations in bankruptcy, however, all tend to have the same effect on the operations of the business going forward. The business that reorganizes in Chapter 11 successfully leaves with a new set of contracts under which it is paying something like the market price for its labor, capital, and material. If a business cannot compete effectively under these circumstances, it is unlikely to survive in a market economy.

Sections 1122 through 1129 establish the structure for negotiations among creditors. These sections set out the procedural rights of all the players and their substantive rights in the event they fail to reach agreement. These various rights, the most important of which are in §1129, embody a general principle known as the *absolute priority rule*. This rule tries to ensure that creditors in bankruptcy are paid according to their nonbankruptcy priorities. The debtor's ability to impose a plan over the creditors' objection by satisfying the absolute priority rule is known aptly as the debtor's *cramdown* power.

Sections 1141 through 1146 govern the discharge of old claims and the implementation of the reorganization plan. Just as the discharge provision of §727 in the case of the individual debtor had to be read in conjunction with the exclusion of individual income from property of the estate under §541, the discharge provision in §1141 must be read in conjunction with the absolute priority rule. Together, the discharge of debt and the absolute priority rule implement the central aim of Chapter 11. They ensure that businesses worth keeping intact remain so, despite the incentives each creditor has to look out for its own interest rather than the collective interest of all the creditors.

The Bankruptcy Forum

The Bankruptcy Code is designed so that the debtor's affairs can be sorted out in a single forum. Unlike a federal court sitting in a diversity case, the bankruptcy court has nationwide jurisdiction. Even a creditor who does not have the minimum contacts with California to make it amenable to suit in state court must still file its claim in the bankruptcy court in California if the debtor has chosen to file its petition there.[21] Proper venue for filing a bankruptcy petition includes state of incorporation.[22] Because many large businesses are incorporated under or have an affiliate incorporated under Delaware or New York law, large bankruptcy cases are often filed there.

A number of constraints prevent the goal of a single forum from being fully realized. Article III of the U.S. Constitution limits what bankruptcy judges can do given that they do not have life tenure. The jury trial right in the Seventh Amendment limits the ability to resolve disputes expeditiously. The sovereign immunity a state enjoys under the Eleventh Amendment might limit the bankruptcy court's power to resolve disputes when the state is asserting its rights as a creditor. Let us look at each of these constitutional limitations more closely.

In eighteenth-century England, the Chancellor appointed commissioners to do much of the work of gathering and administering a bankruptcy estate. Because they were not judges, what these commissioners did cannot be considered an exercise of the judicial power.

[21] See Harder v. Desert Breezes Master Association, 192 Bankr. 47 (N.D.N.Y. 1996).

[22] See 28 U.S.C. §1408.

Modern bankruptcy judges likewise oversee the administration of the bankruptcy estate. They do not enjoy lifelong appointments and cannot exercise "judicial power" within the meaning of Article III.[23] Disappointed litigants have a right to de novo review in the district courts for matters that are not central to the administration of the bankruptcy case.

The Seventh Amendment requires that the right to a jury trial be preserved in federal court for suits at common law when the amount in controversy exceeds $20. Many of the questions in a bankruptcy case, including whether a particular person has a claim against the debtor, would be the basis of suits at common law if brought outside of bankruptcy. It does not follow, however, that all such claims give rise to a right to a jury trial. A bankruptcy court is a court of equity, and it has the right to use "chancery methods" to decide matters that are central to the bankruptcy process.[24] Other actions, such as fraudulent conveyance suits against third parties, retain their common law character and must be tried by jury unless both parties consent to have the judge decide the dispute.[25] Under 28 U.S.C. §157(e), if a right to a jury trial exists, the bankruptcy judge may conduct the trial only by special designation of the district judge and only if the parties again give their express consent.

The Constitution affects the forum in which bankruptcy disputes are tried in a third way. A state can also appear as a simple creditor. For example, it may allege that the debtor owes sales taxes. Alternatively, the debtor may argue that a provision of the Bankruptcy Code, such as §1146, entitles it to a refund of taxes it has already paid. A state is ordinarily immune from suit under the Eleventh Amendment and ordinarily restricts the ability of a litigant to bring it into a forum of its choosing. This limitation, however, matters less than it might seem. Congress's power to enact uniform bankruptcy laws significantly limits the scope of sovereign immunity.[26]

While it may not be possible to resolve the debtor's affairs in a single forum, most of what we shall study plays out in the bankruptcy court and is subject only to appellate review. It is useful to spend some

---

[23] See Stern v. Marshall, 131 S. Ct. 2594 (2011); Northern Pipeline Construction Co. v. Marathon Pipe Line Co., 458 U.S. 50 (1982).

[24] See Barton v. Barbour, 104 U.S. 126, 134 (1881).

[25] Granfinanciera v. Nordberg, 492 U.S. 33 (1989).

[26] See Central Virginia Community College v. Katz, 546 U.S. 356 (2006).

time to see how the rules of procedure bring this about, despite the limitations outlined above.

Federal district courts have original and exclusive jurisdiction over all "cases" under Title 11.[27] The entire process the bankruptcy petition triggers is considered a "case" and thus may be filed only in a federal district court (as opposed to, say, a state court). Section 1334 also gives the district courts original (but not exclusive) jurisdiction over all "civil proceedings" arising under Title 11 or arising in or related to cases under Title 11. A controversy such as a fraudulent conveyance action that takes place in the course of settling a debtor's affairs is considered a "proceeding."

Bankruptcy jurisdiction can extend to parties who are neither creditors nor debtors when the dispute is related to a case under Title 11. The reach of related jurisdiction has been broadly defined. Courts sometimes ask simply "whether the outcome of the proceeding could conceivably have any effect upon the estate being administered in bankruptcy."[28] Courts, however, will typically find that the power does not extend to matters that might lead the losing party to seek indemnification from the debtor.[29] A claim that a creditor has against a guarantor of the debtor that would have no impact on the estate is an example of an action that falls outside the jurisdictional reach of §1334.

Bankruptcy courts are adjuncts of the district courts, and §1334 must be read in conjunction with §157(a) of Title 28. Section 157 allows the district court to "refer" any or all bankruptcy cases to bankruptcy judges. It also provides that the district court may refer any or all proceedings arising under the Bankruptcy Code, or arising in or related to a bankruptcy case, to bankruptcy judges. In all district courts this practice is firmly institutionalized. Bankruptcy petitions are, as a practical matter, filed in the bankruptcy courts. The purpose of this circumlocution is to ensure that the dictates of Article III are satisfied. The bankruptcy judge is not acting autonomously and is not exercising judicial power because the bankruptcy judge is merely an adjunct to the district court. Just as a court of equity can appoint a special master,

---

[27] 28 U.S.C. §1334.

[28] Kelley v. Nodine, 783 F.2d 626, 634 (6th Cir. 1986). See Lindsey v. O'Brien (In re Dow Corning Corp.), 86 F.3d 482 (6th Cir. 1996).

[29] See In re Federal-Mogul Global, Inc., 282 Bankr. 301 (Bank. D. Del. 2002).

the reasoning goes, the district court can choose to delegate bankruptcy cases to bankruptcy judges.

The idea that the district courts have jurisdiction over bankruptcy cases and proceedings is not entirely a formal fiction. Although everything is routinely referred to the bankruptcy courts, §157(d) gives the district judge the power to withdraw the reference in any particular case or proceeding, in whole or in part, for cause. The district court can act either on its own motion or on a timely motion of any party. Although district courts rarely want to hear bankruptcy disputes, they have withdrawn the reference in some important cases.

Withdrawal of the reference is mandatory after a timely motion when "resolution of the proceeding requires consideration of both Title 11 and other laws of the United States regulating organizations or activities affecting interstate commerce." §157(d). This provision has been read narrowly, as it must be, given that so many disputes in a bankruptcy case involve consideration of federal laws that affect interstate commerce. Courts frequently use a substantial-and-material test: withdrawal is mandatory only when the issues presented require a significant interpretation of federal laws, not when what is presented is the straightforward application of federal law to a particular set of facts. A difficult controversy involving the reach of a complex statute is potentially a subject of mandatory withdrawal, but even then the district court may remand to the bankruptcy court for submission of proposed findings of fact and conclusions of law under §157(c)(1).

Once a case is referred to a bankruptcy judge, many decisions are subject only to appellate review by the district court. Section 157 tells us that bankruptcy judges "may hear and determine all cases under the Bankruptcy Code" referred to them, subject to appellate review under 28 U.S.C. §158. *Case* is used in the technical sense here and refers only to the process that begins with the bankruptcy petition. Individual disputes arise during the debtor's course through bankruptcy are *proceedings*. When these proceedings are central to the administration of the case (or, to use the term in Title 28, when they are *core*), the bankruptcy judge is again subject only to appellate review. Core proceedings include confirmation of plans, matters concerning the administration of the estate, and the allowance or disallowance of claims against the estate.

Section 157(b)(2) contains a list of core proceedings, but this list is neither exhaustive nor entirely accurate. As the Supreme Court made clear in *Stern v. Marshall*, some proceedings §157(b)(2) defines as "core" require de novo review by an Article III judge nevertheless.

These include counterclaims against third parties and may also include fraudulent conveyance actions. In such situations, the bankruptcy court can, as with noncore matters, make proposed findings of fact and conclusions of law that the district court then reviews de novo.[30]

Section 157(c)(2) allows the court to refer a proceeding to the bankruptcy judge with the consent of the parties, subject to the review provided in §158. Under 28 U.S.C. §158(a), the district courts "have jurisdiction to hear appeals . . . from final judgments, orders, and decrees" of the bankruptcy court. Consent is routine in large cases heard by highly respected bankruptcy judges. As long as consent suffices to cure the bankruptcy judge's inability to exercise the "judicial power," the problems posed by cases such as *Stern v. Marshall* largely disappear.

The language of §158(a) introduces a complication. It grants district judges "jurisdiction" to hear "appeals." This language implies that bankruptcy judges possess original jurisdiction. It is a matter of hornbook law, however, that parties cannot create subject matter jurisdiction by consent. The consequences go beyond the interests of the parties themselves. State courts must obey the decisions of a judge with jurisdiction. A court with jurisdiction can issue writs of execution and call upon the coercive hand of the state to enforce its orders. Parties can agree to arbitration, but the arbitrator's decision is just so much talk until it is docketed in the district court.

Those who defend the status quo argue that subject matter jurisdiction resides at all times in the district court under §1334. The bankruptcy judge acts under the aegis of the district court. Its orders are in essence decisions of the district court. The distinction between the bankruptcy court's docket and the district court's docket is entirely formal. The former is merely part of the later.

The courts of appeals have jurisdiction to hear appeals from final decisions, judgments, orders, and decrees under 28 U.S.C. §158(d). Determining a final judgment for purposes of 28 U.S.C. §158(d) has proven difficult. Suppose there is a final judgment in the bankruptcy court, and the district court hears the appeal and remands to the bankruptcy court. Courts are divided on whether an appeal can be taken to the court of appeals. Section 158(d) does not tell us explicitly whether it is sufficient that the bankruptcy judge's decision be final or whether

---

[30] See Executive Benefits Insurance Agency v. Arkison (In re Bellingham Insurance Agency, Inc.), — U.S. — (2014).

the district court's decision must be final as well. Most courts recognize that a district court's order generally is not final if it remands the dispute to the bankruptcy court and requires the bankruptcy court to make factual findings or exercise its discretion.[31] Some courts, however, have found that bankruptcy requires a more relaxed standard of finality than ordinary federal civil litigation.[32]

The uncertainty in the meaning of finality in §158(d) can put lawyers in the awkward position of having to choose between appealing a decision that may prove to be interlocutory or waiving the right altogether if it later proves to have been a final order. Section 158(d), however, does not displace the ordinary rules governing appeals from the district court, and §1292(b) mitigates this problem to some extent. This section allows a court of appeals, in its discretion, to review an interlocutory order, provided the district judge finds that at issue is a controlling question of law as to which there is substantial ground for difference of opinion and that an immediate appeal may materially advance the ultimate termination of the litigation.[33]

This review of appellate review of bankruptcy court decisions, however, is somewhat misleading. Appellate review takes time, and most of the important decisions in a bankruptcy case—whether the business should be shut down or whether the managers should be given another month to turn the operation around—are time sensitive and thus essentially unreviewable. How long to wait before taking action becomes a moot point well before the appellate court can hear the case. When a bankruptcy court confirms a plan, those who object may enjoy little appellate review as a practical matter. Even if there are significant issues in doubt, a court may require appellants to post a bond in order to obtain a stay.[34] And if there is no stay, there may be no easy way to unscramble things after the fact. While the issue is not formally moot, it may have become "equitably moot" as a court can fashion no meaningful relief.[35]

[31] See, e.g., In re XMH Corp., 647 F.3d 690 (7th Cir. 2011).

[32] See Buncher Co. v. Official Committee of Unsecured Creditors, 229 F.3d 245, 250 (3d Cir. 2000).

[33] Connecticut National Bank v. Germain, 503 U.S. 249 (1992).

[34] See, e.g., ACC Bondholder Group v. Adelphia Communications Corp., 361 Bankr. 337 (S.D.N.Y. 2007).

[35] Appellate courts, however, may be showing greater reluctance to apply the doctrine of equitable mootness. See, e.g., Bank of New York Trust Co. v. Official Unsecured Creditors' Committee (In re Pacific Lumber Co.), 584

The practical effect of all this is to grant the bankruptcy judge enormous power. From the perspective of financial institutions that have done business with the debtor in the past and expect to continue to do business with it, Chapter 11 is an attractive venue only if the decisions of the bankruptcy judge are predictable. For this reason among others, Delaware and the Southern District of New York have become the venue of choice for many large corporations in bankruptcy.

The Bankruptcy Rules establish the procedures used in the bankruptcy courts. They do not change the substantive rules of the Bankruptcy Code, but they do affect how the issues are shaped. For example, they distinguish the types of hearings that take place before the bankruptcy judge. One type of hearing, called an *adversary proceeding*, is conducted under much the same rules as any other civil dispute. Many sections of the Federal Rules of Civil Procedure that govern pleading, joinder, depositions, interrogatories, and summary judgment have been incorporated into the bankruptcy rules governing adversary proceedings. In Chapter 11 cases, the typical adversary proceeding is a preference or fraudulent conveyance action. For individuals in Chapter 7, an adversary proceeding usually concerns the dischargeability of a particular debt.

Whenever an actual dispute before the bankruptcy court is not an adversary proceeding, it is a *contested matter*. Among the most common is a motion to lift the automatic stay. The procedures for contested matters are more streamlined and are set out in Bankruptcy Rule 9014. For example, no response is required in a contested matter unless the court orders an answer to a motion. The court, however, has the power to invoke the more elaborate rules for adversary proceedings in contested matters when appropriate.

Bankruptcy courts also have the inherent power under §105 to impose sanctions in order to maintain control of their courtrooms and of their dockets.[36] Moreover, Rule 11 or its counterpart under the Bankruptcy Rules, Rule 9011, is available at every stage of bankruptcy litigation. In addition, §362(k) of the Bankruptcy Code explicitly grants

---

F.3d 229 (5th Cir. 2009); Search Market Direct, Inc. v. Jubber (In re Paige), 584 F.3d 1327 (10th Cir. 2009).

[36] See United States v. Mourad, 289 F.3d 174 (1st Cir. 2002); In re Volpert, 110 F.3d 494 (7th Cir. 1997).

the bankruptcy court the power to award actual and punitive damages to an individual injured by any violation of the automatic stay.[37]

Other Insolvency Forums

The layperson often equates bankruptcy with business failure. Bankruptcy, however, is only a small part of the story. Hundreds of thousands of businesses close their door every year. Some have no creditors or owe them nothing. In other cases, creditors walk away without invoking any legal proceeding at all. In the vast majority of cases in which a business encounters financial distress and seeks legal relief, state law remedies prove adequate. For many small businesses, a state law procedure known as an assignment for the benefit of creditors provides a means of selling the assets of a business cheaply and quickly. In some jurisdictions, these take place without judicial oversight. They are especially useful when the business is small and those running the business can work and deal effectively with the senior lender. (Indeed, in many cases, the senior lender is the higher bidder at the sale and keeps the existing managers on.)

Even for large businesses, bankruptcy often proves a costly option that parties want to avoid if they can. In many instances, restructurings or sales are possible outside of bankruptcy. By the time large firms encounter difficulties, the players are investors who specialize in holding distressed debt. There may be few enough so that a deal among them is possible. The fate awaiting each in bankruptcy if they fail to reach a deal forms the backdrop for these negotiations.

In a number of cases, the deal struck has enough loose ends that there is a pre-arranged bankruptcy in which the bankruptcy judge puts her blessing on whatever deal is reached. Understanding what bankruptcy judges are and are not willing to do is again essential.

Those trained in bankruptcy are sometimes called upon to work in wholly unfamiliar territory. Transnational cases arise in which the bankruptcy system of a foreign jurisdiction come into play. A large business may have domestic subsidiaries that are subject to entirely different insolvency regimes, such as insurance companies or banks. During the financial crisis in 2008, bankruptcy professionals were heavily engaged in the bankruptcy of Lehman Brothers, but they were

---

[37] Courts, however, are divided on whether "individual" in this context means only human beings. See In re APF Co., 264 Bankr. 344 (Bankr. D. Del. 2001).

equally involved in the restructuring of AIG, as well as Fannie Mae and Freddie Mac.

Part of the skill of the bankruptcy lawyer is being able to master such new environments quickly. Title II of Dodd-Frank (known as the "Orderly Liquidation Authority") was passed in response to the failure of Lehman Brothers. It is an effort to forge a statutory regime that combines elements of both banking regulation and Chapter 11. As it is new, every lawyer confronting it finds herself in new terrain.

At first blush, the Orderly Liquidation Authority is utterly alien. The necessity for government intervention and the adaptation of a mechanism used for failed banks introduces new terminology and, more importantly, a new decisionmaker. While traditional bankruptcy law reflects a balance of power in which the debtor in possession, the creditors' committee, the lender that is financing the reorganization, and the bankruptcy judge play discrete roles, this regime concentrates power in a single entity, the FDIC. The almost complete absence of a judge is especially striking. The FDIC's powers in this new domain largely track its longstanding powers with respect to commercial banks under the Federal Deposit Insurance Act (FDIA).

Nevertheless, the mechanics of the new receivership process incorporate basic bankruptcy principles. They effectively permit reorganization as well as liquidation, debtor-in-possession financing, asset sales free and clear of existing liens, claw-back of prepetition fraudulent and preferential transfers, and safe harbors for financial contracts. It is possible—indeed essential—for the bankruptcy lawyer called upon to navigate this world to find her way.

CHAPTER TWO

The Individual Debtor and the Fresh Start

Creditor Remedies and Debtor Rights

In our society, extensions of credit are woven into the fabric of everyday life. We become indebted to the electric company every time we turn on a light switch. We routinely use a credit card to buy a cup of coffee. Few of us could pay for our education or buy a house if credit were not readily available. But borrowing carries with it the risk that we shall not be able to repay what we owe. A person might be stricken with a catastrophic illness or lose a well-paying job and be unable to cut back on expenses before being overwhelmed by debt. Families with incomes of $30,000 a year, no matter how well intentioned, are not going to be able to pay off $100,000 in debt. They have no assets beyond clothes, a wedding ring, and some household furniture. There are many honest, decent individuals who through improvidence or bad luck end up owing their creditors more than they can ever repay.

For more than a century, our laws have granted such individuals a fresh start. They can file a bankruptcy petition, discharge their debts, and start over again. More than a million individuals file bankruptcy petitions each year. The overwhelming majority of these cases are short, uncomplicated affairs. The debtors never appear in court, no creditor objects, and the court clerk is the only one who ever sees the file. The system provides enormous benefits to the "honest but unfortunate debtor"[1] while imposing only a small cost on creditors. Having a debt you are owed discharged matters relatively little if there is almost no chance you are going to be repaid anyway. You are better off having the debtor's affairs subjected to scrutiny by a trustee and walking away.

The law that governs the bankruptcy of individuals is complicated not because of the typical case, which again is quite simple and consumes no judicial time, but rather because one must have some way of distinguishing honest but unlucky debtors from those who would

---

[1] See Local Loan Co. v. Hunt, 292 U.S. 234, 244 (1934).

abuse the system. When bad behavior is brought to their attention, bankruptcy judges take action. Section 707(b) of the Bankruptcy Code allows the bankruptcy judge to deny debtors a fresh start if the fresh start would work an abuse of the bankruptcy process. To ensure that unscrupulous individuals do not hide assets, we require those who seek the protection of bankruptcy law to disclose the whereabouts of all assets and submit to questioning from creditors. Debtors who are not forthcoming lose, among other things, their right to a fresh start. See §727. Many creditors will stop pursuing the debtor once they are satisfied that the debtor cannot repay them, independent of whether bankruptcy formally discharged the debt. The procedures that bankruptcy law puts in place reassures creditors that the debtor does not have other assets and that nothing is being hidden from them.

For a long time, Chapter 7 imposed costs on those who used it in such a way that only those for whom the fresh start was intended would use it. To obtain a fresh start, individuals must turn over to creditors all assets other than clothing, wedding rings, and similar types of property that creditors would be unable to reach outside of bankruptcy. For those for whom individual bankruptcy law is primarily designed—lower-middle-class working persons who are hopelessly in debt—the obligation to turn over nonexempt assets imposes comparatively fewer burdens. They do not have much in the way of assets beyond the clothes on the backs and household furniture. In contrast, the same obligation weighs more heavily on those with substantial income who have assembled assets of significant value. For them, the price of bankruptcy is too high if they can pay off existing debt out of future income.

In a world in which the most important asset any of us owns is human capital, however, what we own at any one point in time tells us increasingly less about our ability to pay creditors. A recent law school graduate may have far fewer assets than a line cook with a family yet make three times as much. For the former, a debt of $100,000 is neither unusual nor overly burdensome, while for the latter it is crushing.

For this reason, some argued that bankruptcy law should have an explicit mechanism that gauges whether someone is the honest but unfortunate debtor for whom the law was intended. The law should look explicitly at their income and their ability to repay what they owe. Congress adopted such a mechanism after much debate in 2005. This test, however, affects only a small portion of those who use Chapter 7.

The introduction of means testing had relatively little effect on high-income debtors who could pay much of what they owed. Most courts had already found that the filing of a bankruptcy petition by someone who had the ability to repay debt was itself grounds for dismissing the case.[2] It did, however, impose significant costs on the vast majority of debtors who are not subject to means testing. The problem associated with means testing is one associated with many reform efforts. The game may not be worth the candle. The benefits of catching a few bad actors may not justify the costs everyone else bears.

The Means Test

Section 707(b)(2) blocks access to the fresh start for consumers who make more than most and who have enough disposable income to make substantial repayments to their creditors.[3] It provides a hard-and-fast rule that supplements the discretion that the bankruptcy judge enjoys to dismiss abusive filings by those struggling primarily with consumer debt. The judge determines whether one makes enough to be subject to means testing by taking the debtor's "current monthly income," multiplying it by 12, and comparing it against the "median family income" of others in the same state. Both terms are defined in §101. The "current monthly income" calculation begins with the average income over the six months before the filing. The "median family income" benchmark draws on census data for the state in which the debtor resides, indexed for inflation and adjusted for household size. When the debtor lives alone, the courts looks at the median income in the state for households of one. When the household consists of two, three, or four, we use whichever has the highest median income. When the household consists of five or more, we again take the highest median of two-, three-, or four-person households and then adjust it upward by a fixed dollar amount for each additional household member.

These adjustments represent just one of the many technicalities associated with §707(b)'s means test. But such adjustments (and many others like them) are necessary for the rule to work sensibly. Someone who lives alone has fewer expenses and less income on average than two who live together. Using the median income of a two-person household for a single debtor would make the median income thresh-

---

[2] See, e.g., Zolg v. Kelly (In re Kelly), 841 F.2d 908, 914–15 (9th Cir. 1988).

[3] For an excellent account of how the means test works, see Eugene R. Wedoff, Means Testing in the New §707(b), 79 Am. Bankr. L.J. 231 (2005).

old inappropriately easy for that debtor relative to other debtors. By contrast, the median income for households greater than four is, on average, less than those with smaller households. Simply using that median for larger households would mean that, all else equal, a larger family would be more likely subject to means testing. It makes no sense to have a rule that imposes a lower earnings threshold on larger families, especially given that larger families have greater expenses.

Once a debtor is found to make more than most, we still must establish that the debtor earns enough to be able to pay something back to creditors. The benchmark used here is based on the tables the Internal Revenue Service uses to decide how much delinquent taxpayers are able to pay. In calculating allowable living expenses, for example, the IRS allows one person living alone to spend $315 on food each month. The amount allocated for housing depends on where the taxpayer lives. In New York City, the amount for a household of two or fewer can be as much as $3,524; in Philadelphia the ceiling is $884.

After this benchmark is determined, the bankruptcy judge makes a number of adjustments. Some judges allow for additional expenses not reflected in the IRS tables, such as expenses for the care and support of elderly, chronically ill, or disabled household members who cannot provide for themselves. Incorporating IRS tables designed for different purposes, however, can create challenging questions of statutory interpretation.[4]

Once we determine the debtor's reasonable monthly expenses according to this formula, we subtract the amount from the debtor's current monthly income, as defined in §101, and see whether what remains is sufficient to make substantial payments to creditors. If there is less than $7,475 over a five-year Chapter 13 plan, then the debtor remains eligible for a discharge and a fresh start under Chapter 7. If there is more than $12,475 over the course of a five-year plan, then the debtor whose current monthly income exceeds the median is presumed ineligible for a fresh start. If the income falls somewhere between, we check to see if the amount is sufficient to pay ordinary general credi-

---

[4] Ransom v. FIA Card Services, 131 S. Ct. 716 (2011), illustrates the challenge. With a somewhat strained interpretation of the word "applicable," the Supreme Court reached what seemed to be a sensible result. Debtors were denied the ability to take an allowance for car payments when they owned their cars outright and hence owed no payments on them. Justice Scalia wrote a strong dissent, arguing (characteristically) that a literal reading of the text compelled the opposite result.

tors 25 cents on the dollar. If the debtor can pay that much back according to this metric, then the debtor again is presumptively ineligible. To rebut the presumption, the debtor must establish special circumstances, such as a serious medical condition, that affect the debtor's expected income or expenses and make the debtor unable to repay creditors.

The means test is embedded in a section devoted to bankruptcy abuse, but this is misleading. The means test is focused exclusively on the ability to repay debt. If two debtors' incomes, expenses, and household size are the same, the circumstances that brought about the financial distress are irrelevant. The person who incurred sudden medical expenses or lost a job is treated the same as the spendthrift who ran up credit card debt by taking too many vacations. Ability to repay, as measured by this formula, is all that matters.

But this is not to say that the spendthrifts who escape the means test are off the hook. Debtors who make more than the median are at greater risk of losing their right to a discharge than debtors who make less than the median. The creditors of the former are permitted to ask the judge to find that the debtor's use of Chapter 7 is abusive for some other reason—say, as a means of escaping a covenant not to compete. Debtors who make less than the median are still subject to the risk that the judge will find their use of bankruptcy abusive, but in these cases, either the United States Trustee or the judge must initiate the inquiry; a disgruntled creditor cannot. The ability to put the issue on the judge's radar screen will likely make a difference. Such disputes, however, seem most likely to arise in the business context, and §707(b) is not likely to apply in such situations, as the power to dismiss for abuse is limited to those whose debts are primarily consumer debts.

Whether this rule-based approach to measuring bankruptcy abuse serves its purpose is an open question. Indeed, it is not easy to measure its costs or its benefits. Such a rule, by its nature, does much of its work offstage. Someone who would have otherwise used Chapter 7 may now decide not to file at all. To the extent such individuals are not worthy of a fresh start, the benefits will be largely unobserved. The costs may be equally invisible. Even though few of the individuals who filed before means testing went into effect in late 2005 would have fallen within its scope (perhaps only 10 percent), implementing a means test is costly. Debtors have to provide enough information to show whether they are subject to means testing. The burden of turning over income tax returns and pay stubs increases the cost of every

Chapter 7 filing. The additional time and lawyers' fees might appear small in a single case, but aggregated over a million cases each year they are substantial.

The Mechanics of the Fresh Start

The Bankruptcy Code embeds the individual's right to a fresh start in a statute that is doing many other things at the same time. Section 109 sets out eligibility requirements. Because Chapter 7 is also used to liquidate corporations, the eligibility rules for Chapter 7 are quite broad. They need only exclude insurance companies and other entities that are governed by a different insolvency regime and entities, such as railroads, for which there are special rules in the Bankruptcy Code. Hence, Chapter 7 is available to "persons" other than those listed in §109(b). As we discussed in the first chapter, §101 defines "persons" broadly to include both flesh-and-blood individuals and corporations.

Section 301 states that eligible individuals may commence a case on their own initiative. Section 541 provides that the filing of a petition under §301 transforms assets (including exempt assets) that the debtor owns into property of the estate, but §541(a)(6) creates an exception for the *individual* debtor's future earnings. The language is deliberately limited to individuals, as the future earnings of a corporation are assets to which creditors are entitled. Section 727 provides a discharge, again only to individuals, not to corporations. Section 522 ensures that individuals keep exempt assets.

Section 303 sets out the process for commencing an involuntary case. While involuntary petitions are uncommon today, they were originally the only type of bankruptcy petition that could be filed, and they still serve a purpose. An involuntary bankruptcy provides creditors with a single forum to assemble the debtor's assets and scrutinize financial and other records. It also allows a creditor to unwind a transfer—such as a large payment to another creditor—that would be permissible under nonbankruptcy law but that violates bankruptcy's norm of pro rata distribution.

Once we pass beyond the eligibility requirements, the important provisions can be divided into those designed to prevent abuse and those that ensure the fresh start. Section 727 supplements §707(b) and prevents debtors from receiving a discharge if they have defrauded their creditors or otherwise abused the process. It can come into play even when the debtor makes less than the median income and the misbehavior in question does not come to the attention of the bankruptcy judge or the United States Trustee.

Section 727(a)(2) denies a discharge to debtors who transfer property with the intent to hinder, delay, or defraud creditors. Section 727(a)(3) imposes the sanction if the debtor destroys or fails to keep financial records and thereby makes it impossible for creditors to understand the debtor's affairs. Many debtors who end up in financial trouble, however, are honest individuals who are bad record-keepers. Courts typically do not use the financial records exception to deny a fresh start to such debtors.

History shaped many of the exceptions to discharge under §727. The discharge was originally introduced into bankruptcy law to secure the debtor's cooperation; the intent was not to give the debtor a fresh start but to induce the debtor to cooperate with the creditors and help them assemble the debtor's assets.[5] This explains why a debtor who makes a fraudulent conveyance cannot obtain a discharge but a convicted murderer can. (Whether, however, the murderer can obtain a discharge for the civil claim that the victim's heirs might have is a different question that we confront later.) In addition, §727(a)(8) requires a debtor to wait eight years between one fresh start and the next. This limitation on the right to a fresh start prevents the deliberate wrongdoer from abusing the right. It also works in the debtor's interest because it can make it easier to borrow. Creditors who lend to someone who has just emerged from bankruptcy know that the debtor cannot file a bankruptcy petition before they have a chance to be repaid. Section 727 also ensures that individual debtors complete the credit counseling course that §109 requires.

Other provisions try to ensure that individuals do not use bankruptcy as a delaying tactic. If within 45 days of filing the petition the debtor fails to supply the information needed to determine whether means testing applies, the case is automatically dismissed. §521(i). Rules designed to curb abuse by limiting judicial discretion, however, do not always work as planned. The drafters of §521(i) may not have realized that it is sometimes not creditors, but debtors who want to exit the bankruptcy process. If they want to terminate the bankruptcy over their creditors' objection, they may point to their own failure to pro-

---

[5] The Statute of 4 Anne ch. 17 (1705), which instituted the discharge in bankruptcy, was in fact called "An act to prevent frauds frequently committed by bankrupts."

vide information as grounds for automatic dismissal. The judge may find that she must dismiss the bankruptcy case.[6]

The automatic stay that keeps secured creditors and landlords at bay is sharply curtailed in cases involving individual debtors. It does not apply, for example, to an eviction action involving residential property if the landlord obtains a judgment for possession before the filing of the petition. §362(b)(22). A number of provisions are aimed at serial filers, those who file the petition merely to gain the benefits of the automatic stay. If the debtor filed two or more cases in the previous year, the automatic stay does not even go into effect. §362(c)(3).

Balancing the provisions that prevent individuals from abusing the system are those that ensure that eligible debtors in fact receive a fresh start. The principal provisions at work here are two that we have already mentioned—§541 and §522. We look at each in turn.

Under §541 the debtor may keep assets that do not become property of the estate. Principal among these assets are earnings from future services (§541(a)(6)) and assets held in a trust that the debtor cannot reach under nonbankruptcy law (§541(c)(2)). To understand how hard it can be to determine future earnings, consider the situation of a debtor who is a partner in a law firm whose practice generates substantial income.[7] A partner's future income from a law practice does not derive exclusively from the partner's own future work. Future earnings from a law practice are generated in part by existing assets, such as employment contracts with the associates in the firm. Earnings also come from the partner's past efforts. There are accounts receivable and a client base that has been built over time. A partner's role at a law firm might consist largely of rainmaking; once the client retains the firm, an associate might perform most of the subsequent legal work. Little of the income derived from prepetition clients would qualify as the partner's future earnings within the meaning of §541(a)(6). The court must distinguish revenues that flow from the business and those that flow from the debtor's postpetition contribution of labor.

---

[6] See, e.g., In re Bonner, 374 Bankr. 62 (Bankr. W.D.N.Y. 2007)). Some appellate courts have found their way to giving the bankruptcy judge the power to prevent dismissal under these circumstances. See Wirum v. Warren, 568 F.3d 1113 (9th Cir. 2009); Segarra-Miranda v. Acosta-Rivera, 557 F.3d 8 (1st Cir. 2009).

[7] See FitzSimmons v. Walsh, 725 F.2d 1208 (9th Cir. 1984).

Some courts have valued a practice by asking how much would have been realized in the event that the debtor had sold the practice.[8] But one must identify the kind of nonbankruptcy sale that provides the relevant benchmark. (An outright sale would obviate the need to make an estimate, but if the individual files in Chapter 11 and plans to continue to run the business, an actual sale is not in the cards.) A lawyer or doctor who sells a practice usually, as part of the sale, agrees to vouch for the buyer, introduce him to clients or patients, and perhaps work with him through a transitional period. In addition, the new buyer will ordinarily insist on a covenant not to compete. Hence, the amount for which a cooperative debtor could sell the practice outside of bankruptcy may not be the relevant benchmark. A better approximation might be the amount the practice would fetch if the debtor ceased all connections with the business and remained free to open a competing practice.[9]

Problems also arise with the effect that the discharge has on liens and other rights that third parties have in the debtor's property. Suppose a bank lends a borrower $100,000 and takes a mortgage on the borrower's $150,000 home. The discharge prevents the bank from pursuing its claim against the borrower, but the discharge does not cut off the bank's lien on the property. After the Chapter 7 proceeding is over, the bank can still foreclose on the property if the borrower is in default. As noted in chapter 1 above, liens pass through bankruptcy.

To ensure that a debtor enjoys a fresh start, however, bankruptcy law has carved out several exceptions to the doctrine of lien pass-through. For example, a right of redemption under §722 allows the debtor to extinguish liens on property intended for personal, family, or household use if those liens secure dischargeable consumer debt. (The debtor, however, must pay the secured creditor an amount equal to the value of the property.) In addition, the debtor is entitled to avoid judicial liens in exempt property and nonpossessory money security interests (other than purchase money interests) in some kinds of exempt property such as household goods and tools of the trade under §522(f). Finally, and most important, liens on the debtor's future earnings do not survive bankruptcy. The Supreme Court established this principle

---

[8] See, e.g., In re Prince, 85 F.3d 314, 323 n.5 (7th Cir. 1996).
[9] See Ackerman v. Schultz, 250 Bankr. 22 (Bankr. E.D.N.Y. 2000).

in *Local Loan Company v. Hunt,* which held that an assignment of wages did not survive discharge.[10]

The bankruptcy of Victor Ortiz raised the same problem as *Local Loan Company* in a different guise.[11] Ortiz, a boxer, wanted to escape from a long-term contract with his promoter. The court had to ask if bankruptcy freed him from the unfavorable contract. If Ortiz had foolishly borrowed money from his promoter and lost it all, he would have been able to file a bankruptcy petition and keep his earnings from whatever job he happened to take. Similarly, if a creditor of Ortiz's had garnished his wages, the garnishment would not survive bankruptcy. Conceptually, Ortiz's promise not to fight for any other promoter or indeed any covenant not to compete is the same. The promoter has what amounts to an ownership interest in Ortiz's future income stream. *Local Loan Company* establishes that such interests do not survive bankruptcy.

To be sure, if one can discharge a covenant not to compete in bankruptcy, it will be harder for boxers like Ortiz to find promoters in the first place. Promoters would be less willing to take on new boxers if they are not able to keep them. But this does not distinguish *Ortiz* from *Local Loan Company.* Any limit on the doctrine of lien passthrough reduces debtors' ability to commit themselves and hence makes it less attractive for others to enter into agreements with them.

In this case and in others like it, the structure of the Bankruptcy Code makes it hard to confront such questions head on. Ortiz's agreement with his promoter falls within the definition of an executory contract under §365, but the Code deals with this question imperfectly. We return to this question when we discuss executory contracts in chapter 6 below.

Section 541(c)(2) looks not at future earnings but at a kind of property held in trust that is beyond the reach of both the debtor and the creditors at the time the petition is filed. The paradigm is the spendthrift trust. A parent might establish a trust for a child prone to impulsive spending and provide that the child could not convey future income from the trust in exchange for a fixed sum today. Nonbankruptcy law respects such provisions. Section 541(c)(2) tells us that bankruptcy law respects them as well. If a restriction on the transfer of a

---

[10] 292 U.S. 234 (1934).

[11] Top Rank, Inc. v. Ortiz, 400 Bankr. 755 (C.D. Cal. 2009).

debtor's beneficial interest in a trust is enforceable outside of bankruptcy, it is enforceable inside of bankruptcy.

The Bankruptcy Code does not limit the reach of §541(c)(2) to trusts that are denominated spendthrift trusts. It applies equally to any beneficial interest in a trust that has the crucial attribute of being beyond the reach of the debtor or the debtor's creditors.[12] In addition, §541(b)(7) excludes from property of the estate contributions that a debtor has made to various retirement and benefit programs recognized under ERISA and other federal law. Provisions in §522 ensure further that retirement funds kept in tax-exempt accounts are similarly free from creditor levy.

After discharge, the debtor enjoys, free from the claims of the creditors, everything that the debtor would ordinarily enjoy in the absence of bankruptcy other than property of the estate. Future income is the most conspicuous example, but there are others. Consider the right of a spouse to take a statutory share of the decedent's estate rather than what was bequeathed in the will. The spouse has this right under nonbankruptcy law, and this right is not property of the estate, so the spouse retains this right notwithstanding the bankruptcy.[13]

We turn now to §522. In addition to keeping everything that is not property of the estate and nullifying liens on future income under the principle of *Local Loan Company*, the debtor is able to keep exempt assets. The Bankruptcy Code provides a list of exempt property that debtors can keep as part of their fresh start. States, however, can—and most do—decide on their own which of the debtor's assets should be beyond the reach of creditors in bankruptcy and out. The Constitution gives Congress the power to pass only uniform laws on the subject of bankruptcy. Deferring to state exemption statutes, however, does not prevent a bankruptcy statute from being uniform.[14]

State exemptions vary in detail according to jurisdiction. A few are still firmly rooted in the nineteenth century and include such things as homesteads, church pews, and the family Bible. Most of these statutes have been overhauled in recent years. Modern exemption statutes include pensions and insurance policies. Property that is exempt for pur-

---

[12] Patterson v. Shumate, 504 U.S. 753 (1992). For an example of a case that is close to the line, see In re Hilsen, 405 Bankr. 49 (Bankr. E.D.N.Y. 2009).

[13] See In re Brand, 251 Bankr. 912 (Bankr. S.D. Fla. 2000); In re McCourt, 12 Bankr. 587 (Bankr. S.D.N.Y. 1981).

[14] See Hanover National Bank v. Moyses, 186 U.S. 181 (1902).

poses of §522(b)(2) may extend beyond what a state explicitly calls "exempt." For example, exempt property may extend to all property that the state has put beyond the reach of a debtor's creditors and that otherwise has the attributes of exempt property, whatever label the state (or substantive federal law) applies.

A state may opt to have nonbankruptcy exemptions (both state and federal) govern exclusively. When it does not, §522(b) allows the debtor to choose whether to take advantage of the nonbankruptcy exemptions or keep the property listed in §522(d).[15] The largest exemption in §522(d), apart from the one already noted for tax-exempt retirement accounts, is the federal homestead exemption. It protects about $20,000 of equity that debtors build up in their residences (this amount is adjusted every three years to account for inflation).

Section 522(d)(3) allows a debtor to protect household goods, subject to an overall cap (now a little more than $12,000) and a cap on individual items (of about $500). Again, the exact amount changes over time. Other §522(d) exemptions include the debtor's interest in household goods, health aids, tools of the trade, and a motor vehicle, as well as the debtor's right to receive alimony, support payments, life insurance payments, veteran's benefits, and victim's compensation payments. Some exemptions are limited in scope or amount, while others are not.

Beyond the definition of exempt property, §522 also allows the debtor to "avoid the fixing of" certain liens on such property. This power exists whether the debtor uses the special bankruptcy exemptions or the state and federal nonbankruptcy exemptions. More precisely, §522(f)(1)(a) generally allows the individual debtor to free exempt property from most kinds of judicial liens, including liens created by levy on behalf of a general creditor. Not included are liens that secure an alimony or child-support obligation. Moreover, §522(f)(1)(b) allows the debtor to avoid a nonpossessory, nonpurchase money security interest in specified property.

As noted, most states have their own exemption statutes that work in federal exemption statutes (such as the provisions discussed here covering ERISA plans, tax-exempt retirement accounts, and social security payments). Some state laws put no dollar cap on the property that can be exempt from creditor levy. In Texas, for example, a debt-

---

[15] As we have seen elsewhere (in §109, for example), the dollar amounts are adjusted by regulation every three years.

or's homestead is exempt from creditor levy. Texas limits the size of the homestead (one acre) but not its value.[16] Debtors might use bankruptcy to discharge their debts even though they could pay them in full without great sacrifice, given the equity they have in their homes. One can again argue that a debtor who could pay creditors by selling a large house and moving to a more modest home should not be able to take advantage of Chapter 7. But so long as the debtor lived in the state with the large exemption at the time the loan was taken out, the creditor can take this risk into account. If the debtor moves to a state to take advantage of homestead laws after having incurred the debt, however, then the creditor is at risk. Section 522(p) protects the creditor by capping the amount of exempt property the debtor can keep if the debtor establishes a homestead in the state within 1,215 days of the bankruptcy petition.

Defining Discharge and Nondischargeable Debts

A debtor who files a bankruptcy petition is entitled to a discharge of prepetition claims. The debtor is not free of obligations incurred after the filing of the petition. Moreover, some prepetition burdens remain notwithstanding the discharge because they are not "claims" as defined in the Bankruptcy Code. For example, criminal sanctions, such as imprisonment, survive bankruptcy. A felon enjoys a discharge, but the discharge does not secure release from prison because the state's right to imprison someone is not a claim. Nor can a debtor use a bankruptcy filing to evade a child-custody order.

It is important to understand exactly what it means to discharge a debt. At a minimum, a discharge gives the debtor an affirmative defense to a suit on a prepetition claim. The effect of a discharge, however, is much broader. Section 524 prevents a creditor from making any efforts to collect payment from the debtor once the petition is filed. How the discharge affects future interactions between the debtor and the creditor, however, remains unclear.

A debtor may need to deal with the creditor after bankruptcy. For example, a debtor might seek a transcript from a school that had made loans to the debtor that were discharged in bankruptcy. The school and the debtor battle over whether the school has the right to refuse to give the debtor the transcript. The school has no duty to engage in further dealings with the debtor, but it cannot withhold the transcript

[16] Tex. Stat. Ann. §41.001.

solely because the debtor has not paid a debt that has been discharged.[17]

The discharge applies only to the debtor. Section 524(e) provides that the discharge does not relieve any third party from an obligation on the debt. A typical example is a guarantor whom the creditor can sue directly.[18] Complications arise, however, when the debtor has an insurance policy and the victim of an accident needs to sue the debtor to recover under the policy. The question is whether §524 bars an action against the debtor when the victim seeks to recover only from the insurance company. Most courts have held that §524 does not prevent victims from recovering in such cases. These courts reason that because the debtor is not personally liable, such actions against a debtor do not interfere with the fresh start.[19]

Section 525 limits the ability of two parties, the government and the debtor's employer, to discriminate against those who have filed bankruptcy petitions, even though they may never have been creditors of the debtor. A state's discrimination against a debtor may take the following form. Before filing for bankruptcy, a debtor injures someone in a car accident and fails to pay the judgment that resulted from the subsequent tort suit. The state suspends the debtor's driver's license, and the debtor files for bankruptcy. The tort obligation is discharged, but the state refuses to reinstate the debtor's driver's license. In *Perez v. Campbell*, the Supreme Court confronted a case such as this in which, under the relevant statute, the state would not reinstate the debtor's driver's license until the judgment was satisfied, notwithstanding the discharge.[20] The Supreme Court held that a state statute designed to ensure that tort judgments were paid was inconsistent with bankruptcy's fresh start policy.

The principle of *Perez* has been codified in §525, which prohibits "governmental units" from denying licenses or otherwise discriminating against someone solely because that person is in bankruptcy or has not paid a debt discharged in bankruptcy. One should not extend *Perez* too far, however. For example, the doctrine of *Perez* should not

---

[17] In re Kuehn, 563 F.3d 289 (7th Cir. 2009).

[18] See Terwilliger v. Terwilliger, 206 F.3d 240 (2d Cir. 2000).

[19] See, e.g., Houston v. Edgeworth, 993 F.2d 51 (5th Cir. 1993). These cases arise only when the victim is entitled to the proceeds of the insurance policy (and not the bankruptcy estate).

[20] 402 U.S. 637 (1971).

apply if, under the relevant statute, the state would not reinstate the driver's license until the debtor offered proof of financial responsibility regardless of whether the debtor had paid the tort obligation.[21] This requirement, unlike the one in *Perez*, does not have the effect of inducing the debtor to pay an obligation that has already been discharged.

The reach of *Perez* may be limited for another reason as well. Conditioning a debtor's right to a driver's license on repayment of a debt is ultimately no different from giving a creditor a lien on some other valuable asset of the debtor. We know from the doctrine of *Long v. Bullard* that such liens survive bankruptcy so long as they do not attach to future earnings. In other words, one cannot extend the reach of *Perez* without cutting back on the reach of *Long v. Bullard*.

Although the Bankruptcy Code defines claims broadly and a discharge affects even those who are not creditors, there are limits on the scope of the discharge. A debtor may be eligible for a discharge under §727 but still have some debts that are not dischargeable. Section 523(a) contains a list of nondischargeable debts. Debtors who need to borrow to finance their educations often have no other assets. The only asset they can give to lenders is an interest in their future earnings. They can do this, however, only if such debts are not dischargeable. Section 523(a)(8) provides for this result. Such provisions, of course, do much to explain why means testing is likely to affect only a small number of debtors. Many other rules operate to make bankruptcy unattractive to those who are in fact able to repay their creditors.

Creditors need a chance to participate in the bankruptcy proceeding. For this reason, a debtor does not receive a discharge of an ordinary claim unless the debtor includes the debt on the schedules that must be filed with the court. The debtor must also comply with procedures that ensure that each creditor is notified of the bankruptcy and has the chance to make a timely filing of a proof of claim. §523(a)(3). If a creditor does not know about the bankruptcy and has no chance to share in the assets, it is able to pursue the debtor after bankruptcy. In many cases, however, the debtor has no nonexempt assets; filing a claim is a pointless exercise, and the trustee advises the creditors not to bother, telling them that they will be notified if assets are later found. In such cases, an omitted creditor has not lost any right. As no other creditor was ever given a deadline, there was never a point at which

---

[21] See Duffey v. Dollison, 734 F.2d 265 (6th Cir. 1984).

any filing it might have made would have been untimely. Hence, one can argue that such a debt is discharged along with the others.[22]

The other nondischargeable debts in §523 fall into one of two categories (or sometimes a mixture of both). Either the debt arose out of bad conduct, such as a deliberate tort, or the debt in question is thought to be particularly important. Debts of the latter kind include child support, alimony, and many tax obligations. Those who run their own businesses often have substantial nondischargeable debt because they failed to pay withholding taxes in the waning days of the business. The money that should have gone to the tax collector is used to pay suppliers and workers enough to keep the operation open a few weeks longer. The responsible manager of the business is personally obliged to pay these taxes, regardless of whether the business is a sole proprietorship or a corporation. These tax obligations (depending on when the tax is assessed) are typically not dischargeable. For this reason, as well as many others, taking stock of the debtor's tax position and issuing the appropriate warnings are an essential part of advising a debtor who is in financial trouble.

Section 523(a)'s "bad act" exceptions are aimed in part at curtailing abuse of the bankruptcy system. Section 523(a)(2) states that debts incurred through false pretenses or false financial statements are not dischargeable; §523(a)(2)(c) accordingly limits a debtor's ability to borrow and spend when bankruptcy is imminent and the debtor's good faith is therefore suspect. The *fresh cash doctrine* has been a recurring issue in litigation under §523(a)(2). Suppose a debtor has a loan from a bank. The debtor encounters financial difficulties and returns to the bank for an additional loan, which the debtor obtains through false statements. The bank will argue that if the second loan is consolidated with the first, there is only a single debt and that §523(a)(2) makes the entire loan nondischargeable. Courts are divided on whether the whole loan is nondischargeable or only the fresh cash portion, the part that was obtained with the false statement. Section 523(a)(4) deprives the debtor of the fruits of wrongdoing committed while acting in a fiduciary capacity. The difficulty here is deciding what is and is not done in a fiduciary capacity. One unsettled issue is whether selling collateral and spending the proceeds should trigger this section when

---

[22] See, e.g., Judd v. Wolfe, 78 F.3d 110 (3d Cir. 1996). Not all courts agree, however. See, e.g., Colonial Surety Co. v. Weizman, 564 F.3d 526 (1st Cir. 2009).

state law requires that the debtor hold the proceeds in trust for the creditor. Here, as elsewhere, the deciding factor should not be what state law calls a fiduciary duty but rather what bears the attributes of a fiduciary duty, such as the obligation to maintain separate accounts. Other "bad act" exceptions focus on debts that show particularly reprehensible conduct. Debtors who commit willful and malicious torts, including willful conversions of property, cannot discharge them in Chapter 7.

The list of nondischargeable debts appears to be growing over time. When Congress is presented with the narrow question whether a particular kind of obligation should be nondischargeable, it seems that it should be. It should be remembered, however, that excepting some obligations from discharge, but not others, has the effect of privileging some creditors over others, even though their nonbankruptcy rights may be the same. It is unwise to focus on one type of obligation in isolation. For example, obligations arising from drunken driving are explicitly excepted from discharge while those arising from many other tortious acts are not. Chapter 13, as originally acted, provided a super-discharge that made only a few debts nondischargeable. The same dynamic, however, has played out there, and the two lists now increasingly resemble each other.

A debtor may find that the discharge of a particular debt is not desirable. For example, if a debt is discharged, the creditor may try to collect the debt from a friend or a relative who acted as a guarantor of the initial obligation. Alternatively, the debtor may want to keep a car in which an automobile dealer has a security interest. The discharge will free the debtor from the obligation to pay the dealer, but, under *Long v. Bullard*, the discharge will not affect the dealer's right to repossess the car after the debtor's default as soon as the bankruptcy is over. The creditor may be willing to forgo calling the guarantee or to let the debtor keep the car only if the debtor *reaffirms* the debt. A debtor is always free to repay a debt that has been discharged in bankruptcy. The question of reaffirmation concerns whether debtors can legally bind themselves to repay a debt once it has been discharged.

The rules governing reaffirmations, codified in §524(c), (d), and (k), set forth a two-step inquiry. First, the reaffirmation must be effective under nonbankruptcy law. Second, even if it is, the reaffirmation must meet certain requirements. A reaffirmation, to be effective, must be made before the debtor has formally been granted a discharge. In addition, the reaffirmation must come, in the case of an individual, after the debtor has appeared before the bankruptcy court for a discharge hearing. At this time, the debtor is told that no discharged debt need be reaffirmed. In addition, the consequences of reaffirmation will be set out. This procedure is the bankruptcy equivalent of a *Miranda* warning.

If the debtor is represented by an attorney, the attorney must file an affidavit stating that the reaffirmation agreement is voluntary and does not impose undue hardship on the debtor. In the absence of an attorney, the court must conclude that the agreement will not impose undue hardship on the debtor and is in the debtor's best interest. Courts are generally reluctant to find reaffirmation in the debtor's best interest when the debtor wants to reaffirm in order to keep driving a luxury car. They are similarly reluctant when a debtor wishes to reaffirm in order to keep a creditor from calling on a guarantee that a relative or friend executed in the debtor's favor. Even if all these requirements have been satisfied, the debtor still gets a 60-day cooling-off period, during which the debtor is free to rescind the reaffirmation.

Wage-Earner Plans under Chapter 13

Chapter 7 forces individuals to give up existing assets but allows them to keep future earnings. Chapter 13 reverses things. In a Chapter 13 case, the debtor keeps all assets except a portion of future wages. The portion of the wages that the debtor does not keep is turned over to the trustee for distribution to the prepetition creditors. The main advantages of Chapter 13 are that one can keep existing assets and that one may be able to discharge a greater number of debts.

Over the past decade, Chapter 13 has proved increasingly important for individual debtors in financial trouble, especially debtors who run small businesses. Each year, hundreds of thousands of Chapter 13 petitions are filed and billions of dollars are paid out under Chapter 13 plans. Debtors who file Chapter 13 petitions often face problems quite different from those who file under Chapter 7. Debtors who file under Chapter 13 sometimes do so not only because they need to sort out their obligations to general creditors but also because they have fallen behind in payments to the bank that holds a mortgage on their home. Chapter 13 allows debtors to take advantage of the automatic stay without at the same time giving up nonexempt assets. The decision to use Chapter 13 rather than Chapter 7 also turns on the practices in the different bankruptcy courts. There is enormous variation across districts in how often Chapter 13 is used and how it is implemented.

In contrast to Chapter 7, not every individual debtor is eligible for Chapter 13. Under §109, those whose debts exceed set amounts—a little less than $400,000 and three times that amount for unsecured and secured debt, respectively—may not file for Chapter 13 relief. Chapter 13 is designed for working individual debtors or couples with limited financial affairs, typically consumers or proprietors of small businesses. Individuals with more at stake cannot use it.

As in Chapter 7, a trustee is appointed in every Chapter 13 case. See §1302. The debtor herself, however, is charged with moving the process forward. Under §1321, she must file a plan with the court that sets out the way in which her future income will be used to pay creditors. The plan, which may modify or reduce the debtor's obligations, see §1322(b), must oblige the debtor to pay her creditors from some or all of her future income. Under §1322(a)(1) and (d), plan payments are limited to five years. Payments are generally limited to three years for those who make less than the median income (measured in the same way as in means testing), but this period may be extended to five years on a showing of cause.

The plan must also satisfy a series of important payment conditions. First, the plan must provide for the full satisfaction, in deferred cash payments, of all allowed claims (and administrative expenses) entitled to priority under §507 unless the holder of such a priority claim (or expense) agrees to some other treatment. See §1322. Second, the plan must either consume all of a debtor's disposable income for five years or provide for the satisfaction of all allowed unsecured claims with property (including promises) of a value, as of the effective date of the plan, at least equal to the amount that the creditors would receive from a Chapter 7 liquidation on that date. See §1325(a)(4). In theory, these provisions together ensure that creditors are no worse off than they would be if the debtor filed under Chapter 7, while priority claims may receive even more.

The requirements imposed on Chapter 13 plans protect unsecured creditors in one more way. Under §1325(b)(1), the trustee (or a creditor who is not being paid in full) may insist that the plan require the debtor to pay out all projected disposable income for three years in the case of debtors who make less than the median and five years for those who make more. "Disposable income" is measured differently depending on whether the debtor made more or less than the median income in the period before bankruptcy.

If the debtor made less than the median, disposable income is defined as income not "reasonably necessary to be expended for the maintenance or support of the debtor or a dependent of the debtor." §1325(b)(2). Creditors will not necessarily find it in their interest to insist on such plans. Under §1307 the debtor may convert the case to Chapter 7 or dismiss the case altogether at any time. This power prevents creditors from demanding the dedication of all disposable income when the debtor makes less than the median. Exceptions can arise, however. The debtor may have a debt that is dischargeable in Chapter 13 but not in Chapter 7. Alternatively, a debtor may have already tried to use Chapter 7 but had his case dismissed under §707(b). The "reasonably necessary" standard of §1325(b)(2) is used to determine whether a plan devotes the debtor's entire disposable income to the plan. Like any standard, it lacks clear contours. There is extensive case law, but it developed when the test applied to all debtors, not merely those who made less than the applicable median.

For debtors who made more than the median, payment obligations under Chapter 13 are calculated in a way that parallels the means test in §707(b). The means test, however, looks at income over the six months before the filing of the bankruptcy petition to assess eligibility for Chapter 7's discharge. That amount may be more or less than the money the debtor makes going forward. Section 1325(b)(1) refers to the debtor's "projected disposable income" rather than simply the debtor's "disposable income." The bankruptcy judge may account for changes in income or expenses that are known or virtually certain at the time of confirmation.[23]

One more important requirement imposed in Chapter 13 plans protects holders of secured claims. Within a month of filing the Chapter 13 petition, unless the court orders otherwise, the debtor must commence payments to personal property lessors and secured creditors. §1326(a). If the plan allows the debtor to retain property securing a claim, the plan must provide for full payment of the secured claim unless the creditor consents to less. Recall, however, that under §506(a) claims are bifurcated. A creditor's *secured* claim is limited to the value of the collateral. The balance is the creditor's unsecured claim. Payment on the secured claim may occur over time, if paid with interest. The debtor's obligation under the plan must be secured by a lien on the original collateral. Moreover, the debtor must make equal monthly payments under the plan sufficient to provide adequate protection to the secured creditor. §1325(a)(5).

---

[23] Hamilton v. Lanning, 560 U.S. 505, 524 (2010).

If a plan meets these requirements and otherwise complies with the provisions of Chapter 13—such as the requirements of a plan's good faith, see §1325(a)(3), and feasibility, see §1325(a)(6)—the court must confirm the plan. Keep in mind, however, that even after confirmation, the bankruptcy case still remains open. The debtor's creditors remain stayed from collection by §362 (and an individual co-liable with the debtor generally is protected by §1301). The debtor's postpetition acquisitions and earnings become property of the estate under §1306.

Debtors who successfully complete performance under a Chapter 13 plan hold their property "free and clear of any claim or interest of any creditor provided for under the plan." §1327(c). The debtor receives a discharge under §1328(a) when payments under the plan are complete.

After a Chapter 13 discharge, one can use Chapter 7 or Chapter 11 within six years if the Chapter 13 discharge was granted on at least a 70-percent payout plan. §727(a)(9). Moreover, a discharge granted under §1328(a) is not subject to all the exceptions to discharge that are in Chapter 7. As Congress continues to expand the number of nondischargeable debts in Chapter 13, however, this difference between the two chapters is becoming less important over time.

Debtors who cannot meet payments under the plan may seek to modify the plan under §1329 or request a discharge if creditors have already received as much as they would have received under Chapter 7. The court might grant such a discharge under §1328(b) only if the plan cannot be modified practically and if the debtors failed for reasons beyond their control. Even in such a case, the discharge extends only to debts that could have been discharged in Chapter 7. That is, debtors cannot discharge any debt listed in §523(a). See §1328(c).

A Chapter 13 plan may propose the debtor's retention of collateral for a secured claim and generally "may modify the rights of holders of secured claims." §1322(b). But Chapter 13 protects holders of secured claims from modifications that leave them worse off. The most basic protection is found in §1325(a)(5), which provides that the plan must distribute to the holder of the secured claim property that has a value, as of the effective date of the plan, at least equal to the amount of the claim. Moreover, under the same provision, if the debtor is to retain the collateral, the plan must grant the holder of the secured claim a continuing lien on the collateral until the new obligation is fully paid. Put plainly, a debtor cannot retain collateral unless the plan proposes to pay an amount equal to the value of the collateral, though not necessarily at once. The requirement of a continuing lien supports this full-payment obligation in the event the debtor fails to complete payments under the plan.

Home mortgages often figure centrally in Chapter 13 cases. A debtor who has fallen behind on his mortgage payments is one of those most likely to file under Chapter 13. When a debtor encounters hard times, it may be that outside of bankruptcy she can prevent foreclosure and loss of her home only by paying off a bank's entire loan in full or by reaching a negotiated settlement with the bank. Particularly when the home has fallen in value, the debtor may find the bank uncooperative. The debtor might file for bankruptcy under Chapter 7, but she will find little relief there, as liquidation of the estate will throw the house back to the bank and state law. Chapter 13 offers the debtor breathing room and a last chance to sort things out.

Filing a Chapter 13 petition merely to take advantage of the automatic stay, however, can be found abusive if it is done without any attempt to put in place a plan to restructure debts.[24] One of the most common abuses of Chapter 13 is the serial filing, in which debtors repeatedly file just on the eve of foreclosure, and courts have devised a number of tools to deter the most flagrant forms of misbehavior.[25] Moreover, §1328(f) limits the availability of a discharge in Chapter 13 if it comes too quickly on the heels of a discharge obtained previously.[26]

In addition, Chapter 13 contains a number of special provisions that extend more protection to home mortgage lenders than to other secured creditors. The primary limitation on a debtor's right to affect a home mortgage is the general prohibition on modification of the mortgage. See §1322(b)(2). For other kinds of mortgages, a plan will bifurcate an ordinary undersecured claim under §506(a) into a secured and unsecured claim, then treat each part separately. The plan will provide the holder with two new loan obligations, one on account of the secured claim and one on account of the deficiency. As an unsecured claim, the deficiency may well be paid only a few cents on the dollar. The terms of these loans can differ from each other and from

[24] See In re Felberman, 196 Bankr. 678, 681 (Bankr. S.D.N.Y. 1995).

[25] See Casse v. Key Bank National Association, 198 F.3d 327 (2d Cir. 1999).

[26] The debtor may still seek relief under Chapter 13, even if the discharge is not available, as long as the debtor acts in good faith and can propose a confirmable plan. See Branigan v. Bateman, 515 F.3d 272 (4th Cir. 2008).

those of the original loan. These new obligations replace the old claim, which may be discharged even if the terms of the original loan are never fully satisfied.

Under §1322(b)(2), however, the debtor's ability to modify the rights of holders of secured claims does not extend to rights associated with "a claim secured only by a security interest in real property that is the debtor's principal residence." Section 1322(b)(2) prevents a plan from altering *any* of the terms of the original loan, even if they are not strictly speaking part of the secured claim. An example of such a term would be one that gives the creditor an action against the debtor for the difference between the value of the collateral and the amount of the debt.[27]

Chapter 13 does, however, provide some relief to debtors for their home mortgages. Under §1322(b)(5), a Chapter 13 debtor may cure some defaults on a long-term home mortgage. The cure must occur within a reasonable time and must reinstate the mortgage on its original terms. The exception does not apply if the last mortgage payment becomes due before the final payment under the Chapter 13 plan. In short, Chapter 13 gives debtors a way to keep their homes after a default, even a default that would give the lender a right to foreclose under state law. But during the Chapter 13 plan period and afterward, debtors must continue to pay off the mortgage in full, even if the value of the home has fallen far below the outstanding amount of the debt. The ability to cure only returns debtors to the situation they were in before they defaulted. Unless there has been a change in their circumstances, debtors can quickly find themselves unable to meet these same obligations once again.

When creditors pursue their nonbankruptcy remedies, sooner or later they must have gone so far in the foreclosure process that a debtor can no longer file for bankruptcy and cure outstanding defaults. Section 1322(c)(1) provides that a debtor loses the right to cure defaults once the residence is sold at a foreclosure sale that is conducted in accordance with applicable nonbankruptcy law. Home mortgages can run for 20 years or longer. In most cases, the term of the mortgage is longer than the term of the plan and the rule of modification or cure just described will apply. For the case in which the remaining term of the home mortgage is less than the length of the Chapter 13 plan, §1322(c)(2) provides that "the plan may provide for the payment of

---

[27] Nobelman v. American Savings Bank, 508 U.S. 324, 329 (1993).

the claim as modified pursuant to §1325(a)(5)," notwithstanding the antimodification clause. Chapter 13 thus gives the debtor some maneuvering room with home mortgages that are near the end of their term.

Chapter 13 is beset with a number of interpretative difficulties, many of which arise from the various amendments that have been made to it over time. One that has given rise to numerous disputes is the "hanging paragraph" appended to §1325(a). It declares that "§506 shall not apply" to a claim if the creditor holds a purchase money security interest in a motor vehicle purchased within 910 days of the petition. Presumably, the language was designed to prevent a debtor from stripping down the lien on a recently purchased car and paying the creditor less than the amount of the loan, but the language raises such questions as whether a creditor who repossesses the car is entitled to a deficiency judgment. If §506 does not operate, nothing in the Bankruptcy Code bifurcates the claim into a secured and an unsecured claim. Arguably, without §506, there is no unsecured claim on which to base a deficiency judgment.[28] Many bankruptcy courts adopted this view, but the circuit courts to consider this argument to date have rejected it.[29]

The complexity of Chapter 13 should not obscure two striking features of the way it works in fact. First, there are widespread differences in Chapter 13 practice. From one circuit to the next, from one state to the next, the role Chapter 13 plays varies dramatically. Fewer than one bankruptcy case in six is a Chapter 13 in the Eastern District of Kentucky, while two out of every three is a Chapter 13 in the Western District of Tennessee. Second, Chapter 13 often falls far short of its ambitions. By some accounts, only one plan in three succeeds.

In addition to Chapter 13, a special chapter of the Bankruptcy Code protects small farmers and fishermen. Chapter 12 balances two competing concerns. First, it tries to give family farmers the ability to keep their farms and fishermen their boats even when they owe a secured creditor more than their assets are worth. Second, it tries to ensure that the property interests of the secured creditors are respected and that these creditors receive the value of their secured claim. These two goals might seem incompatible. If a farm is worth less than what

---

[28] See, e.g., In re Payne, 347 Bankr. 278 (Bankr. S.D. Ohio 2006).

[29] See, e.g., DaimlerChrysler Financial Services Americas, LLC v. Miller, 570 F.3d 633 (5th Cir. 2009).

the secured creditor is owed, then giving the secured creditor less than the entire farm seems undercompensatory. The residual interest that the farmer holds has *some* value. To the extent that the interest the farmer keeps has value, the secured creditor would seem to receive less than the full amount of its secured claim. Chapter 12, however, is premised on the notion that a reorganization plan that leaves a farm 100 percent leveraged is permissible.

Farmers have enjoyed special bankruptcy protection throughout the nation's history. The politics of the 1841 bankruptcy statute were tied to the farm crisis that existed at the time. Similarly, the Frazier–Lemke Act protected farmers in the 1930s. A characteristic of much farm relief legislation has been that it remains in effect for only a finite number of years and then must be reenacted. For many years, Chapter 12 had only limited life, but Congress regularly renewed it. In 2005, it was made a permanent part of the Bankruptcy Code. At the same time its protections were extended to fishermen.

CHAPTER THREE

Corporate Reorganizations
and the Absolute Priority Rule

Introduction

We saw in chapter 2 that the animating principle of bankruptcy law for individual debtors is the fresh start, the right to discharge past debts and free future income and other exempt property from the claims of creditors. In this chapter, we see that a different principle—the absolute priority rule—animates the law of corporate reorganizations. The absolute priority rule is so central to Chapter 11 and the negotiations surrounding it that we shall spend the bulk of this chapter trying to understand its origins as well as its shape today.

A corporation in Chapter 11, like an individual in Chapter 7, receives a discharge at the end of the bankruptcy proceeding, but the discharge has radically different consequences in the two cases. In the case of the individual debtor, the discharge works in conjunction with other parts of the Bankruptcy Code to ensure a fresh start. Discharging old debt does not itself keep creditors from reaching the debtor's future income. What matters in the case of an individual is not simply that debts are discharged under §727, but also that future earnings do not become property of the estate under §541. In contrast, a corporation's future earnings *do* become property of the estate. For this reason, the discharge itself does not put future income beyond the reach of those who held rights against it before the petition was filed. The discharge of corporate debt provided for in §1141 must serve a purpose altogether different from the discharge of individual debt in §727.

A limited liability corporation is not a flesh-and-blood individual, but rather a juridical being that owns assets against which many individuals have rights. We must focus on shareholders and creditors and others and ask what happens to their rights in the wake of the discharge. In the case of an individual in Chapter 7, we have to look at the exclusion of an individual debtor's future income provided by §541 to understand the effect of §727's discharge. Similarly, in the case of a corporation in Chapter 11, we have to look to the other parts of the

Code that allocate rights to the corporation's future earnings to understand the effect of §1141's discharge. Section 1141 does not tell us how the earnings of the reorganized business are split among the old creditors and shareholders. Instead, it is the absolute priority rule, as codified in §1129 and other parts of Chapter 11, that determines how those who held rights against the old corporation will enjoy rights in the reorganized corporation.

Before we look at the absolute priority rule, it is important to understand the purpose of Chapter 11 for corporate debtors. In the case of the individual debtor, Chapter 7 is meant to provide a substantive right: it allows an individual to enjoy a new life free of the burdens of unmanageable debt. A corporation is different. We may care about the workers or the shareholders or the creditors, but the corporation itself is merely a legal fiction. It is not a sentient being, and there is no virtue in preserving a corporate charter for its own sake.

Moreover, Chapter 11 cannot remedy the problems of an unsound business venture. Suppose an entrepreneur decides to open a new restaurant in a strip mall in southern California. The restaurant specializes in Chicago dim sum. Customers eat in sequence small plates of food that provide a sample of every ethnic neighborhood in that city. The typical meal begins with a miniature bratwurst. Next is a small deep-dish pizza, followed by mu shu pork, then a small portion of barbeque ribs, and finally a piece of Baklava from Greektown for dessert. As it happens, aging, calorie-conscious baby-boomers in California have little interest either in going to this strip mall or in sampling this kind of cuisine. Chapter 11 can do nothing to make this restaurant or Chicago dim sum a success. It does not matter whether the restaurant has no creditors or dozens of them. No one wants to dine at this restaurant, and bankruptcy law can do nothing to change this. The assets of the restaurant are best put to another use.

Some businesses that cannot pay their debts may nevertheless be enterprises that are worth keeping intact. The archetypal case is a railroad. (As we shall see shortly, reorganizations of railroads in the late nineteenth century were the progenitors of modern Chapter 11.) The assets of a railroad—rights-of-way over narrow strips of land, hundreds or thousands of miles of iron rails, millions of wooden ties, and assorted bridges across the country—have relatively little scrap value. For this reason, a railroad may be worth keeping intact even if it does not carry enough traffic to pay back its construction costs. Building the railroad may have been a mistake, but, once built, the best use of the assets may still be as a railroad. Unlike a restaurant in a bad location that serves bad food, the railroad's assets may have no better use. Nevertheless, everyone has to confront the fact that the railroad cannot pay off its creditors. There needs to be a forum in which the rights of creditors and shareholders are sorted out.

If creditors of the railroad had the right to invoke the rules of various states governing debt collection, any given creditor would have a chance of being paid in full. It could grab the nearest assets of the railroad and sell them for scrap. But a remedy premised on each creditor's pursuit of its own interests could lead to the dismemberment of the railroad. The creditors are better off if the railroad is kept in one piece. They need to enforce their claims against the railroad in a way that preserves the railroad's value as a going concern. The struggle to sort out competing claims to the assets should not keep the assets from being put to their best use.

Ensuring assets are put to their best use requires recognizing that some parties are not going to be paid in full, and a coherent bankruptcy law has to identify them. The basic distributional rule of Chapter 11—the one as central to it as the fresh start policy is to individuals—that emerged was the absolute priority rule. The substantive idea behind the absolute priority rule can be put simply: the filing of the bankruptcy petition brings about a day of reckoning. The assets are assembled and the liabilities are tallied. Senior creditors are paid before junior creditors, and creditors are paid before shareholders. The rhetoric of the fresh start often creeps into discussions of Chapter 11, but one should not be misled by the notion of "rehabilitating" a corporate debtor.

Our bankruptcy law is squarely focused on vindicating legal rights established outside of bankruptcy. Conflating the problem of how to vindicate the bargain among investors in different parts of the capital structure with the idea of the fresh start for flesh-and-blood individuals is a major conceptual mistake that invariably leads to muddled thinking. Ensuring that a viable business continues is a tough task, and the procedures needed to bring it about are correspondingly complicated. The easiest way to understand the ones we have chosen is to understand their origins. Hence, we look first to history.

Equity Receiverships and the Origins of Chapter 11

We can trace the roots of Chapter 11 back to the problems attending the rise of the great railroads in the late nineteenth century. These were the first giant corporations. They connected all parts of the United States and revolutionized the way people lived. Before the railroads, milk would spoil long before it reached the urban marketplace. Ranchers and farmers had only a small market for their meat and produce. The railroad created a national marketplace. The dinner table of New Yorkers included for the first time meat from cattle raised in Kansas and bread from grain grown in Missouri.

Railroads, however, required capital on an unprecedented scale. Laying a single mile of track cost $20,000 or more—sometimes much more. Even by 1860, private investment in railroads exceeded $1 billion. Investment bankers such as J. P. Morgan, August Belmont, and Kidder Peabody had to turn to large commercial centers of Europe for the capital to finance the transcontinental railroads that were to be built over the next three decades. These investment bankers sat on the boards of the various railroads and represented the interests of their European investors.[1] Because they counted on repeated dealings with these investors, they had the incentive to represent them well.

The period between 1865 and 1890 was one of enormous growth for railroads. The period also saw the consolidation of different lines in haphazard and unpredictable ways. More than 75,000 miles of track were laid down in the 1880s alone. This was a time of both increasing competition and increasing government regulation. Competition among the different lines intensified; cartels came into existence and then fell apart. At the same time, the early 1890s brought on one of the United States's worst economic downturns. All these factors created an industry that by the mid-1890s was insolvent. Most of the railroads that had been built could not meet their fixed obligations. More than half the railroads in the United States went through reorganization during this period, some more than once.[2]

The typical railroad needing reorganization had few general creditors. There were different classes of bonds, each widely held by diverse investors, many of whom were in Europe. One bond was secured by track between points A and B, another by track between B and C, a third between C and D, and so on. Points B through Y were in the middle of nowhere, and the terminals at points A and Z connected to solvent railroads owned by the shareholders. The collateral of individual creditors added value to the ongoing railroad. This value, however,

---

[1] See Alfred D. Chandler Jr., The Visible Hand: The Managerial Revolution in American Business 146 (1977).

[2] For a history of railroad reorganizations of the 1890s, see Stuart Daggett, Railroad Reorganization (1908).

could not be realized by foreclosing on the collateral; only through the active participation of all parties could the value of the constituent parts be maximized.

Bringing about a successful reorganization was hard. The value of the railroad had to be estimated against a background of rapid technological and regulatory change. The claim of the many different kinds of bondholders turned on how much their collateral contributed to the earnings of the railroad as a whole. Moreover, many of the investors lived abroad and could not actively participate in the reorganization. They had to rely on their investment bankers and their lawyers to represent them. Although Congress had the power to enact federal bankruptcy law, none was in place during this period. Faced with dispersed interests with uncertain value and no statutory guidance, the lawyers used the equity receivership to reorganize the railroads.

Because the railroads were the first experiments in large aggregations of capital from diverse investors, many of the terms of the investment contracts were left blank or imported mechanically from real estate transactions. The law of equity receiverships had to supply the missing terms, and these had to respond to the distinct problems that arose when the railroad needed a new capital structure. What emerged in the end were the basic features of Chapter 11.

Consider a railroad that owes $100 million to several dozen different kinds of bondholders, each of whom has a security interest in different assets of the railroad. In the aggregate, these bonds cover all the hard assets of the railroad. The railroad also owes a diverse group of general creditors $1 million. The railroad cannot meet payments on the $101 million debt. The bondholders realize that the time has come to restructure the railroad. They call on their lawyers and their investment bankers. The lawyers persuade a general creditor to ask a federal court to appoint a receiver for the railroad. The receiver the court appoints is often the group of manager-shareholders that has been running the railroad. In the meantime, lawyers and the investment bankers form committees, each representing the interests of a different group of shareholders or creditors.

Each bondholders committee then tries to persuade those holding its bonds to deposit them with it and give it the power to assert all the rights of the bondholders in the reorganization. Let us assume that, in our case, 90 percent of the bondholders give their bonds to their respective committees. Similarly, another committee holds 90 percent of the stock. The various committees then meet and create a new committee, the reorganization committee, on which members of each of the other committees sit and that is empowered to act on behalf of the other committees. The reorganization committee now controls 90 percent of all outstanding securities. It then proceeds to form a plan of reorganization.

Under the plan, each participant in the reorganization who holds a $100 bond in some asset of the railroad will give it up in exchange for a $50 bond secured by all the assets of the railroad. The participating shareholders are given the option to acquire equity of the reorganized railroad in exchange for their shares in the old railroad and $1 million in new cash. Through their representatives on the reorganization committee, all the participating creditors and shareholders consent to this plan.

The reorganization committee then borrows $10 million from a bank on a short-term basis. At this point, the receiver conducts a foreclosure sale in which the assets of the railroad are sold to the highest bidder. At the sale, the reorganization committee is the only bidder. It bids $10 million for the entire railroad and takes over the assets of the railroad after it pays the receiver. The receiver takes the $10 million and distributes it to the bondholders. (Nothing goes to the general creditors, because the sale price is not enough to pay the bondholders in full.) Because the reorganization committee itself owns 90 percent of the bonds, the receiver gives back to the reorganization committee $9 million of the $10 million the committee paid to buy the railroad. The receiver pays the other $1 million to the nonparticipating bondholders who did not give their bonds to their committees.

The old corporation is now a hollow shell and the old shareholders dissolve it under state law. Because the legal entity that was the railroad now no longer exists, all claims against it are worthless. The stockholders who did not turn over their rights to the relevant committee are out of luck, as are the general creditors who did not have any chance to participate at all. At this point, the reorganization committee has the assets of the railroad and the $9 million it received from the receiver. The committee now forms a new corporation and transfers all the assets of the railroad to it. The new corporation creates $45 million in bonds and gives them to the old participating bondholders as promised in the reorganization plan. All the stock in the new railroad is given to the old shareholders when they come up with the $1 million in cash they promised in the reorganization plan. With this $1 million and the $9 million the receiver gave it, the committee repays the $10 million bank loan. The reorganization committee now goes out of existence.

If we focus entirely on legal forms, we see a new corporation with a new set of ownership claims against it. In substance, however, the story is quite different. If one collapses the various steps in this elaborate dance, most of the bondholders and shareholders have simply exchanged their old claims against the railroad for new ones that take better account of the condition in which the railroad finds itself. We have exactly the same railroad with the same managers and the same investors, but the ownership rights of the investors have been adjusted so that they are in line with the revenue that the railroad actually earns.

Under Chapter 11 of the Bankruptcy Code, we would say that the railroad's old obligations to its creditors have been discharged. As we noted at the start of this discussion, however, "discharge" in this context means something quite different from what it does in the case of the individual who is given a fresh start. The discharge is only one part of the mechanism that allows the business to acquire a new capital structure.

The debates over the railroad reorganization therefore revolved not around the meaning of a fresh start for corporations but around other issues. First, there was the question of the rights of those who did not participate in the reorganization. In our example, these included 10 percent of the bondholders and the diverse general creditors. The bondholders who did not participate argued that they were given only 10 cents on the dollar, while those who did participate were given 50 cents on the dollar. To the response that they could have participated and enjoyed 50 cents on the dollar if they had wanted, these bondholders would argue that the reorganization forced them to choose between the lesser of two evils. Either their claims would be cashed out at 10 cents on the dollar at a fictitious foreclosure sale or they would have to submit to whatever terms the reorganization committee dictated. None of the individual bondholders had enough of an investment in the railroad to go through the effort necessary to keep the reorganization committee from doing whatever it pleased. As a result, insiders remained in control of the process and ended up in control of the railroad.

The equity receivership thus had to navigate between two dangers: that of insiders taking advantage of the scattered bondholders and that of a few dissident bondholders free riding on the efforts of others to recapitalize the railroad. Under the solution that ultimately emerged in the equity receivership, the judge insisted on an *upset price*, a minimum price that the reorganization committee would have to bid at the foreclosure sale to acquire the assets of the railroad. By ensuring that the upset price was sufficiently high, the minority bondholders would be given an amount commensurate with the value of their nonbankruptcy rights.[3] The defect of this approach in practice was that judges tended to keep the upset price low. They feared that a high upset price would undermine the successful reorganization because it would require the reorganization committee to come up with more cash than it could raise.

The 1978 Bankruptcy Code replaced this way of protecting dissenters in a class of creditors. Congress folded into the corporate reorganization a procedure that had been used in plans under the 1898 Bankruptcy Act. Under the 1898 Act, the debtor would meet with creditors, fill out schedules of assets and liabilities, and subject itself to examination. At this point, the debtor would propose a plan, or *composition*, in which the creditors' claims were scaled back. If the plan was accepted by a majority of the creditors and if the majority held more than half of the outstanding debt, the court would approve it if, among other requirements, the plan was in the best interests of the creditors.[4] Courts interpreted "best interests" to mean that those creditors who did not vote in favor of the plan had to receive as much as they would receive in an orderly liquidation of the business.[5] This method of protecting dissenters in a class of creditors, codified in §1129(a)(7), replaced the use of an upset price in the equity receivership (and its statutory successor in old Chapter X).

More important in the dynamics of modern Chapter 11 are the procedures that emerged in response to the complaints from the general creditors who had no chance to participate in the reorganization at all. It might seem that the general creditors have nothing to complain about. The railroad is worth less than $100 million, the amount the bondholders were owed. Even if the railroad's assets were sold for cash at their fair market value, the general creditors would receive nothing. Given the sorry condition of the business, they are not entitled to anything. This risk is one they should have taken into account when they extended credit to the railroad.

---

[3] See First National Bank of Cincinnati v. Flershem, 290 U.S. 504 (1934).

[4] Act of July 1, 1898, ch. 541, §12b, 30 Stat. 541, 549.

[5] See Fleischmann & Devine Inc. v. Saul Wolfson Dry Goods Co., 299 F. 15 (5th Cir. 1924).

Nevertheless, we must at least have in place procedures that ensure that the railroad is indeed worth less than $100 million. We need to be sure that the senior creditors and the shareholders have not restructured the railroad in a way that slighted others' rights. To ensure the protection of such rights, courts fashioned over the course of many decades a set of rules, loosely identified as the *fair and equitable principle*. Section 1129(b) codifies this principle. It requires that a plan be fair and equitable before it can be confirmed over the objection of a class of claims. To understand what "fair and equitable" means, one must know the sequence of cases from which the principle emerged. The most important of these is *Northern Pacific Railway Company v. Boyd*.[6]

In 1886, a man named Spaulding had supplied $25,000 worth of materials and labor to the Coeur D'Alene Railroad for which he was never paid. The assets of the Coeur D'Alene, after several restructurings, ultimately became part of the Northern Pacific Railroad. Spaulding believed he could hold the Northern Pacific Railroad liable for this debt. Before he acquired a judgment against it, however, the Northern Pacific Railroad became insolvent and went through an equity receivership, out of which emerged a new entity called the Northern Pacific Rail*way*.

Spaulding's successor, a man named Boyd, did not participate in the reorganization of the Northern Pacific Railroad and instead sued the new entity. The dispute finally reached the United States Supreme Court in 1913. The Court found first that the old Northern Pacific had indeed been responsible for the obligations of Coeur D'Alene. The Court then had to ask whether the new Northern Pacific was responsible for the debts of the old.

Boyd argued that the court-supervised sale could not extinguish his rights because the old shareholders remained the shareholders of the new entity. He invoked the common law rule, based on fraudulent conveyance doctrine, that a landowner who purchases back his property at a foreclosure sale takes subject to the claims of junior creditors, even though a third party buying at arm's length would not. Boyd had not participated in the reorganization or relinquished his claims. Thus, he could hold the Northern Pacific Rail*way* answerable for the obligations of the Northern Pacific Rail*road*.

[6] 228 U.S. 482 (1913).

Lawyers for the Northern Pacific Railway argued that the sale had to be respected. The real estate analogy was inapt, they asserted. The Rail*way* was an entity that was distinct from the Rail*road*. One should respect the formal differences, even though the shareholders of the two were the same. The judicial sale was regular in form and free from fraud. The assets had been sold for a fair price and that price was for less than what the secured creditors were owed. Had Boyd participated in the reorganization, he would have received nothing. Recharacterizing the transaction would only foster strike suits and make reorganizations of insolvent railroads impracticable. The Northern Pacific Railway lost below and appealed to the Supreme Court.

In *Boyd*, a divided Court found that the common law principle limiting the effect of debtor purchases at a foreclosure sale existed in the law of corporate reorganizations as well:

> As against creditors, [the sale] was a mere form. Though the Northern Pacific Railroad was divested of the legal title, the old stockholders were still owners of the same railroad, encumbered by the same debts. The circumlocution did not better their title against Boyd as a nonassenting creditor. They had changed the name but not the relation.[7]

Nor did it matter that the assets were worth less than what creditors senior to Boyd were owed:

> [T]he question must be decided according to a fixed principle, not leaving the rights of the creditors to depend upon the balancing of evidence as to whether, on the day of sale the property was insufficient to pay prior encumbrances.[8]

The Court did not go so far as to say that all of real estate foreclosure law should be mechanically transplanted to the law of corporate reorganizations. The Court held only that a complete freezeout of an intervening creditor was not permitted. Indeed, the Court was quick to note its holding was narrow:

> [We do not] require the impossible and make it necessary to pay an unsecured creditor in cash as a condition of stockholders retaining an interest in the reorganized company. His interest can be preserved by the issuance, on equitable terms, of income bonds or preferred stock. If he declines a fair offer he

---

[7] Id. at 506–07.
[8] Id. at 507–08.

is left to protect himself as any other creditor of a judgment debtor, and, having refused to come into a just reorganization, could not thereafter be heard in a court of equity to attack it.[9]

In contrast to real estate foreclosures, a plan of reorganization could include shareholders if the creditor were given a fair offer in a just reorganization. Exactly what these terms meant, the Court did not explain. Lower courts had to identify on their own the contours of the "fixed principle" that should be at work and out of this emerged a set of ideas of what constituted a fair and equitable plan.

After *Boyd*, a plan could not bypass junior creditors unless such creditors consented or had their day in court. Ex post assertions of fairness by a coalition of senior creditors and shareholders would not suffice. The question remained, however, whether or under what conditions a nonconsensual bypass of junior creditors was permissible *even given* their day in court. The Court ultimately confronted this question in *Case v. Los Angeles Lumber Products.*[10]

In *Case*, the debtor was a holding company whose principal asset was the Los Angeles Shipbuilding & Drydock Corporation. This corporation had built ships for the navy during World War I but languished during the 1920s and 1930s. It sought to reorganize itself in 1937. The only creditors were holders of 20-year bonds due in 1944. Holders of more than 90 percent of the face amount of the bonds voted in favor of the plan. The plan gave 23 percent of the stock in the new corporation to the old shareholders. These shareholders planned to continue to play a managerial role in operating the business, but they were not contributing any new cash.

The district court had held that the plan was fair and equitable. It noted that only two bondholders had objected to the plan, and the court did not want to give a couple of dissenters the ability to hold up a reorganization approved by a substantial majority of the bondholders. The court justified the continued participation of the old equityholders on the grounds that the shareholders were willing to assume managerial responsibilities in the company and that they were "the only persons who [were] familiar with the company's operations and who [had] experience in shipbuilding." In addition, the court noted,

[9] Id. at 508.
[10] 308 U.S. 106 (1939).

[m]ost of the present bondholders are widely scattered with small holdings, and their position would be benefited by being associated with old stockholders of financial influence and stability who might be able to assist in proper financing.[11]

The reorganization was brought about from the need for additional capital, not by the threat of foreclosure by existing creditors. Because of a previous workout, interest payments were owed only if earned, and the creditors lacked the power to foreclose until 1944.

When *Case* reached the Supreme Court on appeal, the Court had a vehicle to confront the different interpretations of the "fair and equitable" principle that had been debated in the wake of *Boyd*. Some took the view that the reorganization itself did not need to be seen as a day of reckoning in which junior interests that were underwater had to be wiped out. The equity of an insolvent company trades for a positive price. It has option value. The possibility that the firm will return to health makes the equity worth something. The equity of an insolvent firm is rendered worthless only when there is a recognition event in which all accounts are squared.

It is possible to create a new capital structure in which the option value of underwater interests is recognized.[12] A reorganization does not have to be a recognition event. Indeed, a reorganization regime that recognizes option value has the advantage of forcing investors to focus on the value of the business as a whole rather than on the value of their individual stake. Such a regime of "relative priority" seems to have been part of the equity receivership. Junior investors regularly received a share of the reorganized firm even when it was plain that their stake in the firm possessed only option value. They would receive nothing if all future possibilities were collapsed to present value. This acknowledgement of the option value of out-of-the-money interests emerged from informal norms and practices, rather than through fixed legal rules. Cases such as *Boyd*, seen through this lens, were aimed not at eliminating relative priority, but rather at ensuring that everyone enjoyed the option value of their investment.

---

[11] In re Los Angeles Lumber Products Co., 24 F. Supp. 501, 513 (S.D. Cal. 1938), aff'd, 100 F.2d 963 (9th Cir.), rev'd, 308 U.S. 106 (1939).

[12] For a concrete proposal, see Anthony J. Casey, The Creditors' Bargain and Option-Preservation Priority in Chapter 11, 78 U. Chi. L. Rev. 759 (2011).

The Supreme Court, however, emphatically rejected this approach to priority in *Case*. It held that absolute, rather than relative priority, was the appropriate foundational principle. The reorganization was emphatically a recognition event. Moreover, this principle was one that each individual stakeholder could invoke. It rejected the idea that the approval of the plan by 90 percent of the creditors was enough. Allowing the old equity to continue was a source of mischief. Rather than making it possible to obtain their help after the reorganization, it gave old shareholders an opportunity to hold up other investors. In a business such as a shipyard, shareholders do not control the day-to-day operations. Professionals can be brought in to do the job. Only in the narrowest of circumstances should old equity be permitted to continue in the face of any dissent.

The fair and equitable standard afforded each creditor its "full right of priority" in the business as a going concern. *Case* thus forged a link between the phrases "fair and equitable" and "absolute priority," a link that lawyers, judges, and Congress have accepted ever since.

Once the Supreme Court established this link, it was led to cut back sharply on the shareholders' ability to participate in the reorganization of an insolvent company over a creditor's objection. The absolute priority rule allowed shareholders to participate in the new venture only if they paid fair value for their continuing interest in a reorganized debtor. Moreover, to ensure that the shareholders paid fair value, the Court required that such payments be easy to value. If a creditor objected to an insolvent debtor's plan of reorganization, the plan could not include a distribution to old equity unless each stockholder's participation was based "on a contribution in money or in money's worth, reasonably equivalent in view of all the circumstances to the participation of the stockholder."[13]

Under pre-Code law, a single dissenting creditor could insist that a plan be fair and equitable. This gave one creditor considerable holdup power. Indeed, in *Case* itself, one of the dissenting creditors had a long history of buying claims at a deep discount and holding up reorganizations until he was paid in full. Under the Bankruptcy Code, the "full right" of absolute priority the Court identified now comes into play only if a class as a whole opposes the plan.

The "fair and equitable" language in §1129(b) embodies the absolute priority rule. Those with rights against the assets of a corporation

[13] 308 U.S. at 122.

under nonbankruptcy law receive interests in the reorganized corporation according to the priority they enjoyed under nonbankruptcy law. A creditor who is entitled to be paid before another creditor outside of bankruptcy (by virtue, say, of a security interest) is entitled to be paid first in bankruptcy as well.

Similarly, general creditors are entitled to be paid before shareholders. The effect of the discharge, in other words, is almost the opposite of what we see in the case of the flesh-and-blood individual debtor. In the case of an individual, the discharge (coupled with the exclusion of future income from property of the estate) allows individuals to preserve their right to future earnings in the face of creditors' claims. In the case of a corporation, discharge (coupled with the absolute priority rule) allows creditors to extinguish the shareholders' right to future earnings when the assets are not worth enough to pay the creditors off in full. We will look more closely at the mechanics of §1129 in the next section.

Chapter 11 and the Absolute Priority Rule

Section 1129(b) comes into operation when a reorganization plan fails to garner the acceptance of all adversely affected (or *impaired*) classes of claims and interests and thus fails to satisfy §1129(a)(8). It requires that each class that rejects the plan be treated in a way that is "fair and equitable." These words are a term of art and, standing alone, are sufficient to require absolute priority among the different stakeholders. The section goes on to add specific requirements to ensure that absolute priority is respected. Through them, the core ideas of the judicially created fair and equitable doctrine remain fixed even if the edges of the doctrine continue to evolve.

With respect to a class of allowed secured claims, the fair and equitable principle requires, at a minimum, that one of three tests is met. First, each holder of a secured claim can receive a stream of payments with a discounted present value equal to the value of the collateral. See §1129(b)(2)(A). This stream of payments must be secured by a lien on the creditor's collateral. Second, the collateral can be sold at an auction at which the secured creditor is entitled to bid and offset its claim against the purchase price, provided that the secured creditor's lien attaches to the proceeds of the sale. The third possibility is that the plan provides for the realization of the *indubitable equivalent* of the secured claim. This language is taken from Learned Hand's opinion in *In re Murel Holding*.[14] It has been interpreted quite narrowly.

A common dispute over indubitable equivalent arises in real estate cases in which the plan proposes giving some, but not all of the collateral outright to an oversecured creditor in full satisfaction of its debt.[15] These "dirt-for-debt" plans have on occasion been confirmed when the valuation evidence was particularly strong,[16] but given their reliance on uncertain valuation testimony in high illiquid markets, many bankruptcy judges remain reluctant to enforce them.[17]

To pass muster under §1129(b)(2)(A)(i), a reorganization plan must meet an additional requirement to be confirmed over the objection of a class of secured claims. The plan must also provide a stream of payments equal to the face amount of the secured claim. In most cases, this requirement is redundant. In a world in which discount rates are positive, a stream of payments over time equal in value to a given amount must total more than the face amount owed. Hence, this requirement matters only if the secured claim is for more than the value of the collateral despite the operation of §506(a), which generally equates the two. A mismatch can occur if a secured creditor makes what is called the §1111(b)(2) election. Under this provision, a secured creditor can elect to have its entire claim treated as secured regardless of the collateral's value. As a result, the stream of a plan's payments must not only be equal in value to the collateral, as determined by the judge, but the face amount of the stream of payments in the aggregate must equal the total amount of the claim that the collateral supports. The election is a way in which the secured creditor gives up its deficiency claim and in return limits the extent to which rights can be undermined as a result of judicial undervaluation of the collateral.

Section 1129(b)(2)(B) fleshes out the fair and equitable standard for a class of unsecured claims that rejects the plan. If the plan awards any property to old equity (or to a junior class of claims) on account of the old equity interest (or junior claim), the plan must provide each holder of an unsecured claim with property that is at least equal in val-

---

[14] 75 F.2d 941 (2d Cir. 1935).

[15] Less controversial is turning all the collateral over to the secured party. See In re Sandy Ridge Development Corp., 881 F.2d 1346 (5th Cir. 1989).

[16] In re Bannerman Holdings, LLC, 2010 WL 4260003 (Bankr. E.D.N.C. 2010).

[17] In re Legacy at Jordan Lake, LLC, 448 Bankr. 719 (Bankr. E.D.N.C. 2011).

ue to the amount of the claim. In other words, unless the plan proposes to pay unsecured claims in full, those junior to them must be wiped out if the plan is to be crammed down over objection by the holders of unsecured claims. This provision seems straightforward enough. But complications can arise.

A problem of a different sort arises when the assets are worth less than the secured creditor is owed, the plan calls for giving the entire firm to that creditor, and the secured creditor agrees to share some part of the business with some, but not all of those junior to it. It might seem that if the secured creditor is owed more than the business is worth, it is entitled to all of it and is therefore free to do anything it pleases with it, including giving some of it to junior investors. But when a senior lender makes a "gift," we need to worry about what it is getting in return. It is unlikely to be charitably inclined. Instead, it may be buying a bankruptcy process that favors its interests at the expense of others. There may be more benign explanations. The senior creditor, for example, may be able to enhance the value of the reorganized entity, by ensuring the availability of a critical supplier. Nevertheless, it makes sense to have a presumption against such transfers. As the Second Circuit explained, "if the parties here were less scrupulous or the bankruptcy court less vigilant, a weakened absolute priority rule could allow for serious mischief between senior creditors and existing shareholders."[18]

A parallel issue arises when the business is sold and, as part of the transaction, the buyer agrees to assume some of the old obligations. Courts have tended to approve such assumptions of liability, provided that they are not credited to the purchase price. There is need for caution, however. These transactions raise the same problem as gifts. One needs to worry that payment is being made to grease the skids of the sale.

Equityholders sometimes propose plans in which they receive equity in the reorganized business, even though creditors are not being paid in full and the most senior creditor is unwilling to "gift" part of its interest to them. They justify their continuing participation on the ground that they are contributing new value. They receive new equity on account of the new capital, not "on account of" their old interests.

---

[18] DISH Network Corp. v. DBSD North America, Inc., 634 F.3d 79, 100 (2d Cir. 2010).

Hence, holders of old equity argue, notwithstanding §1129(b), a "new value" plan does not have to pay the unsecured claims in full.

If the equityholders enjoy the exclusive right to buy the equity, however, they have an option, which is itself a form of property. In the last chapter of this book, we shall return to the question of equity participation when a class of claimholders votes against the plan. For the moment, it is worth noting that in the continuing evolution of the fair and equitable principle, courts have further protected creditors by insisting that market benchmarks be used to ensure that equity is paying top dollar.[19]

Section §1129(b)(2)(C) applies to a class of preferred stock interests. Under corporate law, preferred stock, though classified as equity and thus as an interest, is a hybrid between debt and equity, inferior to the former but superior to the latter. The "preference" is typically a right to insist that neither dividends nor any other payments go to the corporation's common shares unless and until the corporation pays the preferred shareholders specified amounts analogous to interest and principal on a debt. The fair and equitable standard requires that a reorganization plan honor these preferences—called *liquidation preferences* or sometimes *redemption prices*—with provision of full payment, though not necessarily in cash. If the plan fails to do this, then the holders of more junior interests, those who hold common stock, may not receive any property on account of their old interests.

For its part, common equity also is protected by the fair and equitable standard of §1129(b)(2)(C), though in a more limited way befitting common equity's status of lowest priority. A plan is not fair and equitable to a class of common equity interests unless the plan provides property with a value at least equal to the value of those interests. This is simply a requirement that creditors not capture the entire value of a solvent debtor. This matters only rarely, as debtors that can pay their creditors usually do not end up in bankruptcy.

As you consider these provisions, keep in mind that the fair and equitable standard is a *class-based* right. The holder of an individual claim or interest can demand at least what it would have received in a Chapter 7 liquidation. If, however, a class votes to make a sacrifice of its priority, a dissenter within the approving class cannot block the plan on the basis of that sacrifice.

---

[19] Bank of America v. 203 North LaSalle Street Partnership, 526 U.S. 434 (1999).

The absolute priority rule sets the ground rules for Chapter 11, but it does not identify all the effects of filing a Chapter 11 petition. For example, a secured creditor may worry that if it works too closely with the debtor in crafting a nonbankruptcy workout, it will be charged with being an insider or be subject to labor laws or environmental laws.[20] Judges are sensitive to the danger of demanding too much of creditors. Nevertheless, third parties are at risk of being classified as insiders if they exercise so much control that it appears that they are distorting the debtor's business decisions and leading the debtor to act in ways that are unsound and contrary to its interests.[21]

A nonbankruptcy restructuring of the debt may also bring unfavorable tax consequences for the secured creditor that can be avoided in bankruptcy. If the secured creditor wants to continue to finance a business, it may be better off doing it under the umbrella of Chapter 11 as a debtor-in-possession (commonly abbreviated as a "dip") lender. Then it would be able to retain significant control, its priority would be respected, and payments to junior debtholders would be suspended. Finally, the secured creditor must face the possibility that a nonbankruptcy workout will only postpone the inevitable. If the secured creditor makes compromises in the workout, it may be worse off in a subsequent Chapter 11 case relative to those who refused to compromise. A long-term secured creditor may be better off in Chapter 11 than it would be if it had to wait and watch while the debtor paid off short-term obligations that were junior to the one owed it.

The ambition of every lawyer whose client files a Chapter 11 petition is to persuade each group of creditors to consent to a plan of reorganization. Whether a group consents depends on its rights under the plan versus the rights it would have if it refused to go along with the plan. The absolute priority rule is central to the law of corporate reorganizations because it is the source of the substantive rights as well as the procedural protections that each participant in a reorganization enjoys. Parties can insist that the priority rights they enjoyed outside of bankruptcy be respected inside. Nevertheless, every junior party, including the shareholders, can invoke elaborate procedures before their rights are compromised. The absolute priority rule allows the

[20] See United States v. Fleet Factors Corp., 901 F.2d 1550 (11th Cir. 1990).

[21] See Schubert v. Lucent Technologies Inc. (In re Winstar Communications, Inc.), 554 F.3d 382 (3d Cir. 2009).

senior parties to insist on full payment, but it also grants all junior parties those procedural protections necessary for a "just reorganization." Resolving this tension between substantive and procedural rights that began with *Boyd* remains central to answering the hard questions that arise under Chapter 11.

The law and practice of Chapter 11 establishes a framework for negotiations. The dynamics of any negotiation are defined by what there is to bargain over and the place of each of the parties in the pecking order. Before a plan of reorganization can take place, we must find out what assets the debtor has and we must know the relative positions of each of the parties. In the next few chapters, we step back from the dynamics of reorganization practice per se and explore how we go about establishing the stakes the parties are fighting over and their rights vis-à-vis one another. Once we understand these, we will return to the reorganization process itself and explore it in greater detail.

CHAPTER FOUR

Claims Against the Estate

We now turn to the way bankruptcy law establishes the debtor's *liabilities* and *assets*—what the debtor's obligations are and what assets exist to meet them. We must determine who gets what. Figuring out the "who" is the problem of claims, which we examine in this chapter. Figuring out the "what" is the problem of assets, which we focus on in the next chapter. In both cases, our starting point is nonbankruptcy law. The *Butner* principle is perhaps most powerful when we look at the subject of claims in bankruptcy. The Supreme Court regularly recognizes "the settled principle that creditors' entitlements in bankruptcy arise in the first instance from the underlying substantive law creating the debtor's obligation."[1] One of the Supreme Court's canonical bankruptcy cases—*Chicago Board of Trade v. Johnson*[2]—tells us to use the nonbankruptcy baseline to identify the debtor's assets.

Establishing a Claim Against the Estate

A creditor often first learns of a bankruptcy filing when it receives notice of it from the bankruptcy clerk. Rule 2002. When a debtor files for bankruptcy, it must fill out schedules that list its liabilities and the names and addresses of its creditors. If you are a creditor and are included on this list, you will be sent notice of the bankruptcy and you will be given a chance to take the appropriate procedural steps to vindicate your rights. Your first step would be to file a form known as a proof of claim. Once that is filed, the claim is "allowed" in the absence of objection. The consequences of failing to file a proof of claim depend on whether your debtor is an individual or a corporation, whether your debtor is in Chapter 7 or Chapter 11, and whether you are listed on the debtor's schedules.

Take first the case of an individual debtor who files a Chapter 7 petition and fails to list your claim. If you do not file a proof of claim, you will not share in the distribution of assets. But if you do not know

[1] Travelers Casualty & Surety Co. v. Pacific Gas & Electric Co., 549 U.S. 443, 450 (2007).
[2] 264 U.S. 1 (1924).

about the bankruptcy, §523(a)(3) prevents your claim against the debtor from being discharged.[3] You can pursue the debtor after the bankruptcy is over.

Your rights against a corporation in Chapter 7 are different. A corporation has no life after bankruptcy. If a corporation files a Chapter 7 petition, you must file a proof of claim to share in the distribution of the debtor's assets regardless of whether your claim is listed or whether you learn of the bankruptcy. To be sure, no corporate debts are discharged in Chapter 7.[4] The discharge, however, is irrelevant. The corporation distributes all its assets in Chapter 7 and then dissolves. At the end of the Chapter 7 case, all the assets are gone and there is nothing left to satisfy your claim.

There is a procedural difference in Chapter 11. A creditor must file a proof of claim only if its claim is not listed in the schedules or is disputed, contingent, or unliquidated. §1111(a); Rule 3003(c). The substantive outcome, however, is the same for a creditor whose claim is not listed or whose claim is contingent. Even though the corporation has a continuing life after bankruptcy, all the debts of the corporation are discharged in Chapter 11, even if they are not scheduled. A creditor who is not listed on the schedules is obliged to file a proof of claim and is left out of the distribution if it fails to do so.

Ordinarily, the treatment of claims is straightforward. The amount each creditor is owed is listed on the schedules and is not disputed. All one has to do is figure out how to divide whatever assets there are among the various claimants. Suppose there are 100 creditors, and all are listed and properly notified. The debtor owes them $10,000. The average claim is $100, but some are owed $10 and one is owed more than $1,000. All the debtor's assets are sold for a total of $1,000.[5] How do we divide the pie, as small as it is? Under pro rata sharing, each creditor receives 10 cents for every dollar it is owed. A creditor that is owed $1,000 gets $100. A creditor that is owed $50 gets $5.

The rule of pro rata distribution provides a way to approximate the rights of each of the general creditors. We do not know what the non-bankruptcy right would be for each creditor because bankruptcy has put a halt to the race among them. We know that without the auto-

---

[3] As we discussed in chapter 2, an exception may exist in the no-asset case. See pp. 46–47 *supra*.

[4] Under §727, only individuals enjoy a discharge in Chapter 7.

[5] Unless specified otherwise, figures exclude the costs of bankruptcy.

matic stay, some of them would have been paid in full and others would have received nothing, but it is not worth the effort to figure out who would have come first. There are other complications. Smaller creditors might have been more likely to be paid in full because they would not have had to seize much to satisfy their claims. For this reason, some might argue that we should give them more than their pro rata share. Large creditors, however, have more to lose and therefore might spend more time and effort monitoring the debtor. For this reason, one could argue that large creditors should receive more than their pro rata share. In the end, we have the pro rata sharing rule because trying to answer arguments like these is more trouble than it is worth. The kinds of distributions in these cases are in the neighborhood of 10 cents on the dollar for general creditors.

It is mistake, however, to think pro rata sharing is the only way to divide assets. An alternative is the solution to the "contested garment" problem offered in the *Talmud*. Assume that there are assets worth $100 and one creditor is owed $100 and another $50. Under pro rata sharing, each would receive 67 cents on the dollar. The contested garment rule begins in a different place. The smaller creditor is laying claim only to $50, half of the pie that is being divided. It has no claim to the other half, so all of it should go to the first creditor. The half that is contested is what should be divided pro rata. Hence, the larger creditor should receive $75 ($50 that is uncontested and its share of the $50 that is contested), and the smaller creditor should receive $25. This method of division is logically coherent and can be extended to an arbitrarily large number of creditors.[6] Working through such schemes is useful if only to remind ourselves that rules to which we have become accustomed should not be seen as inevitable on that account alone.

Returning to pro rata sharing, we will flesh out the story somewhat. Rule 3010 provides that no dividend of less than $5 is paid. It costs that much just to cut the check. Suppose that a fully perfected secured creditor is owed $500. It has a fully and properly perfected security interest on every asset that the debtor has. In this case, the secured creditor gets 100 cents on the dollar, or $500, out of the $1,000 pie. From the remaining $500 we subtract the fees that the trustee gets (and, more important, the fees of the lawyer for the trustee, who is

---

[6] See Robert J. Aumann & Michael Maschler, Game Theoretic Analysis of a Bankruptcy Problem from the Talmud, 36 J. Econ. Theory 195 (1985).

frequently a lawyer at the trustee's firm). Whatever is left is divided among the general creditors pro rata. If the remainder is $150 and the general creditors are still owed $10,000, then the distribution is at the rate of 1.5 cents on the dollar. If you are owed $1,000, you get $15. If you are owed $600, you get $9.

We also need to put a value on disputed claims, such as a lawsuit against the debtor that is in litigation. To see how the Bankruptcy Code handles these claims, it is useful to look at a straightforward example. Assume that a software producer is suing the debtor for unfair competition. If the debtor owes anything, it will owe $12,000. But the debtor argues that all it did was engage in some hardball competition. The liability is an all-or-nothing affair. The software producer's chances of winning in state court are roughly one in three. The trial is still many years away.

Under §101, the software producer is viewed as a creditor who holds a claim against the debtor. The claim, however, is both disputed and unliquidated. After the producer files its proof of claim and the debtor files its objection, the bankruptcy judge may conduct a streamlined trial and decide the merits of the dispute. §502(b). The shortened process makes sense. Even if the producer wins, it is not going to be paid in full. In most Chapter 11 bankruptcies, general creditors are lucky to receive more than 20 cents on the dollar. In deciding the merits of the producer's claim, the bankruptcy judge follows nonbankruptcy substantive rules and bankruptcy's procedural rules. The judge turns to state law to find out what conduct constitutes unfair competition, but the judge may decide factual questions rather than leaving them to a jury. A bankruptcy court is entitled to use chancery methods in putting a value on a claim.

A bankruptcy judge is not, however, required to *fix* a value on the claim. Under §502(c), the judge can estimate the value for the purposes of the bankruptcy proceeding and allow the creditor to reappear if it gets a judgment for a different amount. In the meantime, the creditor participates as if its claim is equal to the estimate. There can even be a distribution according to the estimate, perhaps with some way (such as the issuance of new equity) to increase the distribution after the case is over.

Estimating the producer's claim is not easy. It is a $12,000 lawsuit, but it has only one chance in three of succeeding. Assume that other general creditors are owed $3,000 and that the assets are worth $1,000. If we value the producer's claim at its present probability of success, it would have a claim for $4,000. The producer's claim, even discounted, makes it the largest unsecured creditor. The producer would dominate the bankruptcy proceeding even though in the end its lawsuit would probably not succeed and the debtor would owe it nothing.

Giving the producer a voice according to its present probability of success therefore seems unattractive, but there may be no better alternatives. If the producer prevailed in the end, it would be entitled to 80 percent of the debtor's assets and would virtually be able to dictate the plan of reorganization. Valuing the producer's claim at its present probability of success would be undervaluing it if the producer ultimately wins. By the same measure, we would be overvaluing it if it turns out that the producer loses. Discounting the producer's claim by its present probability of success would give the producer too large a role in some instances and too small a role in others.

It might be useful to view the estimation of claims as a coerced settlement. Outside of bankruptcy, most civil cases are settled. Every settlement reflects an estimate by both parties of their chances of success on the merits. Disregarding concerns about reputation and other complications, the settlement value of the producer's claim against the debtor is about $4,000. It might make sense for a bankruptcy judge to estimate a claim according to its present probability of success. Even though this amount will necessarily be different from the outcome of any litigation, it may match the settlement that we would have seen in the absence of bankruptcy.

There is, however, a good reason to estimate the value of the producer's suit at zero for purposes of determining the kind of role that the producer plays in drawing up the plan of reorganization. The producer should not be allowed to force a settlement on terms more favorable than would be possible outside of bankruptcy. What may be crucial is not that the producer's present probability of success is less than 50 percent, but that it is less than 100 percent. Even though creditors in some sense always deal at arm's length with their debtor, in bankruptcy they are acting as equityholders. They are exercising levers of governance that come with owning a stake in the firm. Someone who possesses only a cause of action, however, should have no control rights. Estimating the producer's claim at zero makes the most sense when the producer is allowed to pursue the claim, unaffected by the bankruptcy process. Courts are most likely to take this approach when the claim is large and the probability of success low.[7]

A person with a personal injury or wrongful death claim has a procedural right in bankruptcy that a contract creditor does not. Unlike a contract creditor, a tort victim has the same right to a jury trial in bankruptcy as would exist under nonbankruptcy law. 28 U.S.C. §1411. As elsewhere in bankruptcy, this additional procedural right may generate substantive consequences. In mass tort cases involving A.H. Robins and Manville, however, the courts limited the scope of the trial right. The courts used §502(c) to estimate the total liability to tort victims. These courts then allowed a fund of this amount to be established that would serve as the victims' sole source of compensation. They confined the scope of the jury trial right to the adjudication of individual claims against the fund.

Apart from these differences, a tort creditor occupies the same position as a contract creditor. Tort victims enjoy no special priority outside of bankruptcy and hence none in. They are simply general creditors with disputed claims. One can argue that as a matter of nonbankruptcy law this is a bad idea. The purpose of tort law is to make businesses internalize the costs of hazardous activities. If creditors through loan covenants or some other kind of monitoring can influence a business's behavior, then giving tort victims a priority right may have the effect of reducing the number of torts the business commits.

Other creditors might complain that there is nothing they can do to make the business more careful. But the risk of having another creditor take priority over them gives them an incentive to think twice about whether there is in fact anything they can force the business to do. If a victim of an accident involving a truck takes priority over a creditor with a security interest in the truck, that creditor will have an incentive to make sure that the truck is properly maintained, that the driver is well qualified, and that the debtor carries insurance. As Samuel Johnson might note, the prospect of being beaten out by another creditor, like the prospect of being hanged in a fortnight, concentrates the mind wonderfully. But existing law does not work this way. Inside of bankruptcy and out, tort victims are general creditors.

Some debtors may have committed some act before the petition that will injure some as yet unidentified person long after the bankruptcy case is over. The technical question is whether the victim has a

[7] See Bittner v. Borne Chemical Co., 691 F.2d 134 (3d Cir. 1982).

claim arising before the filing of the petition for purposes of §101. An aircraft manufacturer has made thousands of planes that are still flying. Some will crash in the future and expose the manufacturer to liability. These as yet unknown victims may not have a prepetition connection with the debtor sufficient to give rise to a claim within the meaning of §101.[8]

The effect of finding that future victims possess claims depends on the kind of case involved. First is the mass tort case in which a corporation is liquidating in Chapter 7. If future victims do not have prepetition claims within the meaning of the Bankruptcy Code, they will receive nothing in Chapter 7 even though they would receive something if the corporation dissolved under nonbankruptcy law. In a nonbankruptcy dissolution of a corporation, a fund usually must be set up to cover any liabilities that appear on the corporation's books. So long as the accountants have recognized the obligation (as they should if matters have deteriorated sufficiently), the tort victim will be able to recover from this fund even though the victim does not know about the injury until after the corporation goes out of existence.

Second is the case in which the business is in Chapter 11 and will have a postbankruptcy life. Here, tort victims may be better off if they do not have a prepetition claim. To be sure, if tort victims lack a prepetition claim, they will be unable to share in the distribution in bankruptcy, but they will be able to pursue the corporation in its postbankruptcy incarnation. Remember that only "claims" are discharged under §1141. Such victims may be able to recover more than they would have received had they participated in the bankruptcy case.

In the wake of the Manville bankruptcy, §524(g) of the Bankruptcy Code was amended to allow the bankruptcy court to enjoin subsequent actions against reorganized corporations and even third parties such as insurers, but this provision by its terms applies only to mass torts involving asbestos. In other cases, the law is less settled.[9] Courts are especially unsympathetic to plans that release nondebtors from liability

---

[8] See Epstein v. Official Committee of Unsecured Creditors, 58 F.3d 1573 (11th Cir. 1995). For an account of how the Code's definition of "claim" should be understood, see Jeld-Wen, Inc. v. Van Brunt (In re Grossman's Inc.), 607 F.3d 114 (3d Cir. 2010).

[9] Such releases are possible under limited circumstances. See Class Five Nevada Claimants v. Dow Corning Corp., 280 F.3d 648, 658 (6th Cir. 2002).

as part of a reorganization.[10] Moreover, even when a debtor attempts to sell assets free and clear of claims against it, the bankruptcy court cannot insulate buyers from potential successor liability under state law.[11]

Several technical complications arise when we try to put a dollar value on each creditor's claim. The best way to understand how the process works is to imagine that the filing of a bankruptcy petition is a presumptive event of default that accelerates all the debtor's obligations.[12] As part of this process, we must decide two basic issues: how interest affects the calculation of claims, and what caps are placed on some types of claims.

Suppose that I borrowed $100 from First Bank last year when interest rates were 7 percent. This year I borrowed $100 from Second Bank at 12 percent. Although I am not in default on either loan, I file a bankruptcy petition. My assets are worth $150. Who gets what? Should the two banks receive the same amount? In the absence of a bankruptcy filing, First Bank is in a worse position than Second Bank. Other things being equal, it would rather have my promise to repay $100 at 12 percent than at 7 percent. In Chapter 7 of the Bankruptcy Code, however, we ignore these differences. Section 502(b)(2) does not allow claims for unaccrued interest. Both banks would have claims of $100. Because the assets are worth $150, each bank would get 75 cents on the dollar. Treating the two lenders equally makes sense. If the debtor defaulted outside of bankruptcy, the obligation to pay back the principal of both loans would be accelerated. At this point, both lenders would be in the same position. Both would have the right to recover $100 immediately. When it ignores differences in the interest rates, all that bankruptcy is doing is treating the filing of a petition as a default. This seems a sensible off-the-rack rule that most lenders would include in their loan agreements.

We can think of Chapter 7 bankruptcy liquidation as financial death. We call in all the loans, gather the assets, and have a general day of reckoning. Sometimes it will not be easy to distinguish principal from unaccrued interest. The simplest case arises when there is a

---

[10] See, e.g., Gillman v. Continental Airlines, 203 F.3d 203 (3d Cir. 2000).

[11] Western Auto Supply Co. v. Savage Arms, Inc., 43 F.3d 714 (1st Cir. 1994); Morgan Olson L.L.C. v. Frederico (In re Grumman Olson Indus.), 467 Bankr. 694 (S.D.N.Y. 2012).

[12] As we shall see in a later chapter, §1124 gives debtors the right to de-accelerate loans in Chapter 11.

zero-coupon note. I borrow $900 and I promise to pay you $1,000 in a year's time. On the face of it, the principal amount of the loan is $1,000 and the interest rate is zero percent. We can be confident, however, that the principal is in fact $900 and the interest rate is 11 percent. In the case of zero-coupon notes, only the principal and interest already owed is accelerated. If I default immediately, you have a claim for $900. If I default in six months, you have a claim for $950. More complicated cases arise when the interest rate is not zero percent but is still substantially below market, and when the note is issued not for cash but in exchange for other securities.[13] Also less clear are cases in which a consumer buys on the installment plan and the interest-rate component is hard to identify.

A common dispute concerns "make-whole" premiums. When a third party leases a machine to the debtor for a fixed period, the lease commonly provides an amount that the debtor must pay if it wishes to terminate the lease early. If the clause is an effort to calculate the depreciation on the machine and the costs the lessor will incur in leasing the machine to someone else, then it is a garden-variety liquidated damages clause. It is enforceable under nonbankruptcy law and hence appropriately treated as a claim inside of bankruptcy. A lender providing capital for a fixed period is sometimes paid early. Such a lender stands in the same position. It may incur a loss as it seeks to find someone else to use the capital on the same terms. For this reason, a loan can have a liquidated damages clause as well. The contract may provide for payment of a fee for terminating the loan early.

If the clause merely makes the lender whole, it is a liquidated damages clause that is enforceable under nonbankruptcy law. Debtors who are seeking to terminate a loan at an unfavorable rate of interest, however, will argue that the "make-whole" premium it is being asked to pay is not liquidated damages, but rather represents interest that the lender would receive if the loan were kept in place. Because claims for unmatured interest are not allowed under §502(b)(2), lenders should not be able to recover them through the guise of a make-whole premium.

In an earlier era in which the riskless rate of interest was large, it was comparatively easy to tell whether the "make-whole" premium

---

[13] See Thrifty Oil Co. v. Bank of America National Trust & Savings Association, 249 Bankr. 537 (S.D. Cal. 2000); Brown v. Sayyah (In re ICH Corp.), 230 Bankr. 88 (N.D. Tex. 1999).

was for the most part merely compensating the lender for unmatured interest. In an era in which the riskless rate is close to zero, it is much harder. Lenders have had success recently in making the characterization of make-whole premiums as liquidated damages clauses stick, but much depends on the dynamics of the individual case.[14]

The Bankruptcy Code also imposes limits on damages that arise from two classes of creditors. Sections 502(b)(6) and (7) limit what both landlords and employees can recover if the debtor rejects a long-term contract with them in bankruptcy. Suppose you lease land to a debtor for $5 a year for a term of years. A year or so later, the bottom drops out of the real estate market. The land falls in value, and now you could rent it out at only $1 a year. The debtor files a bankruptcy petition. Your damages by the ordinary contract rule (the contract–market differential) are $4 for each year remaining on the lease. The Bankruptcy Code, however, limits your recovery. The limit depends on how long the lease lasts. Your cap will never be less than one year's rent ($5). If 15 percent of all the payments remaining turn out to be greater than one year's rent, you get 15 percent of all the payments remaining. But in no event can the amount you get exceed three years' rent. When the rental payments under the lease are constant, your damages are capped by one year's rent if fewer than 6.7 years are left on the lease, 15 percent of the remaining payments if between 6.7 and 20 years are left, and three years' rent if more than 20 years are left.

The usual justification for capping a landlord's damages is that they are hard to measure, but this assertion is not sound. Section 502(b)(6) merely imposes a cap. It does not free you from estimating damages in each case. Moreover, this rationale makes sense only if judges are apt to think damages are too high, but not too low. If there is a ceiling on damages, it would seem that there should also be a floor. A better justification may lie in the landlord's duty to mitigate. Under nonbankruptcy law, the damage measure must take into account the landlord's obligation to try to find someone else to occupy the space. The ability to find another tenant limits the landlord's recovery. Although not tailored to the facts of the individual case, the cap in 506(b)(6) works to the same effect.

---

[14] In re School Specialty, Inc., 2013 WL 1838513 (Bankr. D. Del. 2013); In re Trico Marine Services, Inc., 450 Bankr. 474 (Bankr. D. Del. 2011). Among other things, the creditor must show that the make-whole agreement has been triggered under the terms of the loan agreement. U.S. Bank Trust National Association v. AMR Corp., 730 F.3d 88 (2d Cir. 2013).

Another justification for such limits exists in the case of employees under §502(b)(7). The employees most likely to be affected by the breach of long-term employment contracts are employees with golden parachutes, and they frequently are insider-shareholders. When these contracts are unusually favorable, there may be a significant chance of self-dealing that violates the rights of creditors as a group. The cap in the case of an employee under a long-term contract may be a means of policing misbehavior that cannot be controlled directly.

In considering the merits of capping landlord and employee damage claims, you should bear in mind that this limitation applies only to damages flowing from termination of the agreement. It does not limit the damages landlords or employees might be able to get from other causes, such as the damages that arise if the debtor damaged the premises before filing or terminated an employee without justification.

As mentioned in the beginning of this section, assessing claims against the estate involves asking who is owed what and whether someone has priority. The most common kind of privileged party is a creditor with a perfected security interest. Some priority rights are established in the Bankruptcy Code itself, in §507(a). Workers, for example, enjoy priority with respect to several thousand dollars in back wages and benefits. The tax collector has special priority as well. Special priority rules are hard to defend as a matter of first principle and are often the product of special interest lobbying, but these priorities usually do not play a significant role in large reorganizations. As a practical matter, employees will have to be paid if the business is to remain open, and usually little is owed in the way of back taxes. The typical Chapter 11 case is quite a different matter. Small companies make up the vast majority of the Chapter 11 docket, and the entrepreneurs in charge of them often try to keep the businesses afloat by using money that should have gone to the IRS to pay withholding taxes. The obligations then commonly exceed the value of the estate, leaving general creditors with nothing. For this reason, the rhetoric frequently used to describe Chapter 11—that it protects small general creditors and ensures a fair distribution of assets to them—is misleading, at least in the typical case.

Claims and Equitable Remedies

The drafters of the Bankruptcy Code defined "claim" broadly, but boundary questions can still arise. Assume that the debtor is responsible for spilling toxic waste on property that it no longer owns. State environmental law gives the state's EPA the ability to order the debtor to clean up the site. If the nonbankruptcy law also gives the regulator a right to demand payment for the costs of cleanup, the Bankruptcy Code treats the EPA's rights against the debtor as a claim. Even though the agency has the right to order the clean-up, the right is included in the definition of a claim, as it is "a right to an equitable remedy for breach of performance" and "such breach gives rise to a right to payment."[15]

But if the regulator has only a right to order performance, a court might conclude that it falls outside the ambit of the definition of "claim."[16] Two consequences follow. First, the regulator has no right to any share of the bankruptcy estate, as the estate is distributed only to claimholders. On the other hand, the regulator is free to pursue the debtor in its postbankruptcy life, as only claims are discharged. In some situations (such as a corporation liquidating in Chapter 7), the regulator would definitely prefer having a claim. A corporation in Chapter 7 has no future and receives no discharge in any event. In other situations, such as when the debtor is an individual or a corporation reorganizing in Chapter 11, the regulator would prefer not to have a claim so it can pursue the debtor after bankruptcy. As a matter of first principle, the broadest definition of "claim" makes the most sense, as it allows a day of reckoning in which all of the debtor's obligations are confronted at the same time.

With respect to ordinary property rights, the distinction between equitable remedies not subject to discharge and those that are is easy to grasp. Assume that the debtor bought a diamond ring and it happens that there is a thief in the debtor's chain of title. Under nonbankruptcy law, the debtor does not own the ring. The true owner has the right to go to court and get an order compelling the debtor to return it as an alternative to a damage action.[17] The true owner has the same right in bankruptcy as well. Debtors in bankruptcy have no more right to keep what is not theirs than anyone else. The true owner has an equitable remedy that gives rise to a damage action, but it is not an equitable remedy "for breach of performance." Instead, it is an equitable remedy that vindicates a property right.

---

[15] See §101(5)(B); Ohio v. Kovacs, 469 U.S. 274 (1985).

[16] See United States v. Apex Oil Co., 579 F.3d 734 (7th Cir. 2009).

[17] "Equitable" refers to the nature of the relief, not the historical division between law and equity. The two actions at issue here (replevin and trover) were both common law actions.

Equitable remedies protecting intellectual property rights, such as trade secrets, present the same problem. A franchisor may fear that its franchisees will learn the ropes of the business from it, and then cancel the franchise and reopen the same business under a different name, thereby taking advantage of the tricks of the trade without having to pay for them. It therefore insists upon a covenant not to compete. Can the franchisee escape from such a clause in bankruptcy? Can it terminate the franchise, file for bankruptcy, and assert that its promise not to run a competing business was discharged? Most courts have found that the debtor cannot. The right of the franchisor to enjoin the debtor is not a "claim" and is not subject to discharge.[18] Compliance with the injunction on the part of the debtor requires no expenditure of money. The injunction is not aimed at getting the debtor to perform. The equitable remedy is protecting the trade secrets, property rights, not compensating for a "breach of performance" on the part of the debtor. Hence, it is not a "claim" under §101(5)(B).

Secured Claims

Secured credit, put simply, is a loan supported by a contingent property interest. Outside of bankruptcy, default on the loan satisfies the contingency and triggers the creditor's right to take the property the debtor has pledged as collateral. The creditor then conducts a foreclosure sale. If the proceeds from the sale are greater than the outstanding loan, the creditor remits the excess. If the proceeds from the sale are less than the outstanding loan, the creditor maintains a claim against the debtor for the deficiency. Section 554 allows the bankruptcy trustee to abandon collateral and permit a secured creditor to take the assets and then foreclose under state law. The secured creditor still participates in the bankruptcy process on account of its deficiency claim. Unless the secured creditor agrees otherwise at the time of the loan, that creditor possesses all the rights of an unsecured creditor. Collateral gives a creditor extra rights. Thus, to the extent its collateral falls short of repaying the loan in full, the secured creditor participates in the bankruptcy process as the holder of an unsecured claim.

A trustee may not wish to abandon collateral, however. She may instead intend the debtor to keep the property as part of a reorganization or adjustment of the debtor's obligations. When the collateral is to

[18] See Kennedy v. Medicap Pharmacies, Inc., 267 F.3d 493 (6th Cir. 2001).

remain part of the estate, bankruptcy law provides a procedure that takes the place of a foreclosure sale's valuation of property. Section 506(a) of the Code instructs the bankruptcy court to value a creditor's interest in property of the estate and to designate the creditor's claim a "secured claim to the extent of the value of such creditor's interest." Any remaining claim amount is designated as an unsecured claim. The same process separates into secured and unsecured portions any claim held by someone who enjoys a setoff right. In the most common case, the debtor maintains a deposit account at a bank from which it has borrowed money. The bank has the ability under nonbankruptcy law to "set off" against the loan whatever is in the account. The Bankruptcy Code treats the portion of claim subject to a setoff right as a secured claim and the balance as an unsecured claim. If, for example, the bank had lent the debtor $300 and the debtor has $100 in its account, the Bankruptcy Code gives the bank a secured claim for $100 and an unsecured claim for $200.

In broad strokes, the bifurcation process of §506(a) mimics nonbankruptcy law. The secured creditor receives the full value of her collateral and shares in the debtor's other assets to the extent that the collateral value is less than the creditor's claim. Section 552, however, draws a sharp line at the time of the petition. Property that a debtor acquires after the filing of the petition is not subject to a security interest unless the property is itself proceeds of property that is subject to a security interest. If a secured creditor has a security interest on all the assets of a firm, including its goodwill, it might seem that it would have a security interest in all postpetition assets as well. New assets must necessarily have been acquired on account of the assets already subject to the security interest. In one recent case, however, a secured creditor was unable to meet its burden of showing that postpetition goodwill had not been acquired from other resources.[19]

When the collateral is not sold, however, the court must value the collateral, and this is not a simple task. The secured creditor will argue for a high valuation (and thus a larger secured claim), while the debtor's other creditors, represented by the trustee, will argue for a low valuation. The bankruptcy judge begins with an objective benchmark: the replacement value of the asset. Apart from the cases in which the debtor is an individual in Chapter 7 or Chapter 13, see §506(a)(2),

[19] Official Committee of Unsecured Creditors v. UMB Bank (In re Residential Capital, LLC), 501 Bankr. 549, 612 (Bankr. S.D.N.Y. 2013).

this amount must be adjusted downward. The price a third party would charge for the replacement property would include costs associated with an actual sale, and these should not be counted in determining the secured creditor's rights. For example, the price a dealer would charge if the debtor sought to replace the property would include its costs of shipping and storing the property and any costs associated with warranties it provided. The judge must deduct such costs from the replacement value.[20]

It is essential to distinguish between the rights that a secured creditor enjoys against the debtor by virtue of its claim and the rights that such a creditor enjoys against particular assets by virtue of its lien—its property interest—in those assets. In a simple Chapter 7 liquidation, the lien that the creditor enjoys is unaffected: it passes through bankruptcy. The doctrine of lien pass-through was first set out in *Long v. Bullard*.[21] Recall the example in chapter 1 above. A bank lends a debtor $100 and takes a security interest in a piece of real property that the debtor owns. A recession hits and the property drops in value and is now worth only $25. The debtor files a Chapter 7 petition. The trustee abandons the property, giving it back to the debtor. The Bankruptcy Code provides that the debtor's personal liability to the bank and all other creditors is discharged. The bank remains free to foreclose on the land once it is in the debtor's hands because the lien survives, or passes through, bankruptcy.

Although the question whether liens pass through bankruptcy is straightforward, the extent to which they do is controversial. Return to our example. Assume that immediately after bankruptcy, the debtor is able to raise $25 from friends to pay off the bank. Can the bank insist that even though its claim has been discharged, the lien survives at its original amount of $100? The debtor will argue that the lien was stripped down as it passed through bankruptcy. On the face of it, the debtor might seem right. Section 506(d) of the Bankruptcy Code permits lien strip-down of a claim bifurcated by §506(a): "To the extent that a lien secures a claim against the debtor that is not an allowed secured claim, such lien is void." This language seems to provide that the bank's lien is void to the extent that it exceeds the amount of its secured claim. The debtor originally owed the bank $100, but the

---

[20] See Associates Commercial Corp. v. Rash, 520 U.S. 953, 965 n.6 (1997).
[21] 117 U.S. 617 (1886).

bank's secured claim is for only $25. Hence, the lien is void to the extent it exceeds $25. The debtor could pay the bank $25 and remove the lien on the property.

The bank, however, can argue that §506(d) was not aimed at lien strip-down at all. Rather, the provision was designed to prevent liens from surviving bankruptcy if the underlying claim was disallowed. Consider the following example. A lawyer provides legal services at an exorbitant fee and secures it with a lien on the debtor's property. Another section of the Bankruptcy Code disallows the lawyer's claim, but only §506(d) voids the lawyer's lien. Under this view, the purpose of §506(d) was not to strip down liens but rather to make sure that a creditor's lien fares no better than her claim. Section 506(d) ensures that the lawyer is both denied a pro rata share of the debtor's assets in bankruptcy and prevented from seizing collateral after the bankruptcy is over. The language, aimed at this specific kind of abuse, was never intended to deal with a valid creditor's lien and should not be read to do so.

Stripping down a lien in bankruptcy has the effect after the fact of benefiting debtors at the expense of creditors. If the bankruptcy judge places too high a value on the land, the debtor can surrender the land to the secured creditor. If the bankruptcy judge errs on the low side, the debtor can pay the bank this amount and keep the land. In other words, debtors can systematically take advantage of judicial valuations that are too low but not be stuck with valuations that are too high. Lien stripping runs contrary to established practice in bankruptcy before the 1978 Bankruptcy Act. It also runs contrary to the notion in real estate law that when a debtor defaults, the value of the land is set through a foreclosure sale rather than through a judicial valuation.

The Court accepted the bank's argument against lien strip-down in *Dewsnup v. Timm*.[22] The majority's opinion noted that had it simply looked at §506 "on a clean slate," it would have agreed with the debtor and stripped down the lien to the value of the property. But in light of the historical practice against lien strip-down and a plausible argument that the provision was aimed at an altogether different problem, the majority concluded that strip-down was not allowed.

Because of the special treatment accorded liens in Chapters 11 and 13, *Dewsnup* has limited impact. Nevertheless, it sparked a major debate over statutory interpretation. In a strong dissent, Justice Antonin

---

[22] 502 U.S. 410 (1992).

Scalia rejected the bank's interpretation of §506(d). To have the effect that the bank claimed, Justice Scalia wrote the provision should have been phrased this way: "To the extent that a lien secures a claim against the debtor that is not an allowed claim, such lien is void." In Justice Scalia's view, we should not treat the allowed *secured* claims of creditors like the bank as if they were the same as "allowed claims." The result here may be contrary to preexisting practice, undesirable for creditors, and unsound as a matter of bankruptcy policy, but that should not be enough to deny the statutory language the meaning that both makes sense on its own and is consistent with the way the language is used elsewhere in the Code.

Justice Scalia's approach is rooted in the approach he takes to statutory interpretation. The concept of the allowed secured claim is unique to the 1978 Act and has no statutory or case-law antecedents. These words are carefully defined and repeatedly and consistently used in other parts of the 1978 Act. Courts should assume that drafters knew what they were doing. Competent drafters are unlikely to make such mistakes with stylized terms of art that are a fundamental part of the architecture of the statute. Although Justice Scalia failed to command a majority in *Dewsnup*, his concerns surface frequently both in majority opinions of the Court and in the bankruptcy courts.

CHAPTER FIVE

Property of the Estate and the Strong-Arm Powers

After establishing what claims creditors have, we need to know what assets are available to satisfy them. Outside of bankruptcy, creditors rely on assets that the debtor itself owns. Bankruptcy law ensures that creditors can look to these assets in bankruptcy as well. Through §541(a), creditors are able to enjoy whatever the debtor itself could enjoy, and all these assets become property of the estate. If we are dealing with a limited liability corporation, the creditors are entitled to whatever the debtor has, including future income. Section 541 lets the trustee sell the debtor's equipment, collect money owed the debtor, and bring the lawsuits the debtor has against third parties for the benefit of the general creditors. If we are dealing with a flesh-and-blood individual debtor, matters are slightly more complicated. The fresh start policy requires that we exclude future income from property of the estate and that we allow the debtor to share in property of the estate that is exempt. Section 541 is otherwise quite straightforward. The principal difficulty is ensuring that the bankruptcy process does not expand or contract the property rights the debtor enjoyed outside of bankruptcy.

Creditors outside of bankruptcy sometimes can reach assets that the debtor has attempted to transfer in whole or in part to someone else. Under the Bankruptcy Code, the trustee has analogous powers he can exercise on behalf of the creditors. The trustee can *avoid*—that is, nullify or undo—transfers that the debtor makes with the intent to delay, hinder, or defraud creditors. Similarly, the trustee can void security interests in assets that have not been properly perfected. These assets become part of the bankruptcy estate by virtue of the trustee's *strong-arm power*. This power is based on a sharing rule in which an unperfected secured creditor is treated the same as a general creditor who has not yet reduced its claim to judgment. The operation of the strong-arm power in §544 and §545 is quite straightforward, as is its relationship with §541(a)(1). Whenever there is an asset that the creditors want, we ask first whether the asset is one that the debtor could enjoy outside of bankruptcy. If the answer is yes, the asset becomes property of the estate under §541(a)(1). If the answer is no, we ask next whether the trustee can bring the asset into the estate by virtue of the strong-arm power.

Using both §541 and §544 to identify the assets that creditors enjoy in bankruptcy, however, has created a trap for the unwary. The property brought into the estate through either section standing alone is necessarily less than our intuition tells us should be available to creditors. Judges must resist the temptation to distort the relatively simple tests each section sets out to reach assets that intuition suggests should be available to creditors. Reshaping the tests in this way undermines the operation of the Code in future cases. By remembering that the strong-arm power always works to supplement property of the estate, we avoid the dangers of expecting either §541 or §544 to produce an intuitively sensible result on its own.

Property of the Estate and the Scope of §541

Section 541(a)(1) ensures that in the case of the corporate debtor, creditors are able to reach all of the debtor's property in bankruptcy that they would be able to reach outside of bankruptcy. If a corporate debtor could enjoy a particular right outside of bankruptcy, the trustee enjoys it inside of bankruptcy. It is useful to see how §541 handles the easy cases. Suppose you take some clothes to the dry cleaner. Your dry cleaner also sells used clothing. The dry cleaner, much to your surprise, shuts down and files a Chapter 7 bankruptcy petition. It has thousands of creditors. You are not one of them. The debtor promised to clean your clothes for $5, the market price for cleaning them, due upon completion. The debtor has broken its promise, but if you have suffered no damages, you have no claim against it under nonbankruptcy law. Assume you have no immediate need for the clothes and you can easily find someone else to clean them for the same price. You go to the debtor and try to pick up your clothes and take them somewhere else. The trustee tells you that you cannot have the clothes back.

Can the trustee wave §541 at you and say that your clothes are now property of the dry cleaner's bankruptcy estate? Section 541(a)(1) gives the trustee "all legal or equitable interests of the debtor in property as of the commencement of the case." Does the debtor have a right to your clothes that amounts to an interest in property? What are the debtor's rights with respect to the clothes? Under the Uniform Commercial Code, the debtor has the *power* to give good title to the clothes to a buyer in ordinary course of business. U.C.C. §2-403(2). But the debtor has no *right* to your suit. This disposes of the §541 inquiry.

Under §541(a)(1), we worry about only the debtor's rights. For purposes of this section, we focus on whether it is able to keep the clothes in the face of your assertion of ownership. If the dry cleaner had already cleaned the clothes, it might have a mechanic's lien on the clothes that would give it a property interest in the clothes. The mechanic's lien would allow the trustee to keep the clothes until you paid for the cleaning, but let us assume the trustee has shut down operations and that the clothes have not been and will not be cleaned. In this case, the debtor cannot keep you from taking the clothes back outside of bankruptcy. Hence, the clothes do not become property of the estate under §541(a)(1). Because the debtor has no right to the clothes, the creditors do not have any rights to the clothes under §541(a)(1), either. The rights of the debtor define the outer limits of what the trustee can claim under §541(a)(1).

Cases can arise in which the debtor's ownership of a right is not clear. Consider, for example, an insurance policy. The policy itself belongs to the debtor and is property of the estate. The debtor, however, may not be entitled to the proceeds of the policy outside of bankruptcy. The policy, for example, may provide that the insurance company's obligation runs to the victim of an accident, not to the debtor. The debtor may have no ability to reach these proceeds under nonbankruptcy law. In this event, the proceeds of the insurance are not property of the estate. The victim of the accident, in addition to being a general creditor, may be entitled to pursue the insurance company during or after bankruptcy and to keep the proceeds of the policy rather than sharing them with the other creditors of the debtor.[1]

Section 541(a)(1) gives the creditors only those rights that the debtor itself enjoyed outside of bankruptcy. If a debtor owns a one-half interest in an oil well and files for bankruptcy, only the one-half interest becomes part of the estate, not the entire oil well. This rule is perfectly sensible. Suppose two corporations each have a one-half interest in the same well and both file bankruptcy petitions. We could not allow the trustees of both debtors to be entitled to the entire well.

---

[1] See Houston v. Edgeworth, 993 F.2d 51 (5th Cir. 1993); First Fidelity Bank v. McAteer, 985 F.2d 114 (3d Cir. 1993). Because the insurance policy (as opposed to the proceeds of the policy) is property of the estate, the accident victim should seek relief from the automatic stay. When the victim's right to the proceeds is clear, relief from the stay is routinely granted.

Chicago Board of Trade v. Johnson is the old case that sets out this basic principle.[2] That case revolved around the question of how to allocate the proceeds of the sale of a seat on the Chicago Board of Trade. Its owner, a man named Henderson, went into bankruptcy owing money to many people, including members of the Board of Trade. At the time, the rules of the Board of Trade required a member to pay off any outstanding obligations to other members of the Board of Trade as a condition of selling the seat. The trustee wanted all the proceeds of the seat to come into the estate and the other Board members to be treated as ordinary creditors. The Supreme Court rejected this argument. The general creditors derived their rights from the debtor. If the debtor had the right to the proceeds only after the Board members were paid, then the general creditors had the right to the proceeds only after the Board members were paid. The general creditors could not do any better outside of bankruptcy, so they should not be able to do any better inside of bankruptcy.

Whether state law deemed the seat "property" was irrelevant (in fact, the Illinois Supreme Court had already held that state law did not); what mattered were the attributes of the seat. Outside of bankruptcy, the creditors had no right to reach the proceeds of the sale until the claims of Henderson's fellow Board members had been satisfied. Nonbankruptcy law has the effect of creating priority for one type of creditor over another, and such priorities are unobjectionable so long as they apply consistently outside of bankruptcy as well as inside. *Chicago Board of Trade* remains good law, both for its narrow point about the treatment of seats on exchanges in bankruptcy and for the broad principle it embraces.[3]

If, outside of bankruptcy, the seat can be sold only if it is bundled with the corporation's name, goodwill, furniture, and client lists, then it is subject to the same limitation inside of bankruptcy. The seat becomes property of the estate, but the trustee cannot sell the seat by itself. The nonbankruptcy limitation is recognized in bankruptcy. The most common example of an asset that can be sold only in connection

---

[2] 264 U.S. 1 (1924).

[3] See In re Drexel Burnham Lambert Group Inc., 120 Bankr. 724 (Bankr. S.D.N.Y. 1990).

with another is a trademark. It cannot be conveyed apart from the goodwill associated with the mark.[4]

Let us look at one more possibility. Suppose the seat on the Board is freely saleable, but the Board's rules provide that the seat is forfeited when the debtor files a bankruptcy petition. Is this rule permissible? Although we generally respect rights as defined outside of bankruptcy, we do not allow anyone to opt out of bankruptcy altogether. Bankruptcy law respects restrictions that apply both inside of bankruptcy and out, but those that apply only in bankruptcy are ignored. This "ipso facto" principle is reflected in §541(c)(1) and in §545 with respect to statutory liens and in §365 with respect to executory contracts.[5]

The principle of *Chicago Board of Trade* applies quite broadly. It is useful, for example, when we want to understand the rights that creditors enjoy by virtue of a license that their debtor enjoys. Courts have included in property of the estate everything from liquor licenses to broadcast licenses.[6] The *Chicago Board of Trade* principle ensures that debtors in bankruptcy enjoy the license on the same terms and subject to the same conditions as they did outside of bankruptcy. Suppose a failing airline files a Chapter 7 petition. It has a right to landing slots at a major airport, and another airline would pay a lot to have them. The airline's landing slots are, of course, property of the estate. The airline, however, needs to shut down its operations for a time, and FAA rules provide that an airline loses its slots once it stops using them. Bankruptcy law does nothing to prevent the loss of the slots. This limitation on the debtor's property is one that applies outside of bankruptcy, and hence it applies inside of bankruptcy as well.[7] A debtor's property does not shrink by happenstance of bankruptcy, but it does not expand, either.

---

[4] See, e.g., Vittoria North America v. Euro-Asia Imports Inc., 278 F.3d 1076 (2001).

[5] The Second Circuit has suggested, however, that there is no "ipso facto" principle embedded in the Bankruptcy Code and that courts should invoke it only when the text of the Code explicitly authorizes it. See U.S. Bank Trust National Association v. AMR Corp., 730 F.3d 88, 105–06 (2d Cir. 2013).

[6] See, e.g., Abboud v. The Ground Round, Inc., 335 Bankr. 253 (B.A.P. 1st Cir. 2005); Ramsey v. Dowden (In re Central Arkansas Broadcasting Co.), 68 F.3d 213 (8th Cir. 1995).

[7] See Federal Aviation Administration v. Gull Air, Inc., 890 F.2d 1255, 1261 n.8 (1st Cir. 1989).

A more troublesome case arises when the issuer of the license is also a creditor. Suppose a town decides to auction off a taxi medallion. To encourage small entrepreneurs, the town agrees to finance much of the purchase price. One company makes a winning bid of $11,000 for the medallion. The company makes a down payment of $1,000 and promises to pay the balance over a number of years. The company borrows an additional $10,000 to pay for a used cab. The company's owner is confident that the taxi can generate enough money to pay back the town and the creditors and still leave the owner with a healthy profit. The local economy suffers a downturn, however, and the cab service is less popular than expected. As a result, the company cannot meet its obligations to the town and to the other creditors. It files a Chapter 11 petition. The company is insolvent: it owes $20,000, but the business is worth only $15,000.

The taxi medallion is property of the estate under §541(a) and comes into the estate. Consistent with *Chicago Board of Trade*, however, it becomes part of the estate subject to all its nonbankruptcy limitations. If the company had no ability to sell the medallion outside of bankruptcy without the town's consent, it has no ability to do so inside.[8] At the same time, under §541(c)(1) the town could not cause the medallion to be forfeited in the event of bankruptcy. This rule vindicates again the principle that bankruptcy itself does not expand or limit a debtor's property rights.

As we shall see when we discuss the reach of the automatic stay in chapter 9 below, it is not always easy to draw the line between actions that the government takes by virtue of its position as postpetition regulator and those it takes as the holder of a prepetition claim. In the example above, nothing should prevent the license from becoming property of the estate.

When the regulator is the federal government, disputes may not even be adjudicated in the bankruptcy forum. Judicial oversight of federal administrative agencies may occur first through administrative tribunals and then through the court of appeals.[9] Nevertheless, the

---

[8] The principle of *Chicago Board*, even if not acknowledged explicitly, is also at work in cases in which courts defer to the nonbankruptcy rights of leagues to approve new owners when selling sports franchises. See, e.g., In re Dewey Ranch Hockey, LLC, 414 Bankr. 577 (Bankr. D. Ariz. 2009) (sale of NHL franchise).

[9] See In re Federal Communications Commission, 217 F.3d 125 (2d Cir. 2000).

government cannot vindicate its rights as a creditor by taking advantage of its regulatory powers. The Bankruptcy Code prevents the government from discriminating against debtors in bankruptcy with respect to the licenses or permits it issues. A governmental unit that attempts to exploit its ability to withhold licenses as a lever to enhance its rights as a creditor risks being hoisted by its own petard, as such actions violate the antidiscrimination provision of §525.[10]

The idea that the trustee succeeds to the debtor's rights with all their limitations applies with full force to whatever causes of action that a debtor has against third parties. If the debtor could sue a third party for committing a tort against it outside of bankruptcy, the trustee can bring the suit inside. The third party for its part can assert whatever defenses it would have been able to assert outside of bankruptcy.

Assume, for example, that one of debtor's employees engaged in fraud with the help of its auditor. The trustee will try to bring an action against the auditor, but she will very likely find herself subject to the defense of *in pari delicto*. The auditor will argue that the employee's bad behavior should be imputed to the debtor. Someone who takes part in wrongdoing may not recover damages resulting from the wrongdoing. If the wrongdoing of the employee can be imputed to the debtor (as it might be if the employee was committing the fraud to enrich the coffers of the debtor rather than to steal from it), the debtor may find its path to recovery barred.

The application of *in pari delicto* in any case turns on the particular facts of the case and on the precise shape of the defense under the applicable state's law. If this defense would have worked against the debtor outside of bankruptcy, it works against the trustee inside.[11] Consistent with the *Butner* principle, bankruptcy law takes state-law based causes of action as it finds them, just as it takes other property rights.

The Strong-Arm Power Under §544(a)

Outside of bankruptcy, a general creditor sometimes has greater rights than its debtor and can levy on assets to which the debtor does not enjoy paramount rights. The most common case arises when a

---

[10] See F.C.C. v. NextWave Personal Communications, Inc., 537 U.S. 293 (2003).

[11] Peterson v. McGladrey & Pullen, LLP, 676 F.3d 594 (7th Cir. 2012).

debtor buys a machine from someone who retains a security interest in it but fails to perfect that interest by filing a financing statement. The debtor has no right to keep the machine vis-à-vis its seller if the debtor defaults on its payments. Under nonbankruptcy law, however, a creditor that reduces its claim to judgment can levy on the machine and take priority over the seller. To ensure that creditors can look to the same assets inside a bankruptcy proceeding as outside, the Bankruptcy Code must provide some mechanism to ensure that these assets become part of the estate as well. Section 544(a) serves this function.

Section 544(a) gives the trustee the right to that which the general creditors could have reached under nonbankruptcy law. The trustee has, in the case of personal property, the rights of a hypothetical lien creditor who comes into being and levies at the moment the petition is filed. In the case of real property, the trustee has the rights of a hypothetical bona fide purchaser for value. Section 544(b) enables the trustee to assert the rights that actual creditors would have had under state law, even if a creditor who came into being only at the time of the petition would have arrived too late to have a cause of action. Among the most important of these rights is the right of creditors to set aside transfers that a debtor makes, while insolvent, for less than reasonably equivalent value as well as any transfers that delay, hinder, or defraud creditors. These transfers, known as fraudulent conveyances, are examined in chapter 7 below. Here we will focus on the general structure of §544 itself.

Section 544(a) gives us a measuring rod to determine who prevails in a contest between the trustee and adverse claimants: if an imaginary lien creditor (or bona fide purchaser) as defined in §544(a) would prevail against the adverse interest, the trustee wins. The person whose interest is avoided is reduced to the status of a general creditor. The property itself becomes property of the estate, and all the general creditors (including the erstwhile property claimant) share in it pro rata. There are two important points to keep in mind here: first, the trustee's rights are being measured by those of a *third party*, and second, this particular third party is a *hypothetical* one.

In the case of personal property, the trustee enjoys the powers of a lien creditor. The general creditors can reach not only the debtor's property, but also the property that they could have reached if they had reduced their claims to judgment and levied on the assets that the debtor held. To return to the example of the dry cleaner, you are able to retrieve your suits because you can show both that the debtor had no right to the suits *and that the general creditors had no ability to reach them either.* If the dry cleaner were also in the business of selling used clothing, a buyer in ordinary course of business could have acquired good title to the suits, but a general creditor could not. Hence, the trustee loses under §544 as well as under §541. You are entitled to the suits because you clear both hurdles. The lien-creditor benchmark is easy to use and vindicates the *Butner* principle. General creditors of a dry cleaner have no way to reach suits left for cleaning outside of bankruptcy. Hence, they should have no way inside of bankruptcy either.

The effect of granting the trustee this power is to preserve the relative positions of unperfected secured creditors and general creditors outside of bankruptcy. Article 9 of the Uniform Commercial Code provides that a secured creditor will win against a general creditor if the secured creditor perfects its interest, either by filing a financing statement or by seizing the collateral before the general creditor acquires a lien on it. If a general creditor brings a lawsuit against the debtor outside of bankruptcy, reduces its claim to judgment, and levies on the property before the unperfected secured creditor asserts its rights, the secured creditor will lose. Every general creditor is a potential lien creditor.

Article 9 embraces the principle that the unperfected secured creditor claims an interest in property that is invisible to third parties. Anglo-American law generally does not recognize such ownership interests vis-à-vis third parties unless public notice is given or some other step is taken to cure the ostensible ownership problem that arises from the separation of ownership and possession. Between two competing creditors, the one who is first to cure the ostensible ownership problem is typically the one who takes priority. A general creditor acquires its property interest and cures the ostensible ownership problem in one fell swoop, by levying on the property—by having it physically seized. Hence, outside of bankruptcy the general creditor prevails over the secured creditor if it levies before the secured creditor perfects, but not otherwise.

In short, outside of bankruptcy the unperfected secured creditor and the general creditor are in a race with each other. The outcome of this race is uncertain. The effect of giving the trustee the power to avoid the unperfected secured creditor's interest is to declare a tie. In bankruptcy, the trustee represents the interests of all the general creditors, and an unperfected secured creditor whose lien is avoided becomes a general creditor. (You are not worse off trying to get a security interest and failing than you would have been if you had never tried at all.) To say that the trustee wins is to say that all creditors share equally. The bankruptcy rule, in other words, preserves the nonbankruptcy rule in the sense that in the presence of uncertainty, the creditors share equally.

In the case of real property, the trustee has the rights of a bona fide purchaser for value, not only the rights of a lien creditor. This expanded power may be premised on the notion that the trustee should always win if the competing property owner (typically a mortgagee) has not done everything that it could have done to cure the ostensible ownership problem. Under some state laws, only a bona fide purchaser, not a lien creditor, prevails against unperfected secured creditors with respect to real property. But giving the trustee this right is not inconsistent with the idea that the trustee is simply vindicating the rights of the general creditors. Even though lien creditors may not be able to defeat unrecorded real property interests directly, they may be able to do so indirectly. (A purchaser at the sheriff's sale may take good title and the lien creditors may be able to keep the proceeds.)

The first responsibility of a lawyer representing a lender with a security interest is to ensure that the client has properly perfected its security interest. Under Article 9, this is usually done at the secretary of state's office in the jurisdiction in which the debtor resides. When the debtor is a corporation, it is deemed to reside in the state in which it was incorporated. (Under the pre-2001 enactment of Article 9, the proper place to file was determined by the location of the collateral.) If bankruptcy is already on the horizon, it may be too late, but often it is not. Moreover, mistakes are all too common, and lenders' interests can be unperfected for a number of reasons. Lenders might misspell the debtor's name and thus make the financing statement inaccessible. Moreover, Article 9 does not completely occupy the field. Federal law sometimes preempts Article 9. A prudent creditor who takes a security interest in a copyright, for example, will file both in the appropriate secretary of state's office and with the registrar of copyrights.[12]

Suppose a debtor borrows $100,000 from a finance company on January 1 and grants the company a security interest. The finance company fails to file the financing statement in the proper office. On

---

[12] In all likelihood, state filing is appropriate with respect to unregistered copyrights and federal filing with respect to registered ones. See Aerocon Engineering, Inc. v. Silicon Valley Bank (In re World Auxiliary Power Co.), 303 F.3d 1120 (9th Cir. 2002). But one has to worry about copyrighted works, such as software programs, that are continually updated.

March 1, the debtor files for bankruptcy. Under nonbankruptcy law, lien creditors prevail over (or, as many lawyers would say, *prime*) secured creditors if their lien arises before the security interest is perfected. To perfect its interest, the finance company must file a financing statement in the proper office. Because the company failed to do that, it will lose to a lien creditor on March 1, the date the debtor files for bankruptcy. The trustee has the powers of a lien creditor, so the finance company will lose to the trustee in bankruptcy. There is, however, a small hitch in the literal language of §544. Section 544(a) seems to require that the secured creditor have an interest that is "voidable" by a lien creditor. Under nonbankruptcy law, however, a lien creditor can only make the secured creditor's interest "subordinate" to its own.

Suppose instead that the finance company realizes its mistake before it is too late and files its interest the day before the debtor files for bankruptcy. Under Article 9, the finance company's security interest is perfected on the date it filed. On March 1, could a lien creditor defeat the finance company's interest? The answer is no, it could not. A lien creditor needs to become a lien creditor *before* the security interest is perfected. Because a creditor cannot win if it levies after the security interest is perfected, the trustee cannot win under §544(a). So long as no other part of the Bankruptcy Code allows the trustee to set aside the finance company's property interest, the finance company's security interest will be respected in bankruptcy and it will be paid ahead any of the general creditors.

The finance company's last-minute grab is suspicious, but this kind of conduct is not something to which §544(a) is directed, just as §541(a)(1) is not directed at reaching assets that the debtor could not enjoy outside of bankruptcy. As we will see in chapter 8, the trustee will probably be able to avoid the finance company's interest as a preference under §547. Given that these sections work cumulatively, it is important to resist the temptation to assess the Bankruptcy Code's results prematurely.

The Trustee as Successor to Creditor Claims

Section 544(b) is quite different from §544(a). To use §544(b), the trustee must find a real, live creditor with an *allowable* and *unsecured* claim. Thus, the trustee must find an actual unsecured creditor of the debtor who, on the date of bankruptcy, is able to assert an interest in property that the debtor has transferred to a third party. If this creditor can reach that asset outside of bankruptcy, notwithstanding the transfer (or, to use the language of the Bankruptcy Code, can avoid the debtor's transfer of that asset), the trustee can use §544(b) to step into the shoes of that creditor. The trustee recovers the asset from the third party. The trustee does not then turn over the asset to the creditor who would have reached it outside of bankruptcy. Instead, the asset is placed in the pile of assets that is divided pro rata among all the general creditors. This part of §544(b) is difficult to justify. One must explain why the creditor who had this right outside of bankruptcy must share it with other creditors inside bankruptcy.

The best justification for it is an entirely pragmatic one. Often when the trustee uses §544(b), nearly all the creditors have the right to avoid the transfer. To exclude from the distribution the creditors who would not have shared in the recovery under nonbankruptcy law may impose substantial administrative costs and have only a small effect on the distribution of the assets. Imagine, for example, that the debtor made a bulk sale of its inventory and did not follow the procedures set out in Article 6 of the Uniform Commercial Code. Article 6 allows only creditors of the debtor at the time of the bulk sale to avoid it.[13] There may be few creditors at the time of the petition who were not also creditors at the time of the bulk sale. Nevertheless, the trustee cannot set aside the transfer under §544(a). Under that section, the trustee asserts the rights of a hypothetical lien creditor who came into being only at the time of the filing of the bankruptcy petition. Section 544(b) is therefore needed to allow the creditors to act collectively. Because identifying the few creditors who were not creditors at the time of the bulk sale is difficult, distributing the recovery to everyone may sensibly approximate the nonbankruptcy regime.

A second feature of §544(b) is more troubling. Section 544(b) gives the trustee the power to avoid a transfer in its entirety, even if the party into whose shoes the trustee steps could have avoided only part of it. Consider a corporation that goes through a leveraged buyout. If the leveraged buyout leaves the corporation insolvent, the buyout is a

[13] This illustration is somewhat old-fashioned, as bulk sales laws have been repealed in many jurisdictions in recent years. As we discover in the next section, the revised version of Article 6, in the few jurisdictions that have kept bulk sales law, introduces a complication, ignored here, by characterizing the rights against buyers as damage actions rather than avoidance actions.

fraudulent conveyance.[14] Under state nonbankruptcy law, only creditors who had lent money to the corporation before the buyout would be able to bring a fraudulent conveyance action. The overwhelming majority of the creditors, however, appeared on the scene after the leveraged buyout, having lent with full knowledge of the leveraged buyout. Under state law, then, neither these creditors nor a hypothetical lien creditor who came into being at the time of the petition could bring a fraudulent conveyance action. Only one creditor was owed money at the time of the buyout and is still unpaid at the time of the petition. That creditor is a consumer who bought an oven under warranty and who now has a $1 claim because the oven's light bulb has burned out. This consumer is a creditor within the meaning of state fraudulent conveyance law both at the time of the petition and at the time of the buyout.[15]

Under nonbankruptcy law, this creditor could bring a fraudulent conveyance action at the time the bankruptcy petition is filed. Section 544(b) allows the trustee to step into the shoes of this single creditor. Under nonbankruptcy law, this creditor could never recover more than $1. The trustee, however, faces no such cap. The trustee can set aside a billion dollar transfer on the basis of a single creditor's $1 claim. All that matters is the existence of a single "golden creditor," as she is sometimes called, at the time of the petition who has the power to bring an avoidance action against someone. The amount of that creditor's claim places no limit on the extent of the trustee's power to avoid the transfer. This strange rule originated in *Moore v. Bay*.[16]

The Limits of the Trustee's Avoiding Power

Assume that many general creditors lend money to a corporation. The corporation's shareholders are so casual about maintaining the corporate form and separating their own assets from those of the cor-

---

[14] See Kupetz v. Wolf, 845 F.2d 842 (9th Cir. 1988). We examine the way fraudulent conveyances affect leveraged buyouts and other corporate transactions in greater detail in chapter 7 below.

[15] It does not matter whether the creditor's claim is matured or unmatured, liquidated or unliquidated, fixed or contingent, disputed or undisputed. See Uniform Fraudulent Transfer Act §1(3).

[16] 284 U.S. 4 (1931). The opinion itself is opaque. For an analysis of it under the Bankruptcy Code, see Lippe v. Bairnco Corp., 225 Bankr. 846 (S.D.N.Y. 1998).

poration that the general creditors, under nonbankruptcy law, will be able to *pierce the corporate veil* that shields shareholders from the obligations of the corporation. When they are able to pierce the veil, creditors can sue the shareholders directly and recover what the creditors lent the corporation. If the corporation files for bankruptcy, should the trustee be able to bring the veil-piercing action on behalf of the general creditors? If the corporation itself has the power under nonbankruptcy law to sue its own shareholders and recover from them, the cause of action would be property of the estate under §541. The trustee would be able to assert it for the benefit of the creditors, just as the trustee can bring a contract or tort action that the debtor could have brought outside of bankruptcy. One never reaches the question whether the trustee could bring the action by using one of the avoiding powers.

But if the debtor could not itself bring the action, the trustee likely cannot bring it, either. In *Caplin v. Marine Midland Grace Trust Company*, the Supreme Court examined the trustee's ability to bring damage actions that the debtor itself could not have brought.[17] In that case, the Supreme Court held under the old Bankruptcy Act that the trustee could not bring a damage action on behalf of bondholders against the agent charged with representing their interests.[18] The agent may have failed to monitor the debtor as it was charged to do, but the action the bondholders had against their agent was of no concern to the debtor's other creditors. The fiduciary duty breached in *Caplin* was owed to the bondholders, not to the debtor. A creditor of a debtor ordinarily cannot complain when a third party violates a duty owed to another creditor.

Section 544(b) allows the trustee only to avoid *transfers* that the debtor made or obligations the debtor incurred. It does not give the trustee the right to bring *damage actions*; rather, the trustee can bring damage actions only if the debtor itself would have been able to bring the action outside of bankruptcy. As noted, this issue commonly arises when the debtor has so disregarded its corporate form that its shareholders are liable for its obligations. Veil-piercing actions are in many respects identical to the avoiding actions that the trustee undoubtedly enjoys under §544(a). It is difficult to explain why the trustee should be able to avoid transfers of property that the creditors could have

---

[17] 406 U.S. 416 (1972).

[18] The agent is usually called the *indenture trustee*.

avoided, but not bring damage actions. The purpose of the trustee's strong-arm powers under §544 is to vindicate the rights of creditors as a group. Why the trustee may bring a fraudulent conveyance action against shareholders when the corporation transfers assets to them while it is insolvent, yet not bring a veil-piercing action when the shareholders fail to capitalize the business adequately initially, is a mystery. Nevertheless, as §544 has generally been interpreted, the trustee does not possess the power to bring such damage actions in her own right. She can bring them only if the debtor itself could.[19]

Some federal courts have found that the debtor can bring veil-piercing actions against its own shareholders, and hence the trustee can as well because of §541.[20] State law authority for this proposition, however, is not easy to find. Indeed, the gravamen of the action—that the corporation and the shareholders are one and the same—is inconsistent with the idea that the company can sue the shareholders. At least one state supreme court has repudiated a federal circuit court's opinion that the debtor did possess such a cause of action against its shareholders.[21]

Because the debtor in possession has the same powers as the trustee, allowing the trustee to bring a veil-piercing action creates a conflict of interest in the typical Chapter 11 case. The debtor in possession is ordinarily the group of managers running the business; often the managers are substantial shareholders and thus unlikely to bring an action against themselves. In such cases, an individual creditor or the creditors' committee can ask the court for leave to bring the action for and in the name of the debtor in possession.[22] To obtain permission to bring the action, a creditor or the creditors' committee must establish both that the trustee or debtor in possession has unjustifiably refused a demand to pursue the action and that the cause of action is worth pursuing.[23] Alternatively, either can ask for the appointment of an examiner to bring the action.

[19] See, e.g., Breeden v. Kirkpatrick & Lockhart LLP (In re The Bennett Funding Group, Inc.), 336 F.3d 94 (2d Cir. 2003).

[20] See, e.g., Steyr-Daimler-Puch of America Corp. v. Pappas, 852 F.2d 132 (4th Cir. 1988).

[21] See In re Rehabilitation of Centaur Insurance Co., 632 N.E.2d 1015 (Ill. 1994).

[22] See Official Committee of Unsecured Creditors v. Chinery, 330 F.3d 548 (3d Cir. 2003).

[23] See In re Perkins, 902 F.2d 1254 (7th Cir. 1990).

There is another justification for limiting the trustee's ability to bring damage actions, quite apart from the conflict of interest that arises when we are in Chapter 11 and there is a debtor in possession. Recall the rule of *Moore v. Bay*. It requires the trustee to turn over any avoided transfer or damage recovery to creditors as a group, not those creditors who would have been able to avoid it under nonbankruptcy law. Given the rule in *Moore v. Bay, Caplin* serves to prevent general creditors from sharing in a recovery that only a few creditors would enjoy under nonbankruptcy law.

Whenever such anomalies exist, we should expect related areas of the law to be affected as well. The sharp distinction that *Caplin* and its progeny have drawn between creditor avoidance actions and creditor damage actions led the drafters of Revised Article 6 of the Uniform Commercial Code to recharacterize as a damage action the right creditors have against a buyer who runs afoul of the bulk sales act. This change from prior law was made to take advantage of *Caplin* and limit the trustee's rights in bankruptcy.[24]

Statutory Liens and Constructive Trusts

The different roles that §541 and §544 play becomes especially important when confronting cases involving statutory liens and constructive trusts. Take first the case in which some creditors benefit from a special state statute. Many states, for example, have statutes that protect special interests, such as those of liquor wholesalers. The state statute entitles these creditors to be paid in full before any of the general creditors.[25] Constructive trust cases involve victims of some egregious fraud. The debtor is still holding the money or other property it purloined from the victims, and the victims insist that they are entitled to it before any of the general creditors. The victims argue that the money or other property is held by the debtor in constructive trust.[26] We look at each situation in turn.

The case of the liquor wholesaler is the easier one. As already mentioned, a state statute that applies only when the debtor is in bank-

---

[24] See U.C.C. §6-107 (1988), Official Comment 2.

[25] See California v. Farmers Markets, Inc., 792 F.2d 1400 (9th Cir. 1986); Max Sobel Wholesale Liquors v. Nolden, 520 F.2d 761 (9th Cir. 1975).

[26] See Heyman v. Kemp (In re Teltronics, Ltd.), 649 F.2d 1236 (7th Cir. 1981).

ruptcy (or that is geared to the financial condition of the debtor) should not be respected. States can establish generally applicable priorities, but they cannot dictate federal bankruptcy policy. The Bankruptcy Code tells us this explicitly in §541(c)(1) and in §545(1). Let us assume, then, that the state statute in our case applies inside of bankruptcy and out. The assets that the trustee gathers under §541(a)(1) are subject to this priority claim, but this does not end the inquiry. To say that property of the estate under §541(a)(1) is subject to the claims of the liquor wholesalers is not to say that the liquor wholesalers prime the general creditors. The trustee, in addition to asserting the rights of the debtor vis-à-vis the wholesalers under §541(a)(1), also asserts the rights of the general creditors. Section 545 follows the same principle as §544(a). We need to ask how the liquor wholesalers would fare against the hypothetical person into whose shoes the trustee steps.

We saw in §544(a) that, against secured creditors and other transferees, the trustee asserts the rights of a hypothetical person, acting in good faith, who either levied on the property or purchased at the time of the petition. Section 545 tells us that against the holders of statutory liens, as against those with security interests in real property, the trustee exercises the rights of a bona fide purchaser for value. Hence, one must ask whether the debtor could have sold the liquor free of the claims of the wholesalers. The case law has invented distinctions between such things as "statutory liens" and illegitimate "statutory priorities." In the end, however, these distinctions do not focus on the two-step inquiry the Bankruptcy Code sets out. What matters is whether the wholesaler's priority right is good inside bankruptcy and out and whether that right gives the wholesaler priority under nonbankruptcy law over a bona fide purchaser for value.

The constructive trust cases follow a similar logic. The simplest case arises when I trick you into giving me a $100 bill. I still have it in my pocket when my fraud is exposed and I file for bankruptcy. My many other creditors will argue that the bill should be shared pro rata. But you can counter that when I induced you to part with the $100 bill by fraud, I acquired possession of it, but not ownership. I hold it on your behalf in "constructive trust."[27] You hold equitable title to the $100 bill, and therefore this property interest does not become part of

[27] For this argument to work, it is essential to show that a constructive trust does in fact exist under state law. Because a constructive trust disrupts priorities, bankruptcy judges may be reluctant to find one. See Ades & Berg Group Investors v. Breeden, 550 F.3d 240 (2d Cir. 2008).

my bankruptcy estate. §541(d). My creditors cannot reach it under §541 as it is not an asset that I own.

But to prevail, you must also show that your right to the $100 bill is superior to the rights of my creditors as well. As discussed above, outside of bankruptcy there are some assets that creditors can reach, even though they do not belong to the debtor. Bankruptcy's strong-arm power ensures that they can reach the same assets in bankruptcy. Section 544(a)(1) does this, not by going through specific conflicts between the trustee and various third parties, but by providing a principle of broad applicability: the unsecured creditors of the debtor get to enjoy a pro rata share of any asset that general creditors might have reached under nonbankruptcy law. We ask whether, with respect to any assertion of ownership of personal property, the third party would prevail against a claim of a lien creditor. If the third party would prevail, the asset stays out of the bankruptcy estate.

To find out whether you get the $100 bill back, we apply this benchmark. Put differently, §544(a)(1) requires us to ask whether, under nonbankruptcy law, a lien creditor can levy on assets I hold in constructive trust. If a lien creditor could, then the trustee could as well and $100 bill would come into the estate. But if a lien creditor could not reach the property outside of bankruptcy, the trustee cannot reach it inside. As it happens, a lien creditor cannot attach property that a debtor holds in constructive trust.[28] You get your $100 bill back.

The logic here is straightforward. If a state legislature has decided that your right as the person who unwittingly was defrauded of particular property primes the rights of ordinary creditors, no bankruptcy policy justifies a different outcome. If general creditors have no way of reaching an asset outside of bankruptcy, they should not be able to reach it inside of bankruptcy.

The case law is not as clear as it might be because of a failure to understand that §541(d) and §544(a) work in sequence. Creditors enjoy an asset if they can bring it into the estate under either avenue. Section 541(d) does not keep §544(a) from operating and, more to the point, §544(a) provides a dispositive answer to the question of whether the nonpossessory property interest of the third party should be respected in bankruptcy.

---

[28] See In re Mississippi Valley Livestock, Inc., 745 F.3d 299 (7th Cir. 2014); Restatement (Third) of Restitution and Unjust Enrichment §55, Comment d; Atlas, Inc. v. United States, 459 F. Supp. 1000 (D. N.D. 1978); United Carolina Bank v. Brogan, 574 S.E.2d 112 (N.C. Ct. App. 2002).

In the case of real property, we use a different benchmark—that of the hypothetical bona fide purchaser for value. A debtor who holds an asset in constructive trust has the power (though not of course, the right) to convey good title to a bona fide purchaser for value. Because we have a different benchmark, we have a different outcome, but the basic principle of using a nonbankruptcy benchmark is the same.[29] To find out whether property that does not belong to the debtor might otherwise come into the estate under the strong-arm powers, we use the benchmark §544(a) sets out. Again, rather than going through particular conflicts, the Bankruptcy Code provides us with a generally applicable principle.

The relationship between property of the estate under §541 and the strong-arm powers of §544 is one of the most important and least appreciated in all of bankruptcy law. The trustee enjoys the rights of the debtor under §541. In addition, the trustee can assert the rights that the creditors could assert against the debtor's property outside of bankruptcy under §544. Too often lawyers focus exclusively on §541 and forget that §544 does much of the work.

In this chapter and the one before it, we have seen how the Bankruptcy Code sensibly translates the rights and obligations of a debtor to the bankruptcy forum. In the next chapter, we examine how the Bankruptcy Code handles situations in which the rights and obligations are fused together. These issues—those associated with executory contracts—present a special set of challenges.

---

[29] See Wells Fargo Funding v. Gold, 432 Bankr. 216 (E.D. Va. 2009); Belisle v. Plunkett, 877 F.2d 512 (7th Cir. 1989).

CHAPTER SIX

Executory Contracts

General Nature of Executory Contracts

The previous two chapters looked at a debtor's liabilities and assets—claims against the estate on one hand and property of the estate on the other. A tort action that a third party has against the debtor is a claim; a tort action that the debtor has against someone else is an asset. When the debtor has exchanged promises with a third party, the resulting contract is both a liability and an asset. The debtor's promise to a third party is a liability, while the third party's promise to the debtor is a claim. Section 365 of the Bankruptcy Code deals with such cases and sets out the rules governing them. The section is complicated—often unnecessarily so. Nevertheless, the basic principles at work are sound and can be demonstrated with a few variations on a single set of facts.

Let us start with the following case. I am Debtor Corporation. I pay you $5 and you agree to give me a bushel of wheat in a week. In the interim, I file a bankruptcy petition. My trustee looks at this situation. The $5 I have paid out is gone forever. But the trustee does have a right to get a bushel of wheat from you. If you do not deliver, the trustee is going to sue you. What the trustee has is an asset under §541. All the creditors of the estate are better off with your promise to deliver a bushel of wheat than they would be without it.

Now suppose you give me a bushel of wheat and I promise to pay you in a week. In the interim, I file a bankruptcy petition. What does the trustee find? Your right to get $5 from me is a garden-variety claim. You are one of many creditors, and your claim, like the others, will receive just a few cents on the dollar when the trustee ratably distributes the property of the estate.

Let us combine the first two cases. You and I enter into a contract. You promise to give me a bushel of wheat in a week, and I promise to pay you $5 for it. Here there is both a liability (I have to pay you $5 in a week) and an asset (I have a right to get a bushel of wheat from you). We give the name *executory contract* to this kind of arrangement. It is one in which the debtor has an obligation to a third party and the third party owes the debtor an obligation in return. What matters, of course, is how we treat such a beast, not what we call it.

How does the trustee feel about this contract? It depends on what has happened to the market price of wheat in the interim. Assume that the market price of wheat has gone up, and a bushel of wheat now costs $10. In this case, the trustee is thrilled. The trustee can use $5 to get something in return that is worth $10 (the bushel of wheat). This is a good deal, and the trustee should be able to take advantage of it. You should be held to your bargain: you asked for $5, you will get $5. It is a losing deal for you, but it would have been a losing deal even if no bankruptcy petition had been filed. There is nothing about bankruptcy that should let you off the hook.

The trustee is simply new management.[1] There is nothing about the deal that we entered into that conditioned your obligation to give me a bushel of wheat in exchange for $5 upon the management staying the same. We want to have a rule that says simply this: if the debtor has a good deal that new managers would have been able to enjoy outside of bankruptcy, the trustee should be able to take advantage of it inside of bankruptcy. At first cut, §365 does exactly this. As in the nonbankruptcy world, of course, the trustee has to keep the other side of the bargain. The trustee cannot get the wheat without parting with the $5. The formal process by which the trustee takes advantage of the favorable contract (and lives up to the debtor's obligations under the contract) is called *assumption*. When the trustee assumes the contract and brings it into the bankruptcy estate, the estate enjoys all the benefits of the contract, but bears all its burdens as well.

But what happens if the price of wheat plummets? Now I could buy wheat for $1, and any wheat you have you will be able to sell for only $1. The deal does not look so great. I promised to pay $5 for something that is now worth only $1. It is making deals like this that drove me into bankruptcy. Ridding oneself of a burdensome contract and exposing oneself to a damage action is a power that everyone enjoys. We live in a Holmesian world.[2] The new managers of a corporation can break a contract that the old managers entered into, provided they are liable for damages. The trustee is new management and can breach

---

[1] See Commodity Futures Trading Commission v. Weintraub, 471 U.S. 343 (1985).

[2] See Oliver Wendell Holmes, The Path of the Law, 10 Harv. L. Rev. 457, 462 (1897) ("The duty to keep a contract at common law means a prediction that you must pay damages if you do not keep it—and nothing else.").

a contract if it is in the interests of the estate. The trustee's ability to breach an executory contract (and trigger the third party's claim for damages) is, in the language of the Bankruptcy Code, the ability to *reject*. Rejection of an executory contract is not quite the same as breach of a contract outside of bankruptcy. Rejecting an unfavorable executory contract is akin to abandoning an asset.[3] Little of consequence turns on this distinction, however. For most purposes, you can safely assume that rejection of an executory contract in bankruptcy has the same consequences as breach of the same contract outside of bankruptcy.

Giving the trustee the ability to breach ensures equal treatment among those who are similarly situated. As far as their legal rights are concerned, a party who has a contract with the debtor is in the same situation as someone who has lent the debtor money. Both have the right to sue for damages if the debtor does not do what was promised. An insolvent debtor cannot keep all its promises. Rather than favor one group over another, the general rule of bankruptcy is one of pro rata sharing. Allowing the trustee to reject the debtor's contracts ensures that all those with damage actions against the debtor are treated the same way. At the end of the day, they all have a claim against the debtor and they all share pro rata in the bankruptcy estate.

This, as a very rough approximation, tells you what is at stake in §365. As illustrated above, an executory contract is something that is both an asset and a liability. When a contract is executory, the debtor is obliged to a party and that party is obliged to the debtor. The Bankruptcy Code does not define the term *executory contract*. The best-known and most widely accepted definition is Vern Countryman's. In his view, an executory contract is "a contract under which the obligation of both the [debtor] and the other party to the contract are so far unperformed that the failure of either to complete performance would constitute a material breach excusing the performance of the other."[4]

An executory contract is a good thing for the debtor if the debtor's obligation is less than what the other party owes the debtor in return. Section 365 ensures that the creditors (through the trustee) can enjoy the benefits of an executory contract that is favorable to the debtor. It

---

[3] See Brown v. O'Keefe, 300 U.S. 598 (1937); Sparhawk v. Yerkes, 142 U.S. 1 (1891).

[4] Vern Countryman, Executory Contracts in Bankruptcy (Part I), 57 Minn. L. Rev. 439 (1973).

also ensures that if the contract is unfavorable, the third party stands in the same position it would have been in had the debtor defaulted on a contract outside of bankruptcy. Painted with very broad strokes, the section makes sense. The particular details of §365, however, are harder to reconcile with one another. What we want to do now is look at the more complicated cases. The problems we face under this section fall into two categories. One is the problem that arises when the contract is a bad one and the trustee wants to breach. This is the problem of *rejection*. The other arises when the contract is terrific and the trustee wants to keep a good thing going. This is the problem of *assumption*.

Rejection

Much of the difficulty in reconciling the case law on the rejection of executory contracts stems from the failure of a number of courts early on to distinguish the power of rejection from the consequences that flow from rejection. Some courts, for example, have held that the rejection of an executory contract not only triggers a prepetition claim for damages but also deprives the other party of any benefits of the contract. This result is unsound if the other party would have been entitled to these benefits had the breach occurred outside of bankruptcy. There is no bankruptcy policy in favor of "executoriness."[5] Section 365 is not an avoiding power designed to expand the assets of the estate and give creditors inside of bankruptcy something they would not have had outside. Several examples illustrate this point.

A corporation promises to sell you the Van Gogh that hangs in its lobby for $1 million. Before payment or delivery, the price of works by Van Gogh goes through the ceiling. The business goes broke in the meantime and files a bankruptcy petition. Its assets (apart from the Van Gogh) are worth $1 million. The business owes its creditors (not counting you) $5 million. The managers of the business have been spending too much time buying art and not enough time managing the business.

The trustee wants out of this deal because the Van Gogh can now be sold for $2 million. The trustee reasons that breaching the contract is in the interests of the general creditors because if the business performs on the contract and sells you the Van Gogh, there will be $2

---

[5] See Michael Andrew, Executory Contracts in Bankruptcy: Understanding "Rejection," 59 U. Colo. L. Rev. 845 (1988).

million in assets ($1 million in other assets and the $1 million you fork over) and $5 million in claims. The general creditors will get 40 cents on the dollar. But if the trustee backs out of the deal, the Van Gogh can be sold for $2 million. Then the assets of the corporation are $3 million ($1 million from other assets and $2 million from the sale of the painting). The liabilities are $6 million ($5 million in other claims and $1 million from you for damages for the breach of contract). The damages from the breach of contract is the $1 million difference between the current market price and the amount set in the contract ($2 million minus $1 million). Creditors will get 50 cents on the dollar.

To understand whether the trustee can in fact reject this contract and face only a damage action from you, we need to ask what would have happened if the business's managers had refused to turn over the Van Gogh outside of bankruptcy. You would be able to bring a specific performance action. Vis-à-vis the corporation, you have the right to the painting. Because the Van Gogh is unique, you do not simply get money damages. You get the painting. But you are in a race with the corporation's general creditors. You also need to ask whether you would be able to take the Van Gogh *in the face of their claims*.

We must go through the same process we went through in chapter 5 when we looked at rights that the creditors enjoyed by virtue of §541(a)(1) and those they enjoyed by virtue of the trustee's strong-arm power under §544 and §545. To measure your rights in bankruptcy, you have to worry about how well you would fare not only against the debtor but also against creditors of the debtor who reduced their claims to judgment and levied on the painting. If a lien creditor could prime your right to the painting outside of bankruptcy, you should not be able to insist on getting the painting when the corporation is in bankruptcy. Nonbankruptcy law generally gives priority to the lien creditor. Under U.C.C. §2-402, the property is subject to creditor levy so long as the seller retains possession. You might have a special buyer's lien on these goods if you had already paid for them, but you have not. The rule we have is that your rights to the picture are superior to those of corporation's creditors only after you cure the ostensible ownership problem. For this reason, you should have only a damage claim in the corporation's bankruptcy if you have not taken possession of the picture. Section 365 provides for this result.

Section 365 also applies to leases. Let us take some simple cases. Suppose I have rented a store on Rodeo Drive from you. I am paying $10,000 a month in rent, and I am bound to pay you this amount each year for five years, for a total of $600,000. The market for stores on

Rodeo Drive collapses. The rental value of the store is now much low-er. I file a bankruptcy petition. My trustee can break this lease, just as I was free to break the lease outside of bankruptcy. Outside of bank-ruptcy, you would have an action for the damages you have suffered as a result of my breach. In bankruptcy, the trustee can reject the lease and you are left with an action for damages.[6]

Let us look at the other side of this transaction. I own a piece of re-al property that you rent from me. You agreed to pay me $5,000 a month for six years. The lease obliges me to heat and cool the build-ing, which costs me $2,000 a month. A year into the lease we find ourselves in the midst of a real estate boom. If you were to lease the property from me now, you would have to pay me $10,000 a month. I file a bankruptcy petition. What can my trustee do? More specifically, is there any way that the trustee can take advantage of the dramatic increase in the rental value of the property?

Outside of bankruptcy, I could cut off the heating and cooling of the building. In most jurisdictions, you could respond by either leaving the property and suing me for damages or by remaining in possession of the property and paying for the heating and cooling by deducting it from the rent. If we raise these questions in bankruptcy, we find much the same answers. The trustee can reject the lease and cease heating and cooling the building. Just as you could outside of bankruptcy, you can call off the whole deal and sue for damages. Alternatively, you can exercise your right to pay for heating and cooling out of the rental payments that would otherwise be owed. Your right to stay in posses-sion and offset such costs is given explicitly in §365(h). The trustee's rejection of my obligations under the lease, however, does nothing to dispossess you of the property. You have a right to stay in possession of the property. You have a leasehold interest. This property interest gives you a right to the asset that primes that of any of my creditors. Not even a bona fide purchaser of the property from the debtor can take it free of your right to enjoy the property for the remainder of the lease term. Although the general rule of *Chicago Board of Trade* would itself be sufficient to give us this result, §365(h) makes the point ex-plicitly.

The drafters of the Bankruptcy Code created problems by provid-ing such an explicit rule for real property but not for personal property.

---

[6] Recall, however, that there is a cap on damages from the breach of a lease under §502(b)(6).

Should one infer that, notwithstanding *Chicago Board of Trade*, personal property is to be treated differently? Suppose I lease you a large machine tool. You pay $5,000 a month in rent. This machine now leases for $10,000 a month. I file a bankruptcy petition. The trustee can reject this lease, but what does it mean to reject it? Under non-bankruptcy law, I cannot force you to give the machine back by declaring that I am in breach. I have conveyed a property interest to you. It is a done deal. You are in possession. I can yell "I breach!" all I want, but I cannot force you to give me the machine back. In bankruptcy, the trustee can convert any service obligations I owed you into a general claim you have against my bankruptcy estate. It is just like the heating and cooling obligation in the case of real property. But does rejection mean anything more than that? Does it mean that the trustee can get the machine back? There is no section analogous to §365(h) for personal property. No language says explicitly that you can keep the computer in the face of the rejection.

We could infer that the absence of such language means, in our case, that when my trustee breaks a lease of personal property, you cannot remain in possession. Under the maxim of statutory interpretation of *expressio unius*, one infers from the inclusion of one thing the exclusion of another. One can infer that Congress, by providing explicitly that lessees of real property could remain in possession after rejection, implicitly found that lessees of personal property could not. One can also reach the opposite conclusion, however. An equally plausible view begins with the observation that few cases arise in which the trustee wants to reject a personal property lease. Rejection becomes attractive only when the property increases in value. This is unlikely to happen in the case of personal property. When Congress enacted §365(h), it merely confronted the case that was most likely to arise. Congress may have decided not to trust courts to rely on the principle of *Chicago Board of Trade* in the case of real property, but not have thought about the analogous case of personal property at all. Setting out the rule explicitly in the case of real property does not require the inference that Congress was repudiating the general principle elsewhere. Indeed, why would Congress repudiate so important a doctrine by indirection?

There is an important lesson here. It is one thing to say that the trustee can reject and free the estate from ongoing obligations with respect to a lease or an executory contract. It is quite another thing to identify the consequences that flow in the wake of such a rejection. Rejection does not necessarily return the parties to the position they were in before they entered into the deal. A trustee can reject a lease of property, but that does not mean that the leasehold is extinguished and that the estate regains ownership of the property. Nothing about the nature of "rejection" requires that the trustee be able to undo (or "avoid") what is tantamount to a consummated property transfer. We need to keep this lesson in mind as we look at the rejection of technology licensing agreements, covenants not to compete, and the like.

Let us look at the following problem. A business develops a new soft drink. Your client acquires the exclusive right to sell it in Kalamazoo, paying $10,000 up front and agreeing to pay an additional $1 for each case it sells. (Your client has the formula and manufactures the drink itself. The business, however, promises to run various local and national advertising campaigns.) The soft drink is a big hit in Kalamazoo, but it is a bust in the rest of the country. The business files a Chapter 11 petition. The trustee wants to take away your client's exclusive right to distribute the soft drink in Kalamazoo. If the trustee could do this, the trustee could then enter into a new licensing agreement with your client at a much higher fee. Alternatively, the trustee could sell the right to market the soft drink in Kalamazoo to someone else. The trustee argues that the exclusive distribution right is an executory contract. Moreover, the trustee contends that your client loses the right to sell the drink as soon as the contract is rejected and the business gains the ability to license others to sell it in Kalamazoo. Under the franchising arrangement, each party has obligations remaining that would, if breached under nonbankruptcy law, allow the other to call off the deal. The business has the obligation to provide some marketing support and to pay for some advertising. Your client, of course, has obligations because it has to pay the royalty of $1 per case.

One may be able to argue these obligations do not necessarily make the right to manufacture the soft drink in Kalamazoo part of an executory contract. Take the following example. A business sells you a machine and promises to service it. You promise to pay for the service. The trustee could not bundle this whole package together, call it an executory contract, reject it, take the machine back, and then sell it to someone else on that ground.

This transaction may be no different. Your client bargained for the exclusive right to sell this soft drink in Kalamazoo. Your client already has this right. The business should no more be able to get this right back in its bankruptcy than it should be able to get back a machine it sold to you. The right to sell the soft drink in Kalamazoo does not belong to the debtor anymore. One can argue that it is not the paradigm case in which I promise to sell you wheat and you promise to pay for it, but rather the quite different case in which I have already sold the wheat. Once I have sold the wheat, it is not mine anymore.

But let us assume this is wrong. Assume that what we have in the Kalamazoo case is an executory contract. Even if the distribution right is an executory contract, we still need to identify the consequences of the rejection. The trustee refuses to go ahead with the debtor's obligations under the contract and to advertise the product. But that does not trouble your client much. The soft drink is so popular that no advertising is needed. In any event, your client has a claim for the value of the ads that the business promised and this claim can be offset against any royalties that are owed. But can your client keep on selling the soft drink? This seems to parallel the ability of a lessee to remain in possession. Under nonbankruptcy law, the business would not be able to stop your client from selling the soft drink. The business is the breaching party. It cannot go to court and get your client to stop, just as a lessor of real property on Rodeo Drive cannot file a bankruptcy petition, reject the lease, and evict its tenant. Your client is a licensee who is "in possession." Why should rejection under §365 give the trustee the right to dispossess your client?

What about the debtor's desire to give someone else the right to make and sell the drink in Kalamazoo? Outside of bankruptcy, if the debtor said it was breaking its contract and started giving others the right to sell the soft drink in Kalamazoo, you could get a negative injunction in a hurry. More to the point, the debtor's general creditors cannot have a receiver appointed and assign to others your right to sell the soft drink in Kalamazoo. This case is crucially different from your right of specific performance when the trustee breached and refused to give you the Van Gogh. In that case, you had no right to the painting vis-à-vis a lien creditor. In this case, your rights are paramount. No matter how broadly we define the trustee's strong-arm powers under §544(a), they would not enable the trustee to defeat your client's right to market the soft drink. Outside of bankruptcy, neither the debtor nor its creditors would have the ability to stop your client from making the soft drink. Moreover, your client would be able to enjoin the debtor from marketing the drink. In addition, your client would also be able to enjoin any third party who acquired rights from the debtor, such as a buyer of the business or its assets. Before we conclude that your client should prevail, however, we need to ask whether any other bankruptcy policy enters into the picture. The principal question focuses on how the debtor's discharge will affect your client's rights.

Suppose a store sells you a computer with a warranty and you promise to pay for the computer in 30 days. The store delivers the computer. The store files a bankruptcy petition and rejects its contract with you. The computer is in short supply, and the store would like to reclaim it from you and sell it to someone else. If the trustee rejects the store's executory contract with you, you will have a claim against the store for breach of the warranty obligations. The store's discharge will extinguish your claim, but it will not change your right to keep the computer.

The strong-arm power does the trustee no good here. Using the strong-arm power, the trustee could reach the computer only if the store or a party claiming through the store could reach it. To be sure, nonbankruptcy law calls the rights you have in the machine a "property interest," but what matters is whether the trustee can assert a superior claim to it using §544(a), not whether the right is "property" under nonbankruptcy law. You have a "property interest" in the machine under nonbankruptcy law as soon as the computer is identified to the contract, but your paramount right to it does not arise until later. Given the trustee's strong-arm power, the "property interest" that arises on the identification of the goods to the contract does you no good if you have not paid for the computer and are not in possession of it.

The discharge does not affect your rights, either. Your claim against the store is discharged, but you still retain the computer and the ability to bring actions against the store to enforce the right. (The store could not seize the computer and resist your replevin action on the ground that bankruptcy had discharged your claim.) Discharge affects only general claims that third parties have against the store. Other rights that third parties enjoy pass through bankruptcy.

Similarly, in the case of the soft drink business, discharge affects your client's ability to reach the assets of the business after the bankruptcy is over. It does not give creditors the ability to control a valuable asset (like the right to sell the soft drink in Kalamazoo) that they could not have reached outside of bankruptcy. It should not matter whether the transaction involved a traditional property interest or an intangible right such as a right to distribute a soft drink. We should treat rights like those of the soft drink distributor in Kalamazoo in the same way we treat traditional property interests. So long as neither the debtor nor any hypothetical party claiming through the debtor can upset those rights under nonbankruptcy law, bankruptcy should leave them unaffected.[7]

The law in this area is clear when a traditional property right is in issue. Assume that Debtor sold Blackacre to Buyer. If Debtor later tries to move back onto Blackacre and then files a bankruptcy petition, everyone understands that Buyer's trespass action is a claim and that this claim is discharged. Everyone also understands that the discharge has no effect on Buyer's continuing ownership of Blackacre or on Buyer's ability to bring trespass actions in the future if Debtor tries to move back again. Buyer prevails because Debtor's creditors cannot bring Blackacre into the bankruptcy estate through the use of one of the avoiding powers. Discharge is itself irrelevant.

Return to the case of Victor Ortiz.[8] The boxer had conveyed to a promoter the exclusive right to promote his fights. What happens when he rejects his contract with the promoter in bankruptcy? Does the promoter have the right to prevent him from going to the other promoter? Section 365 is silent on this question. Section 365(g) provides only that rejection of an executory contract constitutes a breach of the contract. It does not set out any other consequences. To determine whether the provision remains enforceable against the debtor, we must determine first whether the right is the sort of equitable remedy that is a "claim" and therefore dischargeable in bankruptcy. As we discussed in chapter 4, it may not be. The promoter's exclusive right to promote Ortiz may be akin to a property interest, a "lien" on Ortiz's human capital, rather than a claim that is dischargeable.

But this does not end the inquiry. As we discussed in chapter 2, the principle of *Local Loan Company v. Hunt* gives individual debtors the right to free themselves from encumbrances on their future earnings. This principle may allow individual debtors to rid themselves of covenants not to compete. In all events, it requires an examination of the penumbra of §541(a)(6), not of §365. Neither §365 nor §101(5)(B) can be a source of an individual debtor's fresh start, as it applies equally to corporations in Chapter 7 that receive no discharge at all.

Congress confronted the consequences that flow from rejection in the case of technology licenses, when the licensor is the debtor and it

---

[7] See In re Printronics, Inc., 189 Bankr. 995 (Bankr. N.D. Fla. 1995).

[8] Top Rank, Inc. v. Ortiz, 400 Bankr. 755 (C.D. Cal. 2009).

seeks to recapture a license it has already issued.[9] In the main, Congress embraced the idea that rejection itself should not allow the trustee to recapture rights that the debtor has already conveyed away. The specific rules governing technology licenses in §365(n) are analogous to the specific rules governing real property in §365(h).

As in the case of §365(h), some might be tempted to draw a negative inference and infer that debtors could recapture intellectual property such as trademarks and franchise agreements that §365(n) does not explicitly cover. Courts, however, tend towards the view that rejection is not an avoidance power and that the third party can continue to use the trademark. Drawing a negative inference is inappropriate, as it assumes a notion of the rejection power that has no basis in history and makes little sense. "Nothing about this process implies that any rights of the other contracting party have been vaporized."[10]

Arguments that justify giving the trustee the power to recapture rights that could never be taken from a third party outside of bankruptcy should not, in principle, rest on the idea that there is a bankruptcy policy in favor of rehabilitating the debtor. The trustee's power to reject executory contracts under §365 is the same in Chapter 7 as in Chapter 11. Nothing in the Bankruptcy Code or its antecedents suggests that the power to reject turns on whether the debtor is liquidating or reorganizing. If it does not, then the debtor's chances of reorganizing successfully should play no role in deciding the contours of §365. The company's ability to regain control of the soft drink franchise should be independent of whether it needs the money to stay in business or whether the trustee is simply distributing the proceeds to the general creditors.

---

[9] Congress acted in the wake of Lubrizol Enterprises v. Richmond Metal Finishers, 756 F.2d 1043 (4th Cir. 1985), an opinion that interpreted the power to reject too expansively.

[10] Sunbeam Products, Inc., v. Chicago American Manufacturing, LLC, 686 F.3d 372, 377 (7th Cir. 2012). A useful discussion of the principles at work can be found in Judge Ambro's concurring opinion in In re Exide Technologies, 607 F.3d 957, 964 (3d Cir. 2010). These recent Circuit opinions repudiate *Lubrizol* and cast doubt on early bankruptcy court decisions that went the other way. See, e.g., In re Ron Matusalem & Matusa of Florida, Inc., 158 Bankr. 514 (Bankr. S.D. Fla. 1993).

Rejection of Collective Bargaining Agreements

When a large manufacturing business enters bankruptcy and has a collective bargaining agreement established in a far different environment, the debtor often seeks to renegotiate the agreement. Collective bargaining agreements have the form of an executory contract. Outside of bankruptcy, however, collective bargaining agreements are strikingly different from ordinary contracts. Collective bargaining agreements set out the relationship between management and labor. Rather than giving rise to a damage action, the failure of either side to abide by its terms is an unfair labor practice. For this reason, a special set of rules governing collective bargaining agreements supplants the ordinary rules for executory contracts when the debtor is in Chapter 11.

Section 1113 mandates negotiations between the debtor and the union. The court can authorize the rejection of a collective bargaining agreement only after the union has rejected proposals that provide for "modifications in the employees benefits and protections that are necessary to permit the reorganization of the debtor." Courts appear divided on what it means for a modification to be "necessary."[11]

It might seem that even the process that §1113 puts in place for re-negotiations in lieu of the ability to reject outright is an inappropriate departure from the *Butner* principle. A debtor in bankruptcy should have no more ability to walk away from a collective bargaining agreement than it had outside. It does not have the option to breach and pay money damages.

But the effect of §1113 is easy to exaggerate. Outside the context of an airline bankruptcy, in which the interaction of the Bankruptcy Code and the Railway Labor Act give rise to some peculiar anomalies,[12] the provision largely sets the framework for negotiations that inevitably take place when a business finds itself in extremis. Section 1113 does not give the court the ability to impose terms.[13] The employees cannot be forced to work under terms and conditions to which

---

[11] Compare Wheeling-Pittsburgh Steel Corp. v. United Steelworkers, 791 F.2d 1074 (3d Cir. 1986), with Truck Drivers Local 807 v. Carey Transportation, Inc., 816 F.2d 82 (2d Cir. 1987).

[12] See Northwest Airlines Corp. v. Association of Flight Attendants-CWA, 483 F.3d 160 (2d Cir. 2007).

[13] The bankruptcy judge, however, does have the ability to order interim modifications under §1113(e).

they never agreed. After rejection, they are free to strike or take other action as if the agreement had expired on its own accord. The rejection process does accelerate the end of the collective bargaining agreement, but labor and management must still come to terms. If the bargaining power that the union had when it negotiated the agreement (perhaps only a year or two before) remains and the union remains willing to use it, management cannot expect to do better than it did before. The new agreement reached in bankruptcy may simply reflect changed circumstances. Union leaders may welcome the ability to blame the bankruptcy process for compromises that are necessary, but extremely unpalatable.

Section 1113 does not contain a provision that parallels §365(g). There is nothing that says explicitly that the rejection of a collective bargaining agreement constitutes a breach of the contract. This has led one court to hold that damage claims are not available following rejection of a collective bargaining agreement.[14] This seems a mistake. There is no need to draw an adverse inference, and, given that employees are entitled to *greater* protections outside of bankruptcy than parties to an ordinary contract, they should not receive *fewer* inside.

Calculating damages, however, is hard. Account needs to be taken both of a reduction in wages and changes in work rules. Because the firm cannot walk away from collective bargaining agreements outside of bankruptcy, one cannot rely on the nonbankruptcy benchmark to calculate damages. A further complication arises because the collective bargaining agreement is a master agreement that controls many individual employment relationships. It may be hard to connect adverse changes to particular employees. For example, consider what happens when a rejection that leads to a renegotiated agreement in which new hires receive lower wages. The change makes the workers as a group worse off, but does not adversely affect anyone who was working at the time of the petition. Notwithstanding these difficulties and uncertainty in the law, agreements reached to resolve §1113 disputes commonly contain some form of compensation to the employees.

Assumption and Limitations on the Power to Assume

We now turn to the *assumption* of an executory contract to look at deals that the debtor has made that are good. Let us recall what our

---

[14] In re Blue Diamond Coal Co., 160 Bankr. 574, 577 (E.D. Tenn. 1993).

basic problem is. There are some things that a debtor has that are mixed assets and liabilities. I can live in this apartment, which is great, but I have to pay rent, which is not so great. I have your promise to give me wheat next week, which is great. But I have to pay you $5 for it, which is not so great. We have been looking at cases in which the burdens outweigh the benefits. Now we want to look at cases in which the burdens are light and the benefits substantial. Can you keep this good deal even though you have filed a bankruptcy petition?

Section 541 tells us that states cannot dictate distributions in bankruptcy. Any priority scheme they create has to be one that applies generally inside of bankruptcy and out. The same principle applies to contracts that the debtor makes with others. Third parties should not be able to change their relationship with the debtor merely because of the happenstance of bankruptcy. A clause that makes the fact of bankruptcy a default (an ipso facto clause) is unenforceable. As in the case of §541, this prohibition extends beyond termination clauses tied to the start of a bankruptcy case and applies to clauses tied to the insolvency or financial condition of the debtor as well. The net must be cast wide enough so that parties cannot do indirectly what they are forbidden from doing directly.

Notwithstanding their unenforceability, ipso facto clauses still abound in formbooks and preprinted contracts. These clauses persist for several reasons. These clauses were generally enforceable before the Bankruptcy Code was enacted in 1978. Though they have long ceased to do any work, they do no harm either. There is no evolutionary pressure to eliminate them, especially as they often appear in conjunction with other language—such as a reference to state insolvency proceedings—that might still be effective.

There is another reason that parties might include them. When your contracting opposite files for bankruptcy, you want to be able to come into court and assert your rights, even if no obligations are then owing. If you make a long-term loan, you do not want to be left helpless while other creditors whose loans are overdue go after whatever assets are available. An ipso facto clause makes this right unequivocal. In principle, it is unnecessary. Bankruptcy automatically accelerates obligations, regardless whether the contract provides for it. A creditor whose loan is due in 10-year's time is treated the same as someone whose loan is due today. This idea that the filing of a petition constitutes a default that accelerates obligations, however, is only immanent in the structure of the Bankruptcy Code. It is not stated in so many words. Ever cautious, lawyers do not want to take the chance that some judge might misunderstand. The ipso facto clause works to prevent this. The chance that a judge would do so is low, but the costs of including an ipso facto clause in a contract are lower still.

Apart from the question of ipso facto clauses, it would seem that the trustee should be able to assume any executory contract that is favorable to the estate. To be sure, the trustee's ability to assume executory contracts requires that the contract has not been terminated before the filing of the bankruptcy petition.[15] If there has been a default and the third party has properly terminated the contract before the petition, there is nothing for the trustee to assume. But apart from this qualification, the ability to assume seems straightforward.

Many of the issues involving the assumption of executory contracts could be handled easily if §365 did not exist at all. Courts would treat a favorable executory contract as property of the estate under §541 and apply the general principle of *Chicago Board of Trade v. Johnson*. Let us go through some examples. You run a Holiday Inn in Camden, New Jersey. You pay Holiday Inn a certain amount of money every month and you are obliged to run your hotel in a certain way. You must have ice machines on every floor. Outside of bankruptcy, your ability to keep the franchise will depend on whether you comply with these conditions. Courts will not second-guess their wisdom or purpose. (This may be a good thing. Judges make for poor hoteliers, and there is always the risk they will regard as unnecessary requirements that are in fact forward-looking. Holiday Inn, for example, insisted on wheelchair accessibility decades before it was required to do so.)

The benefits of being a Holiday Inn are quite substantial. You have the benefit of the company's computerized reservation system; you get a discount on credit card fees. (Credit card companies charge those who accept credit cards for reimbursing them.) You also get extra business from people who have never heard of your hotel before they came to Camden because they know what to expect. If you had exactly the same hotel, but did not have the Holiday Inn sign, your hotel would be worth much less.

Notwithstanding the Holiday Inn franchise, however, your hotel is a complete bust. The idea of a Holiday Inn in Camden seemed like a good one at the time, but not that many people who come to Camden want to spend the night there. You can get more money for the assets

---

[15] Nemko, Inc. v. Motorola, Inc., 163 Bankr. 927 (Bankr. E.D.N.Y. 1994).

if you blow up the building and use the property as a parking lot rather than as a hotel. Let us assume that you have been religious in complying with the rules. You have never let an ice machine run out of ice. When you close up shop, can you sell your franchise to someone else at a better location? We have already talked about this question. The answer should hinge entirely on whether the right you have acquired can be transferred. Whether the franchise can be transferred, like the question that arose in *Chicago Board of Trade* over whether a seat could be sold, should turn on applicable nonbankruptcy rules.

Let us assume that your deal with Holiday Inn ties your franchise to a particular location. Your deal permits you to sell the franchise outside of bankruptcy, but only if you sell the hotel as a going concern. Should this change in bankruptcy? Any bankruptcy policy that justifies a different outcome has nothing to do with giving you a fresh start. You are out of the hotel business. The hotel itself is being converted into a parking lot. If your general creditors can sell the Holiday Inn franchise to some third party who operates a hotel at a different location, they would be better off and Holiday Inn would be worse off. Your creditors would have the proceeds from the sale of the franchise instead of Holiday Inn. In addition, Holiday Inn would lose the ability to choose the new location and its operator. (For example, the new owner might not conform to Holiday Inn's efforts to make each Holiday Inn be like every other and thereby ensure that its guests will not face any unwelcome surprises in a strange place.)

This outcome makes no sense. There is no bankruptcy policy that suggests that we should deprive the Holiday Inns of this world of the revenue from the sale of franchises or control over their franchisees in order to put money into the hands of the general creditors. Giving general creditors more and third parties less, of course, has utterly no bearing on an individual's fresh start.

But consider a different case. Suppose you want to stay in the hotel business. The idea may have been bad, but given the investment you have already made, you are better off using the building as a hotel. Everyone would lose even more if the building were torn down and the land used as a parking lot. The hotel is generating a positive cash flow and cannot generate more in a different configuration. You decide to stay in the hotel business but restructure the debt by filing for Chapter 11. In this case, you should be able to continue to call yourself a Holiday Inn. At most, the filing of a bankruptcy petition brings about a change in management, but because you continue as the debtor in possession, even this change is small. The financial structure of the business changes when it is in Chapter 11, but its operations need not. Unless the guests of the hotel hang around bankruptcy court, they will not notice the slightest change. As far as the franchise is concerned, the bankruptcy case should not make any difference. If, in the course of the bankruptcy case, substantive changes are made, then the consequences should follow inside bankruptcy that would follow outside. Assume, for example, that you are an incompetent manager and the creditors want to replace you with someone else. The control that Holiday Inn would have over the selection of the new manager should be no different from the kind of control they could exert outside of bankruptcy.

If §365 did not exist, we might rely on §541 and the principle of *Chicago Board of Trade* to resolve these questions, and the answers would be straightforward. We are not, however, free to ignore the language of §365 and the complications it introduces. The trouble begins with §365(c), which limits the kinds of contracts that may be assumed:

> The trustee may not assume . . . any executory contract . . . whether or not such contract . . . prohibits or restricts assignment of rights or delegation of duties, if . . . applicable law excuses a party, other than the debtor, to such contract . . . from accepting performance from or rendering performance to an entity other than the debtor or the debtor in possession.

This limitation is inconsistent with §541(c)(1). The trustee should be able to assert control over the debtor's assets and ensure that the creditors can enjoy whatever assets they could enjoy outside of bankruptcy.

With respect to individuals in Chapter 7, §365(c) might seem to bring about a sensible result. An opera singer has a contract to sing with an opera house next year. The singer is slightly past his prime, and the opera house would not engage this singer if it were making the decision now. The singer is deeply in debt and files a Chapter 7 petition. In such a case, there are three players—the debtor, the debtor's contracting opposite, and the debtor's general creditors. Each views the situation differently. The singer wants to be able to sing at the opera house and enjoy the promised fee. The opera company would like the engagement cancelled. The creditors of the opera singer want to be able reach the lucrative fee to recover some of what they are owed.

This case is easy as a matter of first principle. The singer should be able to take advantage of the contract as it is part of his future earnings and therefore his fresh start. The creditors should not be able to reach the fee for the same reason. And *Butner* tells us that the opera house should not be excused from an unfavorable contract by the happenstance of the singer's financial problems.

It might seem that §365(c) exists to ensure that we reach this result. Under it, a trustee cannot assume such a contract, a contract that an individual debtor could not have delegated to anyone else outside of bankruptcy. Applying §365(c) to the opera singer's contract, however, does not mean that the opera singer can take advantage of the contract. Once one assumes that the singer's deal with the opera company is an executory contract that falls within the ambit of §365, the inability of the trustee to assume the contract means that it is rejected and §365(g) deems rejection a breach of the contract. The singer's bankruptcy filing released the opera house from an unfavorable contract. To avoid this outcome, a court might rule that the singer's contract with the opera house is personal to him, thus not subject to the trustee's assumption or rejection. Holding that §365(c) never applies in the case of an individual, however, takes away the only plausible justification for having the provision in the first place.

To make §365 consistent with §541(c)(1) and the *Butner* principle, it would have to take on a radically different form. Contracts for future services by individual debtors should be beyond §365's reach altogether. Moreover, it would need to allow the trustee to assume *every* contract of a corporate debtor.

The law here remains in flux. The most important cases have involved patent licenses. Some courts have found ways to read the statute in a way that allows the debtor in possession to continue to use patent licenses even though nonbankruptcy law provides that they are not assumable. Other courts, invoking Supreme Court opinions that mandate fidelity to statutory text in bankruptcy, have refused to do so.[16]

While §365(c) inappropriately limits the trustee's ability to assume contracts, §365(f)(1) inappropriately expands the trustee's ability to assign whatever contracts the trustee can assume. On its face, it seems to allow the trustee to assign any contract that can be assumed. The power to assume and the power to assign, however, are quite different

---

[16] Compare Institut Pasteur v. Cambridge Biotech Corp., 104 F.3d 489 (1st Cir. 1997), with Perlman v. Catapult Entertainment, Inc., 165 F.3d 747 (9th Cir. 1999), and In re Adelphia Communications Corp., 359 Bankr. 65 (Bankr. S.D.N.Y. 2007).

from each other. If the debtor is to remain intact as a going concern and if the effect of the bankruptcy proceeding is simply to rearrange its capital structure, the trustee's power to assume should not be limited in any way. A state law limitation on transfer should not matter because the appointment of a trustee is in substance merely the substitution of one manager for another.

Section 541(c)(1) provides that, in the case of ordinary assets, a limitation on transfer has no effect on the ability of a trustee to assert the rights of the debtor. In an executory contract, the right in question is linked with an obligation of some kind, but this should not make for a different result. If the debtor had fewer creditors, the debt might have been restructured in a nonbankruptcy workout. There is nothing about the existence of multiple creditors and the need for a collective proceeding to sort out these problems that should change the corporation's ability to enjoy the benefits of whatever contracts into which it has entered.

The power to assign the debtor's rights to some third party, however, is quite different in principle from the power to assume. Under *Chicago Board of Trade*, the trustee should be able to assign a contract to a third party only if it is assignable outside of bankruptcy. Under nonbankruptcy law, the question of assignability is one that is left up to the parties. If the parties specify in their contract that the duty is not delegable, their choice is ordinarily respected, even if the duty would be delegable if they had said nothing.[17] The nonbankruptcy rule presumes that most parties will not allow delegation when performance requires skills that are special or unique, and will allow delegation when they are not,[18] but this is only a presumption.

Section 365(f) neglects the consequences that follow when the nonbankruptcy baseline is merely a presumption. In some environments, such as franchise agreements, parties by contract routinely agree that the franchise is not assignable when the background legal rule provides for the opposite. As with most contract rules, rules on assignment are merely a starting place. Parties can contract around them if they want to. There may be some cases in which the legislature restricts freedom of contract, but in such cases the nonbankruptcy law is again written against a background of freedom of contract. State law, for example, often singles out automobile franchisees for special

---

[17] See, e.g., U.C.C. §2-210.
[18] Taylor v. Palmer, 31 Cal. 240, 247-48 (1866).

protection. Regardless of what the contract provides, franchisees are protected and they are able to transfer their franchisees provided specified conditions are met.

When applied in bankruptcy, however, the state law protecting automobile franchisees takes on a different meaning. All other franchisees are able to transfer their franchises freely once in bankruptcy because state law is silent and the contractual limits are made irrelevant. Automobile franchisees—the ones who were the most able to transfer their franchises out of bankruptcy—are not so lucky. The nonbankruptcy law that gave them the ability to transfer provided certain conditions were made is transformed in bankruptcy into a law that deprives them of the ability to make the transfer unless these conditions are met. The automobile dealers are more able to transfer their franchises outside of bankruptcy, but are less able inside. This shift in relative rights cannot be defended. More importantly, it shows how §365 lacks an internal coherence that we see in other parts of the Bankruptcy Code. We should not be surprised that some parts of the Bankruptcy Code do not make perfect sense. It is important, however, to know where a search for internal coherence will not be successful.

Curing Defaults

Section 365(b) provides that the trustee (or the debtor in possession) can assume a contract even if there have been defaults that would give rise to a right of termination. The trustee must cure past defaults, compensate the third party for losses from the breaches, and provide adequate assurance of future performance. In determining whether assurances are adequate, courts pay particular attention to the debtor's ability to meet its financial obligations going forward and to whether any defaults occurred since the petition was filed.[19]

In some cases, the defaults may not be curable. A franchise agreement may give the franchisor the right to terminate if the franchisee has failed to operate the business for some period of time. Sometimes the same condition that ultimately pushed the debtor in Chapter 11 forced the debtor to suspend its operations just before the bankruptcy. Even if the debtor subsequently reopens, its failure to remain open triggers a default under the "going-dark" clause that is inherently incapable of being cured. Section 365(b)(1) responds to this problem. It

---

[19] See, e.g., In re Texas Health Enterprises, Inc., 246 Bankr. 832 (Bankr. E.D. Tex. 2000).

excuses curing nonmonetary defaults with respect to real estate leases "if it is impossible for the trustee to cure such default by performing nonmonetary acts at and after the time of assumption." The trustee, of course, must comply with such provisions on a going-forward basis.

If the debtor assumes an executory contract, it must assume the entire contract with all its burdens. It cannot pick and choose those parts that are to its liking.[20] Adequate assurance of future performance, however, is a term of art. In *In re U.L. Radio*, the court authorized the assignment of a lease of a television sales and service store to someone who wanted to convert it into a bistro on a budget of $50,000 notwithstanding a use restriction in the lease.[21] The court observed that the primary focus of adequate assurance is the assignee's ability to satisfy financial obligations under the lease. In another case, the court authorized a debtor, whose lease limited it to selling paint and hardware, to assign its lease to a store that sold woman's clothing, even though the landlord had promised another lessee not to let another woman's clothing store operate in the building. The court again found that the landlord was not worse off financially and the bankruptcy proceeding itself insulated the landlord from contractual liability to the other tenant because of the doctrine of impossibility.[22] One may doubt whether $50,000 is in fact enough to convert an appliance store into a bistro in New York City or whether the doctrine of impossibility protects the lessor from actions from a third party. More importantly, however, one needs to ask again what bankruptcy policy justifies ignoring use restrictions in a lease. Courts, however, do not set down hard-and-fast rules in these cases.[23]

Timing and Consequences of Rejection and Assumption

Section 365(d) requires that the trustee make the decision to assume or reject leases of nonresidential real property within 120 days, subject to a single extension of 90 days. Further extensions require the lessor's consent. This strict time limit was introduced into the Bankruptcy Code in 2005 and has changed the dynamics of Chapter 11

---

[20] See In re Crippin, 877 F.2d 594 (7th Cir. 1989).

[21] 19 Bankr. 537 (Bankr. S.D.N.Y. 1982).

[22] See In re Martin Paint Stores, 199 Bankr. 258 (Bankr. S.D.N.Y. 1996), aff'd, 207 Bankr. 57 (S.D.N.Y. 1997).

[23] See, e.g., In re Tama Beef Packing, Inc., 277 Bankr. 407 (Bankr. N.D. Iowa 2002).

cases involving large retailers, whose stores usually occupy leased land. While a seven-month period is long enough for simple cases, it presents significant challenges for debtors that have hundreds of such leases.

Upon assumption, the obligation becomes one of the estate, and the debtor is required to perform. Any subsequent breach will no longer be a prepetition breach. §365(g). Damages will be entitled to administrative expense priority (if it occurs during bankruptcy), or to ordinary damage rules if breached subsequent to the termination of the bankruptcy proceeding. By contrast, upon rejection, the resulting damage action (if any) is treated as a prepetition claim. The debtor, however, does not make the decision to assume or reject immediately and in most cases the debtor continues to enjoy the benefits of the contract or lease. If the debtor ultimately assumes, it presumably has to pay all its obligations at the contract rate, as well as cure any defaults. On the other hand, if the debtor ultimately rejects, the outcome is less clear.

Section 365(d) requires ongoing performance of obligations before assumption or rejection for leases of nonresidential real property and provides more limited protection for personal property lessors as well. Case law suggests that with respect to executory contracts and other leases, the third party is entitled to administrative expense priority, not under the terms of the lease or contract, but "under an objective worth standard that measures the fair and reasonable value" of the contract or lease.[24] There is, however, a dissenting view suggesting that the terms of the lease apply inside of bankruptcy as they do outside.[25]

If the benefits the debtor receives correspond to the costs the other party incurs, this rule would seem to make sense. The trustee would have a chance to assess the situation and the third party would not bear the costs of the delay. The existing rule, however, does not necessarily make the third party whole. Some courts have found that the option value inherent in the right to use the asset does not count as a benefit for which compensation is required.[26] Paying for benefits received is not the same as compensating the third party for all the costs

---

[24] See, e.g., In re Thompson, 788 F.2d 560, 563 (9th Cir. 1986); In re Patient Education Media, Inc., 221 Bankr. 97 (Bankr. S.D.N.Y. 1998).

[25] In re Sturgis Iron & Metal Co., 420 Bankr. 716 (Bankr. W.D. Mich. 2009)

[26] In re Enron Corp., 279 Bankr. 79 (Bankr. S.D.N.Y. 2002).

it incurs between the filing of the petition and the rejection. The starkest case arises when the third party is supplying insurance. Assume that debtor fails to make payments on its fire insurance for the first six months of the bankruptcy. It then decides to reject the contract. What is the benefit that the debtor has received? Can the debtor argue that, given that its building did not burn down, it did not receive any benefit? One would not think so, but exactly this problem can arise in more subtle guises. Assume a software producer has agreed to write the operating system for a new computer Debtor is developing. The operating system is due on July 1 and the computer cannot work without it. Debtor files a bankruptcy petition on January 1. In order to finish the program on time, the software producer must spend $10,000 each month. The trustee rejects the contract on June 1 after deciding that the new computer is not worth developing. The software producer seeks $50,000 in damages for all it spent on the program between the filing of the petition and the time of the rejection. The trustee will argue that because the debtor never used the program (and indeed the program was never finished), the debtor never received any benefit and hence does not owe any damages that deserve administrative priority under §503(b).

There is a second and much more common limitation on the protection that third parties receive before assumption or rejection. Many businesses in bankruptcy have a single secured creditor with a security interest in the debtor's assets. The trustee is entitled to incur expenses and charge them against the secured creditor's secured claim. Third parties, however, cannot do this.[27] For this reason, those in the position of the software producer or the insurer should negotiate with the secured party at the start of the case to ensure that they are paid. It should immediately ask the court to give the trustee a deadline. §365(d).

A negative implication of §365's decision to give the trustee the power to assume is that the third party cannot terminate the contract on the ground of the debtor's breach, as it would typically be able to do outside of bankruptcy. An effort to terminate is simply a nonevent. Section 362 stays everyone from "any act . . . to exercise control over property of the estate." An attempt to terminate might be seen not merely as a breach, but as an effort to exercise control over property of

[27] See Hartford Underwriters Insurance Co. v. Union Planters Bank, 530 U.S. 1 (2000).

the debtor (the "property" being the right of the debtor to the performance of the third party) that violates the automatic stay and may expose the producer to sanctions from the court.[28] When one is in doubt, one should always petition the court for a declaratory order that the proposed action does not violate the automatic stay. If the automatic stay applies, one can ask for relief from it or, in the alternative, one can ask for adequate protection. §362(d).

Financial Contracts in Bankruptcy

The Bankruptcy Code provides a safe harbor for financial contracts. The Bankruptcy Code has elaborate definitions, but it largely exempts forward contracts, swaps, repurchase agreements (repos), and similar transactions from bankruptcy's automatic stay and other provisions. The exception serves to prevent the debtor from exploiting the window that bankruptcy offers to take advantage of forward contracts that prove favorable and enjoy the entire upside, while still being able to rejecting the unfavorable ones and paying damages at only a few cents on the dollar. In the absence of this exception, those on the other side of the transaction, many of whom acquired the contract in order to hedge their own positions, would be exposed to enormous risk.

This account of the safe harbors for financial contracts at first blush seems to prove too much. All executory contracts give the debtor in possession an opportunity to take advantage of its contracting opposite. You promise to sell the debtor a particular component at $100 at the end of the year, and the debtor files for bankruptcy when the market price of that component is at $100. Once given time to decide whether to accept or reject, the debtor has an incentive to delay. If the price falls, the contract can be rejected; you, as seller, will receive a claim for damages, but it will be paid pennies on the dollar. If the price of the component rises, the debtor (and all her creditors) will capture the benefit of paying only $100 for a component that is worth more.[29]

---

[28] See Computer Communications v. Codex Corp., 824 F.2d 725 (9th Cir. 1987) (holding an effort to terminate violated the automatic stay, the court awarded $4,750,000 in general damages and $250,000 in punitive damages). Courts have read this case narrowly, however. See Benz v. Dtric Insurance Co., 368 Bankr. 861 (B.A.P. 9th Cir. 2007).

[29] L.R.S.C. Co. v. Rickel Home Centers, Inc. (In re Rickel Home Centers, Inc.), 209 F.3d 291, 298 (3d Cir. 2000) (stating trustees and debtors in

In the case of an ordinary contract, however, the volatility of the price of the component is typically only one part of the picture, and often it is a small part. The debtor delays the breach-or-perform decision, not because it is exploiting price volatility, but rather because the debtor needs time to decide whether to continue making the product for which the component is used or whether a higher quality or more suitable substitute can be obtained elsewhere. The market price of the component does not change much. The costs that the automatic stay imposes on the seller are small and the benefits to the debtor large.

In the case of a financial contract, by contrast, volatility matters much more. Indeed, for the vast majority of debtors, it is the *only* feature that matters. A financial contract is, almost by definition, a contract in which the counterparties are trading volatility. The counterparties are bearing opposite sides of the risk that market movements will change the price of some underlying asset, index, or other measure of value. If an automatic stay were applied to these contracts, it would fundamentally alter the terms of trade by giving the debtor the ability to gain from favorable price movements and limit its liability for unfavorable ones ("cherry-picking").[30]

Put differently, an automatic stay would give the debtor the option value associated with the volatility in the underlying price. Moreover, the cancelling of financial contracts typically presents few problems for firms that are not systemically important. For the most part, the financial contract brings no firm-specific synergy.[31] More to the point, as long as the market is liquid, as it should be outside of the times of crisis, the debtor can simply recreate the same contract and continue to enjoy whatever benefits the old financial contract provided.

To be sure, it may be very costly to recreate the contract. The conditions that have rendered the debtor insolvent have also probably raised the price it faces to enter new financial contracts. But the same

---

possession have discretion to assume beneficial executory contracts to maximize bankruptcy estate's value).

[30] Edward R. Morrison & Joerg Riegel, Financial Contracts and the New Bankruptcy Code: Insulating Markets from Bankrupt Debtors and Bankruptcy Judges, 13 Am. Bankr. Inst. L. Rev. 641, 642 (2005).

[31] There are, of course, some exceptions. For example, there can be customized contracts between two parties, such as a specialized over the counter hedge that is of particular value to the debtor and that cannot be readily replicated.

market discipline faces any troubled business, which will face different terms of trade when it is healthy than when it is distressed.

A problem arises, however, in the case of systemically important companies whose principal assets include large bundles of financial contracts. Without the protection of an automatic stay, these assets may be destroyed. Recall Lehman Brothers: it was party to about 1.5 million transactions with over 8,000 counterparties when it filed for Chapter 11. If the bankruptcy had not terminated them, they would have been worth billions. As it happened, within two weeks of the petition, 80 percent of those transactions had been liquidated.

It is not simply that Lehman's creditors were worse off than they would have been if the entire package of derivative contracts could have been assumed. When an institution like Lehman is torn apart, entire markets can destabilize. As the institution defaults on millions of contracts with thousands of creditors, counterparties and creditors may too suffer distress and fail (as the Reserve Primary Fund did after Lehman's collapse).[32] And as thousands of counterparties rush to sell collateral and re-hedge positions that were exposed by the institution's default, market prices will experience wild swings in value. These gyrations may severely undermine investor confidence, as we saw in "flight to quality" after the Lehman Brothers' bankruptcy and AIG bailout.

In this setting, the ordinary bankruptcy rule for financial contracts—exempting them from the automatic stay—may no longer be attractive. Indeed, it was precisely the challenges posed by Lehman's inability to preserve the value of its derivative book that was the impetus for key provisions of the Orderly Liquidation Authority in Title II of Dodd-Frank. It gives a short window for the FDIC to transfer the entire bundle of derivatives a distressed systemically important firm has with another entity.

We do not want to permit cherry-picking, but value may exist in the various bundles of contracts that may be impossible to recreate in times of severe economic distress. Title II creates a regime that allows for an intermediate treatment of financial contracts that places them between ordinary executory contracts and financial contracts in the

---

[32] See, e.g., The Orderly Liquidation of Lehman Brothers Holdings Inc. under the Dodd-Frank Act, 5 FDIC Quarterly 31, 33 (2011) available at http://www.fdic.gov/bank/analytical/quarterly/2011_vol5_2/FDIC_Quarterly _Vol5No2_entire_v4.pdf (hereinafter FDIC Report) (highlighting extraordinary negative impact Lehman's bankruptcy had on Reserve Primary Fund).

typical Chapter 11. In this sense, it does not turn its back on Chapter 11 as much as it creates a compromise between two positions that are already embedded in existing bankruptcy law. Those who have advocated adding a new chapter to the Bankruptcy Code to replace Title II of Dodd-Frank typically include a mechanism for financial contracts that works along similar lines.

CHAPTER SEVEN

Fraudulent Conveyances and Related Doctrines

In this chapter, we examine the protections enjoyed by creditors both inside and outside of bankruptcy. These protections, embodied in fraudulent conveyance law and related doctrines, are best understood as protections that most creditors would bargain for when making their loans.[1] In chapter 8, we look at voidable preferences. This bankruptcy-specific policy ensures that when bankruptcy is on the horizon, no creditor engages in gun-jumping.

Fraudulent conveyance law is a feature of state law that the trustee can use by invoking §544(b). Most states have adopted the Uniform Fraudulent Transfer Act (UFTA); some still follow its predecessor, the Uniform Fraudulent Conveyance Act (UFCA), and a few, such as New York, have their own versions of fraudulent conveyance law. The Bankruptcy Code has its own version of fraudulent conveyance law as well, in §548. When transactions span a number of different jurisdictions, the trustee is able to invoke bankruptcy's fraudulent conveyance rules without having to identify which state's fraudulent conveyance law governs. The reach of these laws is largely the same, except that §548 reaches back only two years, while its state law counterparts reach back as long as the relevant statute of limitations permits.

Fraudulent conveyance doctrine encompasses actions that are fraudulent at common law, but its reach is much broader. It is a flexible principle that looks to substance, rather than form, and protects creditors from any transactions the debtor engages in that have the effect of impairing their rights, while ensuring that the debtor can continue to do business and assuring third parties that transactions done with the debtor at arm's length will not be second-guessed.

Some carelessly written opinions leave the impression that, apart from transfers made while the debtor is insolvent for less than reasonably equivalent value, fraudulent conveyance law reaches only those transactions involving actual fraud. More than 400 years of history teaches, however, that this is not the case. Fraudulent conveyance law

---

[1] See Robert Charles Clark, The Duties of the Corporate Debtor to its Creditors, 90 Harv. L. Rev. 505 (1977).

gives the trustee a broad power to void transfers done to deceive creditors or merely give them a false sense of security. Transactions are inherently suspect if done without a legitimate business purpose merely to give the impression that things are better than they are.[2] Even transactions that merely make the debtor's assets less liquid can be a fraudulent conveyance if the purpose was to hinder creditors.[3] By looking to substance, rather than form, fraudulent conveyance law ensures that debtors and their confederates suffer the consequences of being too clever by half.

Fraudulent conveyance law first took statutory form in 1571. Transfers made and obligations incurred with the intent to delay, hinder, or defraud creditors were deemed fraudulent and void as against creditors. The statute underwent a dramatic expansion just a few years after it was enacted. In 1600, or thereabouts, a Hampshire farmer named Pierce conveyed his sheep to a man named Twyne. Twyne allowed Pierce to remain in possession of the sheep, to shear them, and to mark them as his own. A creditor of Pierce's reduced his claim to judgment and had the sheriff try to levy on the sheep that were still in Pierce's hands even though they had been sold to Twyne.

A fight of some kind ensued, and Edward Coke, then the Queen's attorney general, brought a criminal action against Twyne, the buyer of the sheep, in the Star Chamber.[4] The Star Chamber was a court largely reserved for treason trials and other crimes against the state. The Elizabethan fraudulent conveyance statute provided that a share of any assets recovered went to the Crown. The Crown had always enjoyed substantial revenue from those convicted of treason and felony, and fraudulent conveyance law was a useful tool in preventing traitors and felons from putting their property beyond its reach. These concerns may explain why a case involving a creditor levying on sheep was litigated here.[5]

The court in *Twyne's Case* found the transfer of the sheep voidable, not because one could prove that Pierce acted with actual fraudulent intent but because *badges of fraud* were associated with the transaction.

[2] See, e.g., Clow v. Woods, 5 Sergeant & Rawle 275 (Pa. 1819).

[3] See, e.g., Empire Lighting Fixture Co. v. Practical Lighting Fixture Co., 20 F.2d 295, 297 (2d Cir. 1927) (L. Hand, J.).

[4] Twyne's Case, 3 Coke 80b, 76 Eng. Rep. 809 (Star Chamber 1601).

[5] See Garrard Glenn, Fraudulent Conveyances and Preferences §§61–61e (rev. ed. 1940).

A transfer of ownership without a simultaneous transfer of possession was inherently suspect. As the doctrine developed, the badges of fraud ceased to be merely proxies for fraud that was hard to prove and instead covered transactions that, although perhaps not fraudulent, were ones to which creditors would object nevertheless.[6] "Actual intent to hinder, delay, or defraud" remains a term of art. It exists whenever enough badges exist to signal that the creditors' rights are being deliberately undermined.

As fraudulent conveyance law evolved, two badges of fraud gained particular prominence: transfers made while insolvent and transfers for less than reasonably equivalent value. Courts regularly voided transfers that possessed these two features. They saw no need to look for other signs of mischief. Many suspect transactions share these two badges, and innocent ones rarely do. A constructive fraudulent conveyance is merely an actual intent fraudulent conveyance that has two badges so important that there is no need to make further inquiry. Many transactions tagged as "constructive" fraudulent conveyances today are ones that could be set aside as an actual intent fraudulent conveyance. There are enough additional badges, but there is no need to stop and identify them.

"Actual intent" fraudulent conveyances necessarily exist in every Ponzi scheme, frauds in which the malefactors tried to hide their tracks by using newly raised funds to pay off old investors and thus preserve the illusion of legitimacy and profitability. Whether the debtor has actual fraudulent intent is not relevant. As long as transfers are made to sustain the illusion that profits exist when they do not, the transfers are voidable. In contrast to an action for fraud, there is no need to search for or identify any misrepresentations. Nor do creditors need to prove reliance, that they acted (or refrained from acting) because of the transfers, something else an action for fraud would require. The transfers are voidable, unless the transferees can show both that they gave value *and* acted in good faith.

Indeed, in the case of a Ponzi scheme where there is no underlying business, *all* the expenses of the business are intended to maintain the pretense of legitimacy. They serve no other purpose, as there is no economic activity going on. Everything from money used to mail

---

[6] As Justice Cardozo explained in Shapiro v. Wilgus, 287 U.S. 348, 354 (1932), "A conveyance is illegal if made with an intent to defraud the creditors of the grantor, but equally it is illegal if made with an intent to hinder and delay them."

monthly accounting statements to rent paid the landlord are, in this respect, no different from money given to early investors. They are all presumptively fraudulent conveyances.

It might seem that the victim of a Ponzi scheme would have little trouble demonstrating good faith and therefore should be able to keep any transfer to the extent she gave value. She did not know that the person who was masterminding the fraud was up to no good. But Ponzi schemes tend to offer returns that are too good to be true. Someone who invests $100 in return for a 50-percent return in 90 days should know that something unusual is going on. The first lesson of the con artist is that you cannot cheat an honest man. Moreover, the person who cashes out is more likely to be the person who had the most reason to be suspicious. The most naïve and trusting are the ones usually left holding the bag.

At one time, commercial law put a very high threshold on what it took to find an absence of "good faith." The rule was one of the "pure heart and the empty head." You could be as stupid as you wanted, but as long as you acted without actual knowledge of the fraud, you satisfied the test of good faith. The most notorious example is the banker who obtained payment only minutes before two con artists packed their bags and disappeared for good.[7] He did not know exactly what they were up to, but he was content not to ask any questions as long as he got paid. Whether such subjective good faith is sufficient has been contested ever since.

The modern view relies on more objective measures of good faith. You are not judged by your own subjective state of mind. Your good faith can be questioned if you simply engage in a transaction that should have raised eyebrows. You lose the right to assert your good faith even if you have no knowledge of the fraud, as long as you were put on notice that something was amiss and did not follow up.

A case involving a service provider to a Ponzi scheme illustrates.[8] An unwitting investor in a Ponzi scheme mentioned casually and happily to one of the Bear Stearn's senior managing directors at a cocktail party that a particular hedge fund in which he had invested was up 20 percent. This struck the managing director as curious. The hedge fund used Bear Stearns brokerage services, and with Bear Stearns the fund

[7] See Swift v. Tyson, 41 U.S. 1 (1842).
[8] See In re Manhattan Investment Fund Ltd., 397 Bankr. 1 (S.D.N.Y. 2007).

was down so much that it was a concern to its risk managers. The director went back to his colleagues and voiced his suspicions. Bear Stearns then contacted the fund manager. The fund manager (the perpetrator of the fraud) asserted that Bear Stearns was only one of a number of prime brokers that the fund used and that, while investments at Bear Stearns had done badly, others had done well.

Bear Stearns did not go much further than this. The explanation, while bogus, was not completely implausible. No one argued that Bear Stearns knew about the fraud. The question was whether it put on "blinders." Did the cocktail conversation trigger a duty of inquiry that required a more thorough investigation? The District Circuit found the evidence insufficient to deprive Bear Stearns of its good faith defense as a matter of law, and remanded for a jury trial on the question. The jury ultimately found that Bear Stearns had acted in good faith.

The uncertainties associated with an open-ended inquiry into good faith in front of a jury is exactly what led judges, most notably Justice Story, in the nineteenth century to press for a test of good faith that required only absence of knowledge. Modern courts, however, are likely to demand that investors clear a higher hurdle. Investors who receive too-good-to-be true returns should not be surprised to have their good faith questioned. Courts will typically apply some amorphous, multi-factored test, but one should not get caught up in such laundry lists and should use common sense instead.

At a certain point, an investor must start asking questions. The principal issue in the good faith inquiry—and it is largely a factual inquiry—is identifying this point. The reasonable standards of the relevant trade provide the benchmark. A feeder fund is held to the reasonable standards we associate with other professional investors. It should be more keenly aware of suspicious patterns (such as steady earnings year in and year out) than an amateur.

One should be careful not to have too quick a trigger with respect to many modern Ponzi schemes. Fraudulent schemes by their nature lack substance and cannot withstand close scrutiny, but this does not mean that ordinary investors should have been able to see through the fraud. The last decade has seen a dramatic growth in extremely complicated investment strategies, whether through the use of derivatives or flash trading, that are beneath the regulatory radar and are hard for outside investors to understand. Fund managers offer only a general account of their strategy of obtaining consistent above-market returns. They decline to reveal more on the ground that doing so would allow rivals to mimic him and thus destroy the above-market returns. It may be possible for those bent upon fraud to fool others with the same explanation, at least for a time.

After the fact, of course, fraudulent schemes seem silly. But when someone is able to amass large amounts of capital over a significant period of time and yield very good, but not extravagant returns, it is easy to trust the track record and not look deeper. It seems a dangerous business for courts to sort between schemes that investors should identify as scams from those that are legitimate, especially as trading strategies become increasingly complex. If a fund can attract hundreds of millions of dollars over a period of many years, it seems suspect for a judge after the fact to say that everyone should have known better.

For this reason, the good faith issue should not arise with relatively remote and entirely passive investors. Instead, one should expect the focus to be on those who had closer contact, such as feeder funds that made investments on behalf of others and never asked why someone was willing to give them returns inconsistent with those mere conduits usually received. But one should not stop with just these individuals. Anyone who worked with the fund whose suspicions should have been aroused ought to be at risk. In theory, the trustee ought to be able to go after any advisor, any accountant, any secretary who should have asked more questions. They need not have received above market returns. They could simply have been paid their hourly rate. As long as they had a duty to inquire more about what they saw, as long as they knew enough to know that what they saw was not quite right, it is enough to bring their good faith into question and hence make any assets transferred to them for their services voidable.

"Constructive" Fraudulent Transfers

The most common fraudulent action involves the "constructive" fraudulent conveyance, a transfer a debtor makes while insolvent and for which the debtor receives nothing, or too little, in return. The paradigm here is a gift. An insolvent debtor gives a birthday present to a parent. Under fraudulent conveyance law, the creditors can reach the gift that is now in the parent's hands. This transaction may or may not be part of a scheme to defraud creditors, but making these sorts of transactions voidable makes sense. First, it is possible that so many of the transactions in which an insolvent debtor gives away something and receives nothing or too little in return are fraudulent that one is better off voiding them all rather than engaging in elaborate case-by-case inquiries. Second, even if most of these transfers are not fraudulent, so many may be transfers undermine the rights of creditors that we are well off banning all of them.

Fraudulent conveyance law applies to corporations as well as individuals. In the corporate context, "reasonably equivalent value" is given in almost any arm's-length transaction in the marketplace, but transactions with insiders are subject to scrutiny. *Any* transaction that takes assets out of an insolvent corporation and puts them into the hands of shareholders is a fraudulent conveyance. Dividends, stock repurchases, and corporate restructurings (including leveraged buyouts) that have the same effect reduce the pool of assets available to creditors without bringing value to the corporation in return. Hence, when the corporation is insolvent, such transactions are voidable.

UFTA §5(a) and Bankruptcy Code §548(a)(2) reflect the idea that a solvent debtor can do what it pleases with its assets, but one that is insolvent (or becomes insolvent as a result of the transfer) cannot incur obligations or convey assets for less than reasonably equivalent value. Section 4 of the UFCA uses "fair consideration" instead of reasonably equivalent value but operates in the same way.

The way in which these terms are defined determines the scope of fraudulent conveyance laws. Trading one asset for another is an exchange in which there is fair consideration or reasonably equivalent value. Hence, such a transaction is not a fraudulent conveyance, even if the debtor is insolvent. Creditors are stuck with the business decisions its debtor makes so long as the debtor remains in control. Moreover, creditors are powerless to reach assets once they have been placed in the hands of a good faith purchaser for value.

Debtors in financial trouble often try to pay one creditor rather than others. That creditor may be an important supplier or simply a particularly aggressive lender. A transfer to that creditor (called a *preference*) makes the other creditors worse off, but that does not make it a fraudulent conveyance. The UFCA, the UFTA, and §548 ensure this outcome by providing that a transfer on account of an antecedent debt is conclusively presumed to be one for which fair consideration or reasonably equivalent value is given.

This result again makes sense. Outside of bankruptcy, every creditor must rely on its own efforts to obtain repayment. Obtaining payment on a debt is simply the nature of the game when a collective proceeding is not on the horizon. Such transfers on account of an antecedent debt affect how assets are distributed among the different creditors, but they do not affect the pool of assets available to the creditors. Creditors as a group are not worse off when one is paid and others are not. A creditor can challenge a payment to another creditor under the fraudulent conveyance laws only if the payment was made with actual intent to hinder, delay, or defraud. Such cases arise most frequently when the creditor is an insider.[9] To challenge a payment to a creditor, one ordinarily must show that it is a preference, a transfer made on the eve of bankruptcy that violates the collective norms of bankruptcy. We will examine preferences at length in chapter 8.

Creditors are always worse off when the debtor takes assets whose value is certain (such as cash) and exchanges assets whose value is uncertain. A new machine may or may not increase earnings sufficient to offset its costs. Creditors must choose debtors whom they believe able to make competent decisions about how to run their businesses. Lenders know that their debtors will take risks. It is possible that the debtors will not succeed, but creditors are compensated for that risk. Fraudulent conveyance law is limited to actions that we are confident most creditors would forbid if they could. For example, all creditors would agree that the debtor should not hide assets from them when they try to collect. Nor should the debtor be able to give away money when the debtor already lacks the money to pay off creditors in full.

The concept of reasonably equivalent value must be interpreted sensibly to ensure that fraudulent conveyance law does not extend too far. Suppose a creditor forecloses on property, and the property is sold at a properly run foreclosure sale. The debtor is insolvent and allows its right to redeem the property to lapse. The debtor's loss of this equity of redemption is itself a transfer of property as defined in §101 of the Bankruptcy Code. A court, however, does not inquire into whether the foreclosure yielded a reasonable price in this particular case. A regularly conducted, noncollusive foreclosure sale necessarily yields reasonably equivalent value.[10]

Determining whether a corporate debtor is solvent at a given time requires answering a simple question: would a solvent buyer at the relevant moment be willing to pay a positive price to take on all the debtor's assets and all the debtor's liabilities?[11] Assume that a debtor has guaranteed a $10 million debt of its parent corporation and other-

---

[9] See, e.g., Bullard v. Aluminum Co. of America, 468 F.2d 11 (7th Cir. 1972).

[10] See BFP v. Resolution Trust Corp., 511 U.S. 531 (1994).

[11] See Covey v. Commercial National Bank, 960 F.2d 657 (7th Cir. 1992).

wise has no other obligations. The debtor's assets are worth $1 million. If you were solvent, whether you would pay to acquire the debtor's assets and liabilities would turn on whether the chance that you will be called upon to honor the guarantee was greater or less than one in ten. No one would agree to acquire an asset worth $1 million if it came with a 50–50 chance of having to pay $10 million. But a buyer might acquire the asset if the chance that it would have to pay $10 million were, say, only one-in-twenty. Hence, the debtor is insolvent in the first instance and solvent in the second.

The insolvency test is based on the idea that when a corporation's assets are greater than its liabilities, the shareholders are the residual claimants. They enjoy each additional dollar the corporation brings in, and they lose each additional dollar the corporation loses. Because they are the residual owners, they internalize the benefit of making the right decisions and the cost of the wrong ones. When a corporation is insolvent, the shareholders enjoy some of the upside if the corporation's fortunes improve enough, but they bear none of the downside risk. By adding an insolvency requirement, we ensure that creditors are able to upset only those transactions where the shareholders do not internalize the costs of their decisions. Creditors are assumed to trust the shareholders to make decisions when the shareholders themselves are the first to lose when they make bad decisions. If they want to limit the shareholders further, they must bargain for such protections in their loan agreement.

The insolvency requirement, however, is underinclusive. A corporation can be solvent and the shareholders can still have the incentive to engage in transactions that run contrary to the creditors' interest. Assume that a corporation owes its creditors $10. One asset is $10 in cash and the other is a lottery ticket that has a one-in-ten chance of paying $101. If the corporation decides to use the cash to make a dividend of $10, the corporation would still be solvent. Its remaining asset—a lottery ticket worth a little more than $10—is greater than its $10 in liabilities. But the dividend would dramatically change the creditors' chances of being repaid. The insolvency test is not sensitive to lenders' concerns about both the magnitude of a debtor's assets and liabilities and the chances that each might change. If a creditor wants to be able to object because the value of the debtor's assets was subject to variance, it has to bargain for such a right. The off-the-rack protection of fraudulent conveyance law cannot be carefully fitted to every debtor.

Whether a company is insolvent at any given moment depends on what is known at that time, not on what is known in hindsight. Consider the case in which a corporation's sole asset is an oil-drilling venture. Its only creditor is owed $100. At the time the corporation declares a dividend, the corporation is drilling 10 wells. There is a 90 percent chance that at least one of them will strike oil. If any of the wells is successful, the company will be worth at least $1,000. There is, however, a 10-percent chance that none of the wells will produce. In this event, the corporation will be worthless. A year passes and all the wells prove to be dry holes. Can the creditor attack the dividend on the ground that the corporation was insolvent at the time of the dividend? No. The determination of insolvency must be tied to what was known at the time the dividend was made. At that time, a solvent buyer would have paid a positive price for the oil wells. This is sufficient. To work effectively, fraudulent conveyance law must focus on the position of the parties at the time of the initial transaction.[12]

When the transaction in question involves a publicly traded corporation, one can often draw inferences from the market. If the business is able to raise equity in the public markets and if its bonds are trading at par, one should conclude that the business is solvent, even if its product ultimately proves a hopeless failure in the marketplace.[13] To rely on market data, however, whether for showing either solvency or reasonably equivalent value, it is essential that the relevant information reach the market. Managers cannot conceal the financial condition of the business, issue a dividend before the bad news comes, and then assert that the business was solvent on the basis of market data.[14] And if the market capitalization of the company—the combined value of its bonds and its stock—is less than the outstanding debt, we should similarly have a strong assumption of insolvency.[15]

As noted in chapter 5, fraudulent conveyance law, working in conjunction with §544(b) and the doctrine of *Moore v. Bay*, is conspicuously defective in one respect. Existing law may not sufficiently distin-

---

[12] See Lippe v. Bairnco Corp., 249 F. Supp. 2d 357 (S.D.N.Y. 2003).

[13] Statutory Committee of Unsecured Creditors v. Motorola, Inc. (In re Iridium Operating LLC), 373 Bankr. 283 (Bankr. S.D.N.Y. 2007).

[14] For cases in which failures to disclose hindered the use of market measures of solvency, see Tronox Inc. v. Kerr McGee Corp., 503 Bankr. 239 (Bankr. S.D.N.Y. 2013), and VFB LLC v. Campbell Soup Co., 482 F.3d 624 (3d Cir. 2007).

[15] In re TOUSA, Inc., 680 F.3d 1298 (11th Cir. 2012).

guish present and future creditors. Suppose a corporation issues a huge dividend to its shareholders, and the dividend leaves the corporation insolvent. Anyone who was a creditor at the time of the dividend should, of course, have a fraudulent conveyance action against the shareholders. But what about the creditors who came on the scene after the dividend? Unless they lent because they were misled by the past financial health of the corporation, they are no different from creditors who lend to a corporation that has become insolvent through a market reverse. Ordinarily, those who lend to thinly capitalized corporations have no right to reach that corporation's shareholders in the event it fails. Such a right typically exists only when the corporate form has been abused. If creditors want shareholders to become liable for the corporation's obligations, they must insist on a guarantee, as indeed many do.

Shareholders and §546(e)

From the perspective of its creditors, a corporation receives nothing in return when value leaves corporate solution and ends up in the hands of its shareholders. Whether styled as a dividend or a stock repurchase or something else altogether, the corporation never receives anything of value to its creditors back from the shareholders. Hence, if the transaction leaves the corporation insolvent or with unreasonably small capital, there is a fraudulent conveyance.

The Bankruptcy Code works easily and unambiguously with respect to the simple two-party case. Section 548(a)(1)(B) allows the trustee to avoid a dividend from Firm to Shareholder if Firm was insolvent at the time of the transfer was made and if the dividend was made within two years of the filing of the bankruptcy petition. Section 544(b) allows the trustee to take advantage of state fraudulent conveyance law outside the two-year window and avoid any dividend that falls within the state's relevant statute of limitations. Section 550 allows the trustee, in the event that a transfer is avoided, to "recover, for the benefit of the estate, the property transferred, or, if the court so orders, the value of such property, from . . . the initial transferee of such transfer." Shareholder is an "initial transferee" and hence the trustee can recover from Shareholder the cash transferred to her or its value.

None of this is hard or controversial. Creditors are entitled to be paid first, and when a firm is insolvent, payments to shareholders serve no purpose other than to divert assets to someone not entitled to them. Several obstacles, however, prevent the trustee from pursuing shareholders with fraudulent conveyance actions. Quite apart from the difficulty of tracking them down, §546(e) prevents the trustee from avoiding a transfer that is a "settlement payment." Transfers made to shareholders during the course of a leveraged buyout are often formally repurchases of shares of stock and other transactions that may fall within the definition of a "settlement payment."[16] As a result, ordinary public shareholders are typically not at risk when their position is bought out in a leveraged buyout.

Matters become more complicated, however, when a major player is bought out during a leveraged buyout. If the transaction does not involve publicly traded securities and especially if the transaction itself does not comply with the securities laws, the transfer may not count as a settlement payment.[17] Even if it does, there are two other potential avenues of recovery that can be used if the stakes are large enough.

First, the exception of §546(e) does not extend to transfers made with "actual intent" to delay, hinder, or defraud under §548(a)(1)(A). Many transactions usually brought as "constructively fraudulent" transfers that could equally have been brought as "actual intent" cases as additional badges of fraud are often easy to find. Again, an "actual intent" fraudulent conveyance requires only additional badges, not actual fraud. When insolvency and lack of reasonably equivalent value are manifest, there is usually no need to think about the other badges. The obstacle that §546(e) puts to the usual path of recovery changes this.

Second, and potentially more important, §546(e) prevents only *the trustee* from bringing fraudulent conveyance actions. Fraudulent conveyance actions live outside of bankruptcy in state law. Although bankruptcy suspends their ability to bring these actions, creditors can argue that they can reawaken them when the bankruptcy is over. Section 546(e) applies only to the trustee, not to them. It does not extinguish whatever rights they have. Although their state-law actions are stayed during the bankruptcy, they can be asserted after it is over.

Those subject to these fraudulent conveyance actions argue that §546(e) does more than suspend the individual rights of creditors. It exists to protect the integrity of the securities markets and can serve this purpose only if it preempts both the trustee during bankruptcy

---

[16] Enron Creditors Recovery Corp. v. Alfa, S.A.B. de C.V., 651 F.3d 329 (2d Cir. 2011).

[17] In re Grafton Partners, 321 Bankr. 527 (B.A.P. 9th Cir. 2005).

and creditors after bankruptcy from using fraudulent conveyance law to unsettle such transactions.

Bankruptcy courts confronting two of the largest failed leverage buyouts ever (Lyondell and Tribune) have allowed the creditors to proceed after bankruptcy.[18] The crux of the argument may turn in the end on the extent to which the creditors can argue successfully that they are bringing the actions in their own right and are not simply the trustee wearing a different hat.

The Fraudulent Conveyance Net

In practice, much of the complexity of fraudulent conveyance doctrine arises because multiple parties are involved. Although the outcomes are often as clear, threading the statutory needle is harder. To understand these dynamics, it is useful to put questions about §546(e) to one side and return to the simple example in which Firm is hopelessly insolvent and seeks to distribute value to Shareholder.

The distribution to Shareholder is, of course, voidable. Moreover, Shareholder cannot hope to escape fraudulent conveyance liability by having Firm pay Old Lender, one of Shareholder's creditors. The transfer is again a fraudulent conveyance within the meaning of §548(a). Whether Firm transfers value to Shareholder or to Old Lender, Firm is receiving nothing of value in return. Its trustee can pursue Shareholder. Section 550 provides for this explicitly, as it allows the trustee to recover from "the entity for whose benefit such transfer was made." When a creditor such as Old Lender is paid money to extinguish an old debt, then its debtor (Shareholder in this case) is an "entity for whose benefit such transfer was made."

There is not much legislative history for the "entity for whose benefit" language, which was added at the last minute, nor did the 1898 Act use this language in the context of fraudulent conveyance law. Nevertheless, the language did appear in the old Act's preference provisions, and the Supreme Court relied on this language to strike down a transaction notwithstanding a formal structure designed to evade the

---

[18] See Weisfelner v. Fund 1 (In re Lyondell Chemical Company), 503 Bankr. 348 (Bankr. S.D.N.Y. 2014); In re Tribune Company Fraudulent Conveyance Litigation, 499 Bankr. 310 (S.D.N.Y. 2013).

statute's strictures.[19] You make a transfer for someone's benefit if you pay off that person's creditor.[20]

Under these facts, Firm's trustee also can bring an action against Old Lender. Old Lender is the "initial transferee" within the meaning of §550. It is irrelevant that, in accepting the payment, Old Lender gave value to Shareholder by extinguishing the debt. Old Lender gave no value *to Firm*. This result is not troubling. Old Lender received payment from someone who was not its debtor. It stands in a position no different from that of anyone else who receives a gift. By their nature, gifts are fraudulent conveyances when the person doing the giving is insolvent. You cannot expect to keep gifts when they come from someone who is broke.

The next variation is only slightly more complicated. Instead of Firm paying Old Lender directly, Firm issues a dividend to Shareholder. Surveying his desires and obligations, Shareholder then decides to give the money to Old Lender. In this case, Old Lender is not an "initial transferee," but a "transferee of such initial transferee" within the meaning of §550(a)(2). Section 550 limits the ability of the trustee to reach transferees of the initial transferee by prohibiting the trustee from recovering from them when they "take for value, including satisfaction . . . of . . . an antecedent debt, in good faith, and without knowledge of the voidability of the transfer avoided."

In contrast to the safe harbor in §548(c), which is limited to value given *to the debtor*, §550(b)(1)'s safe harbor allows Old Lender to point to the value it gave its transferor (Shareholder in this case). That none of the value reached the debtor (Firm in this case) does not matter. The principle that animates §550(b)(1) is seen throughout commercial law. As a general matter, good faith purchasers for value are privileged

---

[19] See National Bank of Newport v. National Herkimer County Bank, 225 U.S. 178, 184 (1912) (famously observing that "circuity of arrangement" will not save an otherwise voidable transaction). For an excellent analysis of the "for whose benefit" language in §550, see Larry Chek & Vernon O. Teofan, The Identity and Liability of the Entity for Whose Benefit a Transfer is Made Under Section 550(a): An Alternative to the Rorschach Test, 4 J. Bankr. L. & Prac. 145 (1995).

[20] Bonded Financial Services, Inc. v. European American Bank, 838 F.2d 890, 895 (7th Cir. 1988) ("If [Firm] had sent a check to the Bank with instructions to reduce [Shareholder's] loan, the Bank would have been the initial transferee and [Shareholder] the 'entity for whose benefit.'"); In re Columbia Data Products, Inc., 892 F.2d 26, 29 (4th Cir. 1989).

characters. If you buy goods from someone with voidable title, such as someone who bought with a rubber check, you have greater rights than your transferor. Your seller had no right to keep the goods, but you can as long as you bought in good faith and for value.[21]

Being a good faith purchaser is not a universal trump. It does you no good if there is a thief in your chain of title. But such protections often make sense, and they make sense in this case with Old Lender. Any other rule puts good faith transferees at risk of a fraudulent conveyance somewhere in their chain of title. The creditors for whose benefit fraudulent conveyance law exists are better positioned to make sure that their debtor does not give away assets than subsequent good faith purchasers are able to guard against such mischief. Subsequent transferees have no easy way to know how their transferors acquired their assets. The purpose of the exception also identifies its natural limits. Once someone knows enough about their transferor's acquisition of assets to raise suspicions, she is on inquiry notice and loses the protection of §550(b)(1).

Courts have confronted the question of whether the trustee might also bring an action against Old Lender on the ground that, even if Old Lender cannot be reached as a transferee of the immediate transferee, Old Lender is "the entity for whose benefit such transfer was made." Assume, for example, that the dividend happened only because of the pressure that Old Lender was putting Shareholder for payment. Old Lender did not know anything about Firm or Shareholder's extraction of a dividend from it, but Shareholder would never have arranged for the dividend otherwise. One can argue that the dividend was made for Old Lender's benefit. If this argument works, then a fraudulent conveyance attack lies against Old Lender regardless of its good faith and lack of knowledge about the voidability of the transfer from Firm to Shareholder.

Courts have largely resisted this argument. Creditors are entitled to insist on being paid. Requiring them to inquire how their debtor acquired the resources to pay them is inconsistent with the idea that, outside of bankruptcy, each creditor must look after its own interests if it wishes to be paid. Allowing such a broad scope to the "for the benefit" language would undermine the ability of §550(b)(1) to provide sensible cover to bona fide purchasers for value. Creditors of Shareholder, like anyone else who transacts with her in good faith, for value,

---

[21] U.C.C. 2-403(1).

and without knowledge of the fraudulent conveyance, should be able to sleep comfortably.

The most straightforward way to ensure that the "for whose benefit" language does not undermine the policy of protecting those who act in good faith and without knowledge is to assume that, whatever "for the benefit of" means, it does not apply to subsequent transferees.[22] If the trustee wishes to recover from a subsequent transferee, she must navigate §550(b)(1) and show an absence of good faith or knowledge of the voidability of the transfer. There is nothing inherently wrong with taking this approach, but one should not think that it avoids the problem entirely. Cases arise in which it is not easy to determine whether someone is a transferee.

Another type of three-party transaction takes place when the debtor needs to borrow in order to make a dividend. Assume Firm borrows $100 on a secured basis from New Lender and then gives Shareholder a $100 dividend, rendering itself hopelessly insolvent. As we have seen, the dividend to Shareholder is a simple fraudulent conveyance. How Firm acquires the cash does not change the fact that taking cash out of corporate solution is a fraudulent transfer.

Nothing changes when Firm gives a security interest to New Lender and asks it to give the cash directly to Shareholder. Whether New Lender gives the money to Shareholder directly or whether New Lender gives it first to Firm and then Firm passes it on to Shareholder makes absolutely no difference. Shareholder receives a transfer from Firm whether it is done directly or indirectly. In both cases, value has left Firm once the dust settles. Courts often ignore the path that the money takes when they find Shareholder liable.[23] It is enough that a comparison of the world before and after the deal shows value going from Firm to Shareholder.

Courts look to substance.[24] They routinely collapse the various steps and view what has happened as, in substance, a transfer from

---

[22] *Bonded Financial Services* established this proposition. See Bonded Financial Services, Inc. v. European American Bank, 838 F.2d 890, 895 (7th Cir. 1988). Others have followed its lead. See, e.g., Danning v. Miller (In re Bullion Reserve of North America), 922 F.2d 544, 548 (9th Cir. 1991).

[23] Nordberg v. Sanchez (In re Chase & Sanborn Corp.), 813 F.2d 1177, 1181–82 (11th Cir. 1987) ("[T]he court must look beyond the particular transfers in question to the entire circumstance of the transactions.").

[24] See, e.g., Wiebolt Stores, Inc. v. Schottenstein, 94 Bankr. 488, 502 (N.D. Ill. 1988) ("[A] court should focus not on the formal structure of the

Firm to Shareholder. The issue of collapsing various transactions usually arises in the context of a leveraged buyout,[25] but the principles animating these opinions apply to any transaction in which shareholders orchestrate a transaction in which value flows from the corporation to them.[26]

Matters become only slightly more complicated if, instead of borrowing the money, Firm guarantees a loan that Shareholder takes from New Lender and supports the guarantee with a security interest in its assets. The easiest way to analyze this transaction is to find that the guarantee and the security interest supporting it are transferred to New Lender for the benefit of Shareholder. The trustee can recover from Shareholder under §550. But one can also recharacterize the transaction as one in which Firm has given the guarantee directly to Shareholder. (A path of this sort happens when Firm becomes an accommodation party on a negotiable instrument that Shareholder then transfers to New Lender.) One still has to establish the value of what has been transferred, but as long as the debtor is insolvent when burdened by the guarantee, the existence of the fraudulent conveyance is easy to establish.

Collapsing the transaction to ensure that those in Shareholder's position are held liable is routine once the predicate facts are made out. The harder part of this hypothetical is whether New Lender received a fraudulent conveyance. The key to holding New Lender liable lies in whether, from its perspective, the transaction had two steps or only one. No action should lie against New Lender if it gave $100 to Firm and had no reason to believe that Firm would pass the money on to Shareholder. Everything turns on whether New Lender can argue successfully that the two steps of the transaction—the loan from it to Firm and the dividend of the loan proceeds to Shareholder—are distinct. Clear dividing lines are not available, but the extreme cases are easy. If New Lender knows that Firm will use the loan to make a dividend, then this transaction is the same as one in which New Lender

transaction but rather on the knowledge or intent of the parties involved in the transaction.").

[25] See, e.g., Rosener v. Majestic Management, Inc. (In re OODC, LLC), 321 Bankr. 128, 138 (Bankr. D. Del. 2005).

[26] See Boyer v. Crown Stock Distribution, Inc., 587 F.3d 787, 793 (7th Cir. 2009) ("Now whether one calls it an LBO or not is not critical. . . . [I]f the dividend was part and parcel of the transaction that fatally depleted new Crown's assets, it was part and parcel of a fraudulent conveyance.").

conveyed the money directly to Shareholder. It is subject to a fraudulent conveyance attack because it received a promise of payment from Firm and a security interest in its assets and, in substance, provided nothing in return *to Firm*.

In practice, New Lender is most at risk when the trustee can show that the entire transaction bears sufficient "badges of fraud." This is not hard if, for example, if the dividend was concealed from the other creditors and Firm was hopelessly insolvent. Putting together a sufficient evidentiary record might not seem easy in the mine-run of cases. Those involved in large-scale corporate transactions should know better than to write emails to the effect that the loan with New Lender is necessary in order to hinder, delay, and defraud Firm's existing creditors, but people can be astonishingly loose-tongued.

Sorting this question out, however difficult, does not implicate §550. Once New Lender's security interest is avoided, there is no need for the trustee to seek to recover anything from New Lender. The security interest and the obligation disappear.

Combining the two three-party cases introduces few new wrinkles. Firm goes to New Lender and grants it a security interest in its assets and promises to pay it $100, and, in exchange, New Lender promises to give the $100 to Shareholder. Shareholder in turn gives the $100 to Old Lender. The presence of Old Lender may impose additional evidentiary burdens on the trustee, but the basic principles are the same. Assume that Firm's trustee can show that when Shareholder paid Old Lender, Old Lender was fully aware of all the details of the transaction and indeed was responsible for initiating it. Old Lender knew both that the transaction took place while Firm was insolvent or rendered Firm insolvent and that Firm received nothing in return of promising to repay New Lender and giving it a security interest in its assets.

Under these facts, Old Lender may be liable. Its intimate involvement in the transaction empowers the court to conclude that Firm's undertakings were for its benefit within the meaning of §550(a)(1). Alternatively, one can argue that it was a subsequent transferee of the money that passed from Firm to Shareholder and its knowledge of the details of the transaction keeps it from invoking the protections of §550(b)(1).

When a court finds that Old Lender is a subsequent transferee, it needs to assess Old Lender's good faith and knowledge of the underlying transaction. "Good faith" turns on whether there were sufficient facts to put Old Lender on inquiry notice and whether it engaged in sufficient diligence. This good faith inquiry lacks hard edges. It turns on both Old Lender's own sophistication and the size of the transaction. Moreover, the relevant knowledge is not of the voidability of the transaction, but rather of the predicate facts underlying it.[27]

The "for whose benefit" inquiry is not the same as the one under §550(b)(1), but in practice it usually amounts to the same thing. To conclude that Firm's promise to New Lender and grant of a security interest was for the benefit of Old Lender, the court has to assess Old Lender's involvement in the overall transaction. The court has to identify the elements that distinguish Old Lender from the dry cleaner that presses a customer for payment when it knows it to be financially distressed. From the perspective of fraudulent conveyance law, nothing is wrong with collecting what you are owed, even if payment is outside the ordinary course. But the more you become involved in Shareholder's plan to use the assets of Firm to pay the debt, the easier it is to say that Firm's actions were for your benefit.

Old Lender's good faith and absence of knowledge are likely going to be essential to showing that the transaction was not for its benefit. A court is unlikely to conclude that a transaction was for the benefit of a creditor in the position of Old Lender if it lacked the relevant knowledge and lacked the duty to inquire further. Correspondingly, it is unlikely that the trustee can attack Old Lender as a subsequent transferee who lacks good faith without also being able to show that the initial transfer was for Old Lender's benefit.

The case will rarely arise when Old Lender has sufficient knowledge to deprive it of the benefit of §550(b)(1), but not be sufficiently instrumental in shaping the transaction to lead a court to find that the transaction was for its benefit. When Old Lender has knowledge of the source of Shareholder's new-found ability to repay an enormous debt, it is most unlikely to have been an innocent bystander. Knowledge and participation go hand-in-hand. The "for the benefit" language and the good-faith and knowledge tests of §550(b)(1) both advance the same policy objective of putting some monitoring burdens on those in the position of Old Lender without undercutting the policy of protecting good faith transferees.

Fraudulent conveyance law is, in the first instance, an *in rem* remedy. At its core, fraudulent conveyance law merely allows levying credi-

---

[27] Brown v. Third Nat'l Bank (In re Sherman), 67 F.3d 1348 (8th Cir. 1995).

tors to treat a transfer as if it had never been made.[28] They are free to levy on the debtor's sheep even if someone else now claims to be their owner. Even when multiple paths of recovery are available, the trustee can recover under only one of them. Section 550(d) limits the trustee to a single satisfaction. The trustee's causes of action are at an end, for example, once she extinguishes the obligation to New Lender and the lien supporting it.[29]

Understanding fraudulent conveyance law when multiple parties are involved remains remarkably unexplored. Many variations of the basic problem are possible. Consider, for example, a problem that might arise when there are multiple tiers in a corporate group. Shareholder owns 100 percent of the equity of ParentCorp. ParentCorp is hopelessly insolvent. ParentCorp's only asset is the stock it holds in SubsidiaryCo, and SubsidiaryCo has no creditors and only a single asset (Machine), which is worth $100.

Seeking to side-step ParentCorp's creditors, Shareholder asks SubsidiaryCo to sell Machine directly to her for $1. SubsidiaryCo agrees. Six months later, ParentCorp files for bankruptcy. Can the trustee recover Machine from Shareholder? Shareholder argues that the creditors of ParentCorp cannot complain. *Their* debtor (ParentCorp) never owned Machine. More to the point, the party that made the transfer (SubsidiaryCo) never had any creditors. To be sure, the transfer was not for reasonably equivalent value, but those without creditors can do what they please with their assets. They are allowed to make gifts. Nor was the transaction one that aimed to hinder, delay, or defraud *SubsidiaryCo's* creditors. SubsidiaryCo had no creditors.

The first instinct of some in confronting such cases is to think about veil-piercing and substantive consolidation, subjects to which we are about to turn. If the veil could be pierced between ParentCorp. and SubsidiaryCo, the transactions could be avoided.[30] But cases can arise in which the separateness of each of the corporate entities has been meticulously respected. In such cases, the presence of the fraudu-

[28] See 13 Eliz. ch. 5 (1570).

[29] See Schnittjer v. Linn Area Credit Union (In re Sickels), 392 Bankr. 423 (Bankr. N.D. Iowa 2008) ("Avoidance of the lien constitutes a complete recovery for the bankruptcy estate. No further recovery is allowed or necessary to remedy the avoidable transfer or put the estate back into the financial condition Debtors enjoyed prior to the transfer.").

[30] The court used such reasoning in Asarco LLC v. Ams. Mining Corp., 396 Bankr. 278, 316 (S.D. Tex. 2008).

lent conveyance is the sole ground for collapsing the two entities. One must again focus on the way in which fraudulent conveyance law looks to substance rather than form. A court should be able to recharacterize the transaction as consisting of two steps, rather than one. The transfer from the SubsidiaryCo to Shareholder is substantively the same as one in which the subsidiary transfers Machine to ParentCorp and ParentCorp transfers it to Shareholder. This second transfer is a dividend by an insolvent debtor and voidable.

The hardest cases arise when the affected creditors are at the parent level and the transfer takes place entirely in the subsidiary. Shareholder owns the equity of ParentCo. ParentCo is hopelessly insolvent. ParentCo's sole asset is 100 percent of the equity of SubsidiaryCo, which has no debt. Shareholder approaches Friend and asks Friend to help him acquire the resources to relocate far away from ParentCo's creditors. Friend agrees. Friend loans $100 to SubsidiaryCo and takes a security interest in all its assets. SubsidiaryCo declares a $100 dividend to ParentCo, which in turn makes a $100 dividend to Shareholder. Shareholder uses the money to buy a plane ticket and disappear to parts unknown. ParentCo and SubsidiaryCo file for bankruptcy. Although Friend's conduct falls short of that needed to bring an action against him for aiding and abetting Shareholder's actual common law fraud,[31] the obligation SubsidiaryCo incurred would have been an "actual intent" fraudulent conveyance vis-à-vis ParentCo's creditors if Friend had lent to ParentCo directly and ParentCo were obliged to repay.

The trustee argues that SubsidiaryCo's obligation and grant of a security interest to Friend should be set aside. The court in the *Tribune* reorganization suggested that neither the obligation nor the security interest is avoidable, at least if substantive consolidation is not in the cards.[32] The dividend from ParentCo to Shareholder is as clear a fraudulent conveyance as one might hope to find, but the grant of the security interest to Friend is another matter altogether. SubsidiaryCo did not have any creditors. The transfer to Friend made the creditors of ParentCo worse off. It diminished the value of the equity ParentCo had in SubsidiaryCo. Nevertheless, fraudulent conveyance law entitles

---

[31] Merely aiding and abetting a fraudulent conveyance, even an "actual intent" fraudulent conveyance, should not generate tort liability in the absence of genuine, old-fashioned common law fraud. See Freeman v. First Union Nat. Bank, 865 So. 2d 1272 (Fla. 2004).

[32] See In re Tribune Co., 464 Bankr. 126, 172 (Bankr. D. Del. 2011).

them to complain only if property *of their debtor* is transferred. They can complain about the dividend that went from ParentCo to Shareholder, but not to SubsidiaryCo's transfer of the security interest to Friend.

While this logic seems impeccable, it is decidedly odd that someone can knowingly participate in a transaction aimed at hindering, delaying, and defrauding a creditor, but be insulated from a fraudulent conveyance action because of the accident of corporate structure. Given that courts have used fraudulent conveyance law for centuries to resist manipulations of form that allow debtors to thwart their creditors, one should not be surprised to find them using it here, at least if presented with a set of facts similarly egregious to those involving Shareholder and Friend.

Equitable Subordination

Sometimes a creditor may acquire a great deal of control over the debtor and may use this control to benefit itself at the expense of other creditors. At some point this creditor may go too far and thereby forfeit its right to take priority over others (if it is secured) or even lose its ability to share with them pro rata. When all the debtor's assets go to one secured creditor, the only chance that the general creditors have to recover anything is to find some defect in the claim of the secured creditor. If the secured creditor's interest has been properly perfected and cannot be avoided under the strong-arm powers, the trustee will sometimes examine that creditor's conduct to see whether a claim of *equitable subordination* can be made out.

The origins of the equitable subordination doctrine can be found in *Pepper v. Litton*:

> In the exercise of its equitable jurisdiction the bankruptcy court has the power to sift the circumstances surrounding any claim to see that injustice or unfairness is not done in administration of the bankrupt estate.[33]

In *Pepper v. Litton*, the dominant shareholder of a corporation had caused the corporation, before the bankruptcy, to confess judgment on a long-dormant wage claim he had against it. Justice William O. Douglas noted that the dominant shareholder had manipulated the corporation's affairs so that an unsecured creditor would receive noth-

[33] 308 U.S. 295, 307–08 (1939).

ing. For this reason, he found that the debtor's action failed the test of "whether or not under all the circumstances the transaction carries the earmarks of an arm's length bargain."[34]

Courts possess some leeway in shaping equitable subordination doctrine under §510(c)(1), but they cannot go so far that they effectively alter the priorities that Congress has provided for different kinds of claims.[35] Claims of equitable subordination against non-insiders are often brought and rarely succeed. Creditors acting within the scope of the powers given to them in their loan agreements are safe.[36]

The cause of action is a close kin to fraudulent conveyance actions. Those few that are successful typically target conduct that might have given rise to a "badges of fraud" attack. It often involves creditors who know that their loans enable insiders to drain assets out of a troubled firm.[37]

There is nothing inherently wrong with insiders or shareholders also being creditors of the corporation. Indeed, they are among the ones most likely to be willing to extend credit to the corporation, particularly when it is in trouble. But if they want to enjoy the status of creditors or secured creditors, they must cut square corners.[38] A creditor who enjoys the benefit of an insider guarantee or who otherwise is in a position to exercise control over the debtor is also at risk.

Courts often begin with a three-part test set forth in *In re Mobile Steel Co.*—the subordinated creditor must have engaged in inequitable conduct, the misconduct must have injured other creditors or conferred an unfair advantage on the subordinated creditor, and equitable subordination is not inconsistent with the other provisions of the Bankruptcy Code.[39] Like most other multi-part tests in the law, this one is not terribly illuminating. The heavy lifting tends to be done by the meaning the judge attaches to "inequitable" and "unfair," and in interpreting these words, there is plenty of play in the joints. The basic

[34] Id. at 306–07.

[35] United States v. Noland, 517 U.S. 535 (1996).

[36] Smith v. Associates Commercial Corporation, 893 F.2d 693, 702 (5th Cir. 1990).

[37] Official Committee of Unsecured Creditors v. American Tower Corp. (In re Verestar, Inc.), 343 Bankr. 444 (Bankr. S.D.N.Y. 2006); Credit Suisse v. Official Committee of Unsecured Creditors (In re Yellowstone Mountain Club, LLC), 2009 WL 3094930 (Bankr. D. Mont. 2009).

[38] See Stoumbos v. Kilimnik, 988 F.2d 949 (9th Cir. 1993).

[39] 563 F.2d 692, 700 (5th Cir. 1977).

lesson of these cases for creditors is simple: the lender who turns a blind eye to insider mischief or who does more than it was authorized to do in the original loan agreement is asking for trouble.

While a creditor faces risks by shutting down a debtor prematurely, the same creditor faces risks from doing the opposite as well. A creditor can exercise so much control over the debtor, in effect propping it up, that other creditors are worse off than they would have been if the creditor with control had simply shut down the debtor's operations. Courts, however, have rejected the idea that such conduct alone constitutes a tort.[40] A bank that extends credit to a failing business or fails to exercise default rights may show bad judgment, but that alone does not constitute the violation of a duty that gives rise to a tort action.[41]

Substantive Consolidation

When the debtor is part of a larger corporate group, the trustee may have an additional place to turn to enhance the bankruptcy estate. The trustee may be able to combine the assets and liabilities of the debtor with those of a related corporation. A subsidiary's parent, for example, may have fewer liabilities and more assets than the subsidiary. If the assets and liabilities of both corporations were combined, the creditors of the subsidiary would enjoy a larger pro rata share. Putting the assets and liabilities of two related corporations into a single pool is known as *substantive consolidation*. Substantive consolidation must be distinguished from cases that are jointly administered. Related corporations frequently file bankruptcy petitions at the same time, and the different bankruptcy cases can be administered together. Assuming conflicts of interest do not stand in the way, these separate corporations can pool their resources by hiring the same professionals and the like.

Substantive consolidation is quite a different affair. To the extent that the creditors of one corporate entity benefit from substantive consolidation, the creditors of the other are made correspondingly worse off. To justify substantive consolidation, one must justify not only the benefit that one set of creditors receives but also the harm that other

---

[40] See Seitz v. Detweiler, Hershey & Associates (In re CitX Corp.), 448 F.3d 672, 681 (3d Cir. 2006) (Ambro, J.) (deepening insolvency not a valid stand-alone theory of damages for negligence).

[41] See Trenwick American Litigation Trust v. Ernst & Young LLP, 906 A.2d 168 (Del. Ch. 2006).

creditors suffer as a result. When a corporate group files for bankruptcy, however, substantive consolidation simplifies matters considerably. The creditors among themselves might willingly consent to a plan in which the different entities were lumped together. But hard questions arise when some creditors resist.

The following hypothetical reflects the common pattern. Premium Paint is one of the largest manufacturers, distributors, and retailers of paint and paint-related merchandise in the Midwest.[42] It consists of six separate corporations. Premium Paint Co., Inc., is a publicly traded Delaware corporation. Its only function is to serve as a holding company for its various subsidiaries. With some overlap, the remaining corporations work as follows: RetailCo operates most of the retail paint and paint-related stores. NewRetailCo operates the balance. Formerly owned by a competitor, Premium acquired NewRetailCo several years ago and assumed all of its debt, including a number of long-term unsecured notes. Putting intercorporate obligations to one side (of which there are many), NewRetailCo is in the best financial shape of any of the subsidiaries.

ManufacturerCo manufactures paint and paint-related items. DistributorCo is the distribution subsidiary for paint manufactured by ManufacturerCo. RealtyCo owns or manages real estate holdings, including those where RetailCo and NewRetailCo operate the retail paint stores.

The six corporations operate as a consolidated entity, with the subsidiaries and parent all being dependent on one another to make a functional whole. Separate books and records are kept for internal purposes, but the debtors have always done their reporting to the SEC on a consolidated basis. The institutional creditors that lend to any entity typically secure cross-guarantees from the others. Cash from each entity is swept every day into the same account. Intercompany accounts are kept, but no cash changes hands and no accounts are ever closed out. Assets such as computer software are shared, as is office space. Employees of the different entities work together in planning new products and advertising campaigns. Overhead costs are divided among the different entities according to a formula that was established years ago.

---

[42] These facts are loosely based on In re Standard Brands Paint Co., 154 Bankr. 563 (Bankr. C.D. Cal. 1993), and, to a lesser extent, those in Flora Mir Corp. v. Dickson & Co., 432 F.2d 1060, 1062 (2d Cir. 1970).

Invoices do indicate the separate corporate status of the different entities in fine print, but other communications are less clear. All the entities use the Premium Paint logo on their stationery, on their advertising, and on press releases. They usually also include their own names. RetailCo's letterhead, for example, says, beneath the Premium Paint logo, "RetailCo, a member of the Premium Paint Group." DistributorCo's letterhead says, beneath the same logo, "DistributorCo, a division of Premium Paint." "Divisions" at Premium Paint, however, do not always correspond with discrete legal entities. ManufacturerCo is divided into several product lines (such as Premium Outdoor and Premium Metallic), and occasionally these have identified themselves as "divisions" of Premium Paint, even though they are part of ManufacturerCo and not separate legal entities.

The boards of directors of each subsidiary consist entirely of officers of the parent. The debtors, however, have always paid meticulous attention to corporate formalities, such as holding meetings and keeping minutes. Institutional lenders know they are dealing with different legal entities, as do the largest trade vendors. There is disclosure of the corporate structure in an exhibit to Premium Paint's 10-K and some discussion of some of the entities in the body of the 10-K and footnotes to the company's financial statements. Nevertheless, most trade vendors and the public at large are not aware of the different corporate entities. On-the-ground employees are not always completely aware of them either and sometimes blur the lines in accounting for costs and recording intercompany transactions.

When such a corporate group files for Chapter 11, the plan that emerges often consolidates the claims against all the entities, while the separate entities themselves are preserved (often for tax reasons). Consolidation for the purposes of distribution avoids the complications that arise from sorting out the many intercorporate balances and the rights that various creditors have against the different entities. Competing groups often reach agreement with one another, and the court approves what is, for practical purposes, a consensual plan.

But what happens if the negotiations fail? Can the plan still be confirmed even if what is proposed is only a "deemed" consolidation in which the entities are to retain their separate identities after the Chapter 11 is over? Someone who wants to argue that substantive consolidation is appropriate in a case such as Premium Paint usually begins with *Auto-Train*.[43] *Auto-Train* itself discusses substantive consolidation only in dictum and purports to follow the cases in the Second Circuit. Teasing out of it a test for substantive consolidation that is distinctly different from that of the Second Circuit, as lower courts have done, seems a mistake.

That case, at least as read by lower courts, suggests that substantive consolidation requires a three-part inquiry. First, those proposing substantive consolidation have to show "a substantial identity between the entities to be consolidated." The consolidated financial statements and a seamless interaction between the various entities that we see in Premium Paint may be sufficient to make such a showing. Second, the proponent needs to show that "consolidation is necessary to avoid some harm or to realize some benefit." Here again, sorting out the messy intercorporate transactions and protecting the vast majority of creditors who thought they were dealing with a single business seem to satisfy this test.

At this point, the burden shifts to the opponent of consolidation to show that "it relied on the separate credit of one of the entities and that it will be prejudiced by the consolidation." Under our facts, only the noteholders of NewRetailCo will be able to argue that they relied on the separate form of NewRetailCo. So long as these creditors consent to the plan, there may be no one around to rebut the presumption of consolidation. Even if a few of these noteholders do dissent, they may not be able to show that the harm to them outweighs the benefits that everyone as a group enjoys from the consolidation.

The old noteholders of NewRetailCo may have to contend with two additional arguments as well. First, the typical case today does not involve substantive consolidation in the traditional sense. The entities still retain their separate identity after the reorganization. (Indeed, the failure to do this will trigger tax liabilities.) What we have instead is substantive consolidation for distributional purposes only. The proposed plan pays out different claims as if the entities were consolidated, but the entities are not actually consolidated. If the premerger noteholders of NewRetailCo as a class approve the plan, an unhappy noteholder holding a claim in that class may be out of luck. Given that other members of its class accepted their distribution under the plan,

---

[43] Drabkin v. Midland-Ross Corp. (In re Auto-Train Corp.), 810 F.2d 270, 276 (D.C. Cir. 1987).

the dissenter can insist only on receiving what it would receive in a Chapter 7 liquidation, which may be little or nothing.

A second avenue of defense exists, and it is available even if the dissenting noteholders as a class reject the plan. Assume that NewRetailCo has assets of $100. The old noteholders are its only creditors, and they are owed $100. The plan proposes paying everyone 40 cents on the dollar. The noteholders are worse off in the absence of intercorporate liabilities, for if NewRetailCo were in Chapter 11 by itself, they would be paid in full. But intercorporate liabilities cloud the issue considerably. NewRetailCo owes for the paint it has bought from ManufacturerCo. There is the back rent owed RealtyCo. NewRetailCo owes DistributorCo for advertising and other expenses. There are disputes about whether the formula used to apportion overhead still makes sense. Workers paid by other divisions may have worked for NewRetailCo. If NewRetailCo and the other entities enter into a comprehensive settlement of intercorporate obligations in which NewRetailCo has net obligations of $60 or more, the dissenting creditors will be unable to show that substantive consolidation prejudices them.[44]

The *Auto-Train* test, as received in other courts, has morphed into long laundry lists. Such lists are too often messy and confusing affairs put together with too little thought. But one can take the array of tests and factors and argue that substantive consolidation is plausible in a case such as Premium Paint, where everything, including cash, is centrally managed and controlled and where the different legal entities function as a single whole rather than being merely a collection of discrete businesses under one corporate umbrella. We have substantial identity, benefits from consolidation, and relatively few who can show reliance on corporate separateness. The harm that creditors suffer from the plan may be modest relative to the benefits of a fast and efficient reorganization, especially if intercorporate transfers make their payout under a stand-alone plan uncertain.

When the goal is to confirm a plan and see a business's rapid exit from Chapter 11, there is a natural tendency to gloss over the legal niceties involving the corporate form of related entities.[45] *Auto-Train*

---

[44] See In re Genesis Health Ventures, 266 Bankr. 591 (Bankr. D. Del. 2001).

[45] See, e.g., In re Worldcom, Inc., 2003 WL 23861928 (Bankr. S.D.N.Y. 2003).

and its progeny have now evolved into a doctrine that is altogether different both from veil piercing, substantive consolidation's first cousin outside of bankruptcy, and from the doctrine long articulated in the Second Circuit.

The Second and Third Circuits, however, have put forward a much different approach in *Augie/Restivo* and *Owens Corning* respectively.[46] They have held that substantive consolidation is appropriate in only two circumstances. One is that the affairs of the entities are so closely entwined that each lacks a separate existence for all practical purposes. Substantive consolidation in this context is simply the bankruptcy analog for piercing the corporate veil. The two doctrines are not quite the same. Veil piercing allows the creditors of a subsidiary to reach the assets of the parent, but does not at the same time allow creditors of the parent to reach the assets of the subsidiary. By contrast, substantive consolidation puts all the assets in a common pool and creditors of the various entities share in it pro rata. Nevertheless, both apply when the debtor has disregarded separateness so significantly that creditors treated the different corporations as one legal entity.[47]

The second circumstance is that keeping the entities' affairs separate is impractical. Here we need to look at the costs of sorting out the affairs of related corporations if they are treated as one entity and if they are treated as several. Even though the corporations are sufficiently separate that we would not pierce the corporate veil outside of bankruptcy, their affairs may be so entangled and their assets so meager that unscrambling the mess may simply not be worth the cost. When the administrative costs of sorting out the obligations of the various corporations dwarf the benefits to any group of creditors from keeping the corporations separate, it is in everyone's interest to consolidate them.[48]

In one Second Circuit case, the court confronted a situation in which there were multiple subsidiaries and "a multitude of intercom-

---

[46] Union Savings Bank v. Augie/Restivo Baking Company, Ltd., 860 F.2d 515, 518–19 (2d Cir. 1988); In re Owens Corning, 419 F.3d 195 (3d Cir. 2005) (Ambro, J.).

[47] Substantive consolidation is not limited to combining the assets of corporate entities, nor do both need to be in bankruptcy. See, e.g., Alexander v. Compton (In re Bonham), 229 F.3d 750 (9th Cir. 2000) (consolidating assets of a debtor individual and a nondebtor corporation).

[48] See In re The Leslie Fay Companies, 207 Bankr. 764 (Bankr. S.D.N.Y. 1997).

pany transactions, many without apparent business purpose."[49] The court found these alone "grossly insufficient" to allow substantive consolidation, especially when the objecting creditor, like the noteholders of NewRetailCo in our example, came into being before their debtor became part of the corporate group.

A court that follows *Augie/Restivo* and *Owens Corning* is not likely to allow substantive consolidation under the facts of Premium Paint. Under the first test, such factors as common control, consolidated financials, and modern cash management would not be enough trigger corporate law veil-piercing and alter-ego actions outside of bankruptcy. Indeed, the court in *Owens Corning* questioned whether there could ever be such a thing as "deemed" substantive consolidation. The entities cannot be both so intertangled as to justify consolidation and yet so distinct that it was both possible and desirable to keep them separate after bankruptcy. Even when there are complicated intercorporate transactions, it is often possible to settle them or set up a mechanism in the plan for resolving them without going so far characterizing what one is doing as substantive consolidation.[50]

The Supreme Court or an appellate court such as the Seventh Circuit might even reject the doctrine of substantive consolidation outright. The power of the court to order substantive consolidation is not well grounded in the statute.[51] Substantive consolidation emerged through a series of judicial opinions under the Bankruptcy Act. In the view of some, such substantive powers continue under the Bankruptcy Code only to the extent that they grow out of particular provisions of the Bankruptcy Code. Substantive consolidation is, as the words suggest, a *substantive* power. Courts have told us again and again that we cannot derive substantive powers from §105. Whatever powers exist must come from substantive provisions of the Bankruptcy Code itself.

There is still another reason to question the continued viability of substantive consolidation. In *Grupo Mexicano de Desarrollo v. Alliance*

---

[49] Flora Mir Corp. v. Dickson & Co., 432 F.2d 1060, 1062 (2d Cir. 1970).

[50] In re New Century TRS Holdings, Inc., 390 Bankr. 140 (Bankr. D. Del. 2008).

[51] Section 1123(a)(5)(C) suggests a plan can provide for the "consolidation of the debtor with one or more persons," but this cannot sensibly be read as a grant of power. It cannot, for example, give the debtor the ability to merge itself with any third party it pleases, whether that party wants the merger or not. The source of such a power must come from elsewhere.

Bond Fund, Inc., the Supreme Court found that in the absence of explicit congressional authorization, district courts lack the power to issue preliminary injunctions to protect the rights of general creditors.[52] The reasoning of *Grupo Mexicano* reaches beyond its narrow holding and suggests that federal courts cannot create new powers as courts of equity. Courts lack the power to "create remedies previously unknown to equity jurisprudence." Equitable powers are limited to those that have a long history. New rules can "radically alter the balance between debtor's and creditor's rights which has been developed over centuries through many laws—including those relating to bankruptcy, fraudulent conveyances, and preferences."

Substantive consolidation did not develop over "centuries." Substantive consolidation emerged as a distinct power of the bankruptcy judge only in the 1960s and 1970s. Earlier cases involved either fraudulent conveyances or other nonbankruptcy principles such as veil piercing, none of which is sufficient in a case such as Premium Paint. The first use of the term "substantive consolidation" in a reported opinion was not until 1975—the same year in which the remedy at issue in *Grupo Mexicano* emerged.[53] Substantive consolidation stands distinct from the preference, fraudulent conveyance, and other bankruptcy powers that existed in 1789.

Nevertheless, substantive consolidation may have more traction than this discussion seems to suggest. On a set of facts much like those in our hypothetical, the court in *WorldCom* allowed substantive consolidation even though it purported to follow *Augie/Restivo*. Two factors proved decisive. First, as often happens in bankruptcy practice, the major parties reached a deal with each other. The court did not face the concerted opposition that would lead, among other things, to a strongly contested appeal of the decision. Second, and much more important, was the sheer size and number of intercorporate transfers. In a single month, there were over 600,000 transactions. Millions of transactions flowed through intercompany accounts, and these aggregated a *trillion* dollars. When a corporate group merely functions as a single whole, courts may be quick to find "substantial identity." They may be easily persuaded that creditors relied on the debtor as a single legal

---

[52] 527 U.S. 308, 330–31 (1999). See, e.g., J. Maxwell Tucker, *Grupo Mexicano* and the Death of Substantive Consolidation, 8 Am. Bankr. Inst. L. Rev. 427 (2000).

[53] See In re Continental Vending Machine Corp., 517 F.2d 997 (2d Cir. 1975).

entity.[54] Such reasoning is hard to resist in a case such as *WorldCom* when confirmation will lead to a quick exit from bankruptcy and the creditors overwhelmingly support the plan. For this reason, the prudent lender should document reliance on corporate separateness as part of every extension of credit.

[54] See, e.g., In re Standard Brands Paint Co., 154 Bankr. 563, 573 (Bankr. C.D. Cal. 1993).

CHAPTER EIGHT

Preferences

Preferences Under §547: The Basic Elements

The descent of a healthy business into insolvency and then bankruptcy is usually a long, slow process. Bankruptcy law has a set of rules to prevent creditors from trying to grab assets when bankruptcy is on the horizon. The rules that prevent creditors from receiving *preferences*—eve-of-bankruptcy transfers to creditors that distort bankruptcy's pro rata sharing rule—are embodied in §547 of the Bankruptcy Code.

A creditor would much rather be paid off in full than work things out with everyone else and ultimately take fewer than 100 cents on the dollar. If we allowed creditors to keep payments they extracted when they knew bankruptcy was imminent, bankruptcy might do more harm than good. The prospect of a bankruptcy proceeding might have the effect of accelerating and exacerbating the creditors' race to the assets. To guard against this prospect, we need a bankruptcy rule that has the effect of turning back the clock and returning people to the positions they were in before bankruptcy was on the horizon.

Although its rules are complicated, the basic purpose of preference law is quite straightforward and quite different from the role of fraudulent conveyance law. Recall that a transfer to a creditor on account of an antecedent debt is typically not a fraudulent conveyance. The antecedent debt counts as fair consideration or reasonably equivalent value. Preferences to creditors are themselves unobjectionable so long as a collective proceeding is not in the works. Every creditor is "preferred" when it is paid, and paying a creditor is an ordinary part of commercial life. Section 547 is designed to root out only preferences that are made on the eve of bankruptcy and hence interfere with the collective norms of bankruptcy law.

Section 547(b) defines a transfer as presumptively preferential if it is made by an insolvent debtor to or for the benefit of a creditor on account of an antecedent debt within 90 days of filing a bankruptcy petition, provided the transfer leaves the creditor better off than if the transfer had not been made. Such a transfer is presumptively preferential (and therefore voidable by the trustee) because it is likely to be a "last-minute grab." It is probably the result of opt-out behavior. Because an insider is likely to know more about the debtor and be able to see the prospect of bankruptcy before others, transfers made on account of antecedent debts while the debtor was insolvent are suspect for the entire year before the filing of the petition, provided again that the transfer makes the insider better off. Insiders are typically those who actively manage the company or own its equity. Those who lend at arm's length are not. A creditor who exercises too much control, however, may be found to be an insider, especially if it brings about operational decisions that work to its advantage and to the disadvantage of others.[1]

Like any other bright-line rule, §547(b) is both under- and overinclusive. Some creditors will see bankruptcy coming and act outside the 90-day preference period; others will be paid within the 90-day period knowing nothing of the imminent bankruptcy petition. Section 547(c) cuts back on the breadth of the rule by insulating some transfers from preference attack, but nothing is done to reach deliberate opt-out behavior that takes place outside the 90-day preference window. As a result, §547 is subject to manipulation. A big creditor can twist the debtor's arm, extract payment or obtain a security interest for what it is owed, and then prop the debtor up for 90 days. A review of the case law reveals a large number of filings 91 or 92 days after a big transfer to a major creditor. This does not seem a coincidence.

Let us look at how §547(b) plays itself out. The most obvious preference is that of a debtor who pays cash to a creditor a few days before filing a bankruptcy petition. A preference also exists if the debtor gives a general creditor a security interest in its assets just before it files a petition. Even though the trustee cannot strike down the last-minute transfer of a properly perfected security interest using the strong-arm power of §544(a), the trustee can void such a transfer under §547. The security interest gives the creditor priority over other general creditors and, assuming the debtor is insolvent, makes it better off.

Section 547, however, covers more than transfers of cash or security interests. For example, assume that a manufacturer buys a season's worth of fuel oil from a supplier and pays in advance. The supplier delivers the fuel on schedule. Spring comes and the supplier files a

---

[1] See Schubert v. Lucent Technologies Inc. (In re Winstar Communications, Inc.), 554 F.3d 382 (3d Cir. 2009).

bankruptcy petition. The supplier's trustee may have a preference attack. The manufacturer became a creditor of the supplier when it paid for the oil in advance. The supplier had an obligation it owed the manufacturer. Each shipment of fuel discharged some of that obligation and was therefore a transfer on account of an antecedent debt owed the manufacturer. So long as the supplier was insolvent at the time it shipped the fuel, each shipment is a preference. There are exceptions to §547(b) in §547(c), but none apply here. There is an exception for payments in ordinary course transactions in §547(c)(2), but here the "transfer" was a shipment of fuel, not a "payment."

There cannot be a preference unless the transfer to or for the benefit of a creditor is made on account of an *antecedent* debt. In every case involving a potential preference, we must ask two questions: when was the debt incurred and when was the transfer made? We do not have a voidable preference unless the first event took place before the second. A lender who makes a loan just before the filing of the bankruptcy petition and simultaneously takes and perfects a security interest in the debtor's property does not receive a preference. The transfer of the security interest to the creditor is on account of a debt, but it is not on account of an *antecedent* debt. Consider another example. You are about to file a bankruptcy petition. You go to a lawyer and ask her to handle your bankruptcy. The lawyer asks for a retainer of $10,000. There are rules in the Bankruptcy Code (such as §329) dealing with compensation of a debtor's lawyer, but is this transaction objectionable so far as preference law is concerned? Isn't the lawyer grabbing assets while bankruptcy is on the horizon? The lawyer is, but this does not matter. Before a lawyer agrees to represent you, the lawyer is not your creditor. When you pay the retainer, you are paying for future services. You are a creditor, not a debtor, in this transaction. You have not made a transfer *on account of an antecedent debt*, the sine qua non of a preference.

If the debtor has enough money to pay everyone in full, there is typically not going to be a race to the assets. All the creditors believe they will be paid in full. Hence §547(b) applies only if the debtor is insolvent at the time of the transfer. Under §547(f), a debtor is presumed insolvent during the 90 days before the filing of the petition. Most debtors are in such bad shape at the time of the petition that they became insolvent well outside the 90-day period. Bankruptcy petitions are more often filed too late than too early, and insolvency is rarely litigated in preference cases. There is, however, no presumption of insolvency between 90 days and one year before the filing of the petition in the case of an insider. In this situation, the trustee carries the burden of showing that the debtor was insolvent at the time of the transfer, and whether the debtor was insolvent a full year before the filing of the petition may not always be evident.

Section 547(b)(5) requires that the transfer make the creditor better off than it would be in a Chapter 7 liquidation. Imagine that you are a fully secured creditor. You have lent Jones $1,000 and you have a fully perfected security interest in Jones's red Porsche. Jones pays you in full 10 days before filing for bankruptcy. Is the repayment a voidable preference? Jones was insolvent at the time he paid you, and his payment is a transfer on account of an antecedent debt to you, a creditor, within 90 days of the filing of the bankruptcy petition. The payment, however, does not make you any better off. In bankruptcy, you would, in theory, be paid in full because your security interest in the Porsche would entitle you to priority. We are going to look at this idea more closely later. A secured creditor would much rather be paid in full before the start of the petition than have a fully secured claim in bankruptcy. Nevertheless, the common understanding of §547(b)(5) ensures that transfers to fully secured creditors are not voidable preferences.

The extent to which we apply §547(b)(5) to other transactions is unclear. If the debtor had not made the transfer, the creditor might have behaved differently. For example, it might not have made the debtor another loan or shipped it new supplies. We do not know the extent to which a creditor can make such arguments about what the world would have looked like if the transfer had not been made. The exceptions to the preference power in §547(c) protect the creditor in those cases that matter the most (such as an additional extension of credit after a payment that, in hindsight, turns out to be preferential). Courts, however, may point to these exceptions as a rationale for interpreting §547(b)(5) narrowly.

Let us recap §547(b). The six requirements that must be met before a preference is voidable are that (1) a transfer is made (2) on account of an antecedent debt (3) to or for the benefit of a creditor (4) while the debtor was insolvent (5) within 90 days of the filing of the petition (6) that left the creditor better off than it would have been if the transfer had not been made and it had asserted its claim in a Chapter 7 liquidation. If a transfer is preferential, §550 tells us that the trustee can recover the amount transferred from either the initial transferee or the party for whose benefit the transfer was made.

Section 547 provides only a weak deterrent against opt-out behavior. The trustee can recover the amount of the transfer and interest on the amount of the transfer, but interest generally runs only from the time that the trustee asks for the transfer back, not from the time of the transfer. The person who receives the transfer enjoys the time value of the transfer from the time it receives the preference until the trustee demands its return. If you see the debtor sinking, why not grab while the grabbing is good? The debtor may survive for 90 days, in which case you are in the clear. Even if the debtor does not survive that long, the trustee may not find you. Even if the trustee does find you, you need only give the property back. You suffer no penalty for having received a preference.

With these basic principles in mind, most preference problems are straightforward. You lend Jones $1,000. The loan is payable on demand. You leave the country for six months. You return, completely unaware that Jones's financial situation has deteriorated substantially. You ask for repayment. Jones obliges you even though Jones is now hopelessly insolvent. A week later Jones files a bankruptcy petition. Is this a voidable preference? Section 547(b) is a per se rule: although it is aimed at opt-out behavior, it does not require us to ask whether there was opt-out behavior in any given case. Hence, the transfer from Jones to you is a voidable preference. It does not matter what your motives were or that you were completely unaware of Jones's financial straits.

In making intent irrelevant, the Bankruptcy Code differs from its antecedents. Under the 1898 Act, a transfer was a preference only if the creditor receiving the transfer knew, or had reason to know, of the debtor's insolvency. This intent-based test generated a huge amount of litigation. Under the Bankruptcy Code, some creditors are subjected to a voidable preference attack even though there is no opt-out behavior. It may be better to pick up the few creditors who were genuinely unwitting, however, than to litigate the many cases of creditors who tried to grab assets but deny it after the fact with cow-eyed innocence.

Let us look at a variation on the facts above. You return from your trip and ask for your money back. Jones refuses. You sue, reduce your claim to judgment, and have the sheriff levy on the Porsche. You get your $1,000 back, but only with Jones kicking and screaming all the way. The sheriff seizes and sells the Porsche 10 days before the filing of the petition. What do we do about this case? In the past, preferences were thought objectionable because the debtor was picking and choosing among its creditors, and the debtor should not be allowed to favor some creditors over others. From this perspective, the transfer should not be voidable. You simply won the race to the assets fair and square. If another creditor did not like it, it could have joined the race or it could have filed a bankruptcy petition and put a stop to it. Modern preference law, however, focuses on the behavior of creditors and asks whether they were trying to opt out of an impending bankruptcy. It does not matter that the property was taken from the debtor involuntarily. There was still a transfer within the meaning of §101.

Let us focus on another requirement of §547(b), the requirement that there be a transfer of an "interest of the debtor in property." Suppose you take your $1,000 watch to a jeweler to be repaired. You pay the jeweler in advance for the work. Three weeks later, you pick up your watch. The jeweler files a bankruptcy petition a month later. Can the trustee argue that the jeweler's return of the watch was a voidable preference? The jeweler transferred the watch to you within 90 days of the filing of the petition, while insolvent, and on account of an obligation previously incurred. The transfer, however, is a preference only if the watch is property of the debtor within the meaning of §547(b). It might seem obvious that the watch does not belong to the jeweler, but we have to be careful. While in the possession of the watch, the jeweler had the power to convey it to a buyer in ordinary course. To reject the argument that the watch is not the jeweler's, we have to be able to explain why this power is insufficient to make the watch the jeweler's property for purposes of §547.

The answer ultimately lies in the trustee's powers under §541 and §544(a). We can first ask what would have happened if the jeweler had still possessed the watch at the time of the bankruptcy petition. The watch would not become property of the estate under §541(a)(1) because the jeweler has no right to keep the watch in the face of your claim. Moreover, the trustee could not bring the watch into the estate under §544(a) because a hypothetical lien creditor would have no ability to levy on the watch while it is in the jeweler's hands. That the jeweler could have conveyed good title to a buyer in ordinary course should not matter. The trustee should be able to avoid the transfer only if the transfer took assets out of the reach of creditors.

Other cases can arise in which the answer is not so intuitive, but the general principle is straightforward. It was well stated in *In re Bullion Reserve of North America*: "[P]roperty belongs to the debtor for purposes of §547 if its transfer will deprive the bankruptcy estate of something which could otherwise be used to satisfy the claims of creditors."[2] If the item at issue is money in an account from which the debtor's creditors could have sought payment, it is property of the debtor. It does not matter that, for example, the funds are in an account held not by the debtor but by a related entity.[3]

But if a debtor holds personal property in constructive trust, its creditors cannot reach it.[4] Hence, investors in a Ponzi scheme who recover their original investment within the preference period are not subject to an avoidance action if they can show they were paid back with the same assets they contributed to the scheme in the first place. The debtor only held these assets in constructive trust. They were never subject to creditor levy. The payment did not diminish the pool of assets available to them. The Supreme Court decided precisely this question in litigation that followed in the wake of Charles Ponzi's own bankruptcy.[5]

Let us look at one more case dealing with the meaning of "interest of the debtor in property." A parent corporation owes money to a lender. The parent is insolvent, but one of its assets is its stock in a subsidiary and the subsidiary is solvent. The lender presses the parent for payment. Rather than use its own money, the parent has the subsidiary pay the lender. The subsidiary owes the lender nothing, so its transfer to the lender is for less than fair consideration. The subsidiary, however, is solvent and it is able to pay all *its* creditors in full. The transfer, therefore, is not a fraudulent conveyance so far as the subsidiary's creditors are concerned. Moreover, the transfer cannot be a fraudulent conveyance so far as the parent's creditors are concerned, either. The transfer is on account of an antecedent debt and thus, from the parent's perspective, is supported by fair consideration.

The transfer might appear to be a preference. It is a transfer to the lender, on account of an antecedent debt, made while the parent is insolvent, within 90 days of the filing of the bankruptcy petition, and the transfer makes the lender much better off. The parent's other creditors are made worse off. If the transfer had not taken place, the subsidiary would have more assets and the parent's equity interest in the

---

[2] 836 F.2d 1214, 1217 (9th Cir. 1988).

[3] See Southmark Corp. v. Grosz, 49 F.3d 1111 (5th Cir. 1995).

[4] See In re Mississippi Valley Livestock, Inc., 745 F.3d 299 (7th Cir. 2014).

[5] See Cunningham v. Brown, 265 U.S. 1 (1924). The ability to trace is crucial. For a discussion of the interaction between constructive trusts and the rights of lien creditors, see pp. 108–11 *supra*.

subsidiary would be worth much more. Nevertheless, bringing a preference attack and recovering the money from the lender will not be easy. The trustee can assert that the transfer from the subsidiary to the lender is voidable and can be brought into the *parent's* bankruptcy estate only by showing that the parent transferred *its* property when it had the subsidiary make the transfer. If one looks only at form, the *parent* made no transfer. The parent's creditors were injured only because the value of one of its assets (its equity interest in the subsidiary) went down. No assets, however, actually left the parent's hands.

If one looks to substance rather than form, the transaction does amount to a transfer of property. Assume that the parent had given some of its shares in the subsidiary to the lender. Transfer of the shares is a transfer of property of the debtor within the meaning of §547. Nothing changes if the subsidiary now repurchases the shares from the Lender. This scenario, in which there is undoubtedly a preference, is identical in substance, though not in form, to one in which the subsidiary pays cash directly to the lender. The transfer from the subsidiary to the lender is a preference to the extent that one can recharacterize the transaction and treat it like one that is economically the same in substance but different in form.[6]

Secured Creditors and Voidable Preferences

You lend Jones $1,000. Jones's fortunes take a turn for the worse. You come to Jones and ask to be paid ahead of everyone else before Jones goes into bankruptcy. Jones does not have the money and so turns you down. Besides, if Jones granted your request and then entered bankruptcy, any cash you received would be on account of an antecedent debt and would thus be a voidable preference. Suppose Jones offers instead to give you a security interest. Can you take him up on it and not worry about the impending bankruptcy?

No. When bankruptcy is on the horizon, changing your status from general creditor to a secured creditor is itself a form of opt-out behavior. One can argue that taking a security interest should not be treated the same way as a naked seizure of assets because taking a security interest affects only how the pie is divided among creditors. It does not actually destroy value in the same way that seizure of assets does. Ex-

---

[6] See Harry M. Flechtner, Preferences, Postpetition Transfers, and Transactions Involving a Debtor's Downstream Affiliate, 5 Bankr. Devs. J. 1 (1987).

isting law, however, treats them the same. You are improving your position in anticipation of bankruptcy in the same way (although not to the same extent) that you would if you were paid off. In both cases, you are receiving an interest in property within the 90-day period, while Jones is insolvent, on account of an antecedent debt. By receiving the transfer you are ensuring that you get paid in full, which puts you in a much better position than if you had not tried to improve your place in line. This transaction is, of course, a voidable preference. The two of you cannot use a security interest to circumvent bankruptcy's pro rata sharing rule.

Suppose Jones needs additional money to keep his unincorporated business alive. Jones's existing creditors, however, refuse to throw good money after bad. Jones comes to you. You agree to lend, but only if Jones agrees to give you a security interest in his machine, the only piece of equipment his business owns. Is this a voidable preference? Of course not. No gun-jumping has taken place. Jones transferred an interest in the machine to you, but did not make the transfer on account of an *antecedent* debt. Jones did it in order to get the money in the first place. You were not opting out at the time you took the security interest; you were opting *in*. Jones gave up something (an interest in the machine) but got something in return at the same time (cash). Jones's creditors cannot complain. If they think that Jones is so far gone that they should take control, they should throw Jones into bankruptcy. Until they do, Jones is free to borrow money in arm's-length transactions and encumber assets that would otherwise go to the general creditors.

A secured creditor avoids a preference attack by ensuring that the security interest is transferred to it within the meaning of §547(e) at the same time it extends value to the debtor. Remember our discussion of §544(a). If you are a secured creditor, but have not perfected your interest, you are at risk. All you have done is bargain for the ability to repossess without having to go to court, provided you can repossess without a breach of the peace. Vis-à-vis other creditors, you are no better than a general creditor. You are still in a race to get a priority right. The relevant time is not the moment that you enter into a security agreement with the debtor, but rather the moment that you perfect your interest (typically through a public filing) and acquire priority over a lien creditor. So far as other creditors are concerned, a preexisting but unperfected secured creditor who perfects on the eve of bankruptcy has grabbed assets just as much as an unsecured creditor who takes a security interest and perfects on the eve of bankruptcy. The crucial factor is not the existence or the nonexistence of the security interest, but rather the existence of the priority right. If we are measuring your rights against the rights of the other creditors, it makes sense to date the time of the transfer from the time that you acquired the priority right. You should be able to enjoy your security interest only if you acquired your priority right a long time ago, or only if you acquired your priority right at the same time you extended credit.

The plight of the secured creditor who wakes up and discovers that its security interest is not perfected is a common one. A bank will make a loan and everyone will shake hands and pass out cigars. The loan documentation will be filed away and forgotten. Only when the deal starts to go sour does anyone look at it again. Indeed, the lawyers handling the workout may not even come into the deal until after things have taken a turn for the worse. At this point, their first job is to check out the paperwork. Should they be able to correct the paperwork without having to worry about a voidable preference attack? Of course not. The workout lawyers have been called in because the debtor is sinking fast and bankruptcy is on the horizon. They are in the picture because the race to the assets has begun and they are trying to win it. It is exactly this kind of opt-out behavior that §547 tries to prevent.

Section 547 does allow a short grace period for perfecting the security interest. Assume that Jones is in big trouble and borrows $1,000 from you. Jones gives you a security interest in his machine, but you take five days to file the financing statement. You were not trying to opt out; it just took some time to get all the paperwork in order. In §547(e), the Bankruptcy Code tries to distinguish between the case in which you wake up and discover that your interest is not properly perfected and the case in which the filing in the ordinary course comes a little while after the security interest attaches. Section 547(e) provides for a grace period of 30 days. A transfer takes place at the time it is effective between the parties, provided that you perfect within 30 days. The grace period collapses only the time of perfection and the time of attachment. You still have to ask when the debt was incurred. If the debt was incurred before the security interest attached, there is a presumptive voidable preference, regardless of whether perfection took place at the same time.

Suppose Jones borrows $1,000 from you on January 1. On that day, you take a security interest in his machine, and Jones signs a written security agreement. Five days later you file your financing statement. Six weeks later Jones files a bankruptcy petition. There is no voidable preference. The debt was incurred on January 1. Because the filing was made within 30 days, §547(e) provides that the transfer of the security interest from Jones to you took place on that day as well. If you had waited until February 5 to file, there would be a voidable preference, because the act that makes the transfer good as against lien creditors took place outside the 30-day grace period. Problems also would arise if you lent the money on January 1 and filed on January 1 but Jones did not sign the security agreement until January 5. A transfer does not take place for purposes of §547(e) until it is effective between the parties and, under Article 9 of the Uniform Commercial Code, a security interest is not effective between the parties until the debtor signs a written security agreement. The transfer in this case took place on January 5, after the debt was incurred. To survive a preference attack, you would have to show that you fit under one of the exceptions to the trustee's preference power. These are in §547(c), and it is to them that we now turn.

The Safe Harbors of §547(c)

The Net Result Rule. Section 547(c)(4) protects lenders who make a new loan after an old one is paid off. The typical case is a revolving credit arrangement. Suppose you lend Jones $1,000 for 30 days, and Jones pays you back at the end of 30 days. You lend Jones $1,000 again for another 30 days, and so on. At the time Jones files a bankruptcy petition, you have been repaid a $1,000 loan three times during the 90 days before the filing of the petition. Under §547(b), each of the transfers would be preferential. Each of the repayments was on account of an antecedent debt and each made you better off than you would have been if you had not been repaid and everything else remained the same. It would not make sense, however, to allow recovery of all three $1,000 payments. The purpose of the credit arrangement was to limit your risk to $1,000 at any one time. You made the subsequent loans only because Jones paid off the earlier ones. The transfers made you better off only to the extent of $1,000, the most you would have lost if any of the transfers had not been made.

You might argue that two of the $1,000 transfers are not preferential because of §547(b)(5). These two payments did not make you better off than you would have been if the payments had not been made. If the payments had not been made, you would not have extended new credit. In other words, §547(b)(5) forces us to ask what the picture would look like if Jones had not made the transfer. This is not necessarily a picture in which everything else looks the same. If Jones had not repaid the old loans, you would not have made the new loans. Thus, $2,000 of the $3,000 you received did not make you better off, because these payments induced you to extend $2,000 in new credit.

You need not, however, rely on §547(b)(5) here. This case is specifically covered in §547(c)(4). One looks at the *net result*—the extent to which you were preferred, taking account of the new value you extended to Jones *after* repayments on old loans.

Section 547(c)(2). Section 547(c)(2) excepts from preference attack routine payments to creditors. These are payments that are made in ordinary course on debts incurred in ordinary course or according to ordinary business terms. Without §547(c)(2), the trustee would have the power to avoid many routine transactions. You receive your phone bill on the fifth day of the month and you regularly pay it on the twentieth day of the month. Without §547(c)(2), there might be a preference action against the phone company. The transfer occurs on the day you make the payment. The debt, however, is incurred when you use the phone service, which is during the prior month. It is a transfer on account of an antecedent debt, but there is no opt-out behavior. It is the ordinary way you go about paying bills. Section 547(c)(2) serves to except these sorts of payments from the trustee's avoiding powers. Section 547(c)(2), however, deals only with *payments*. It does not apply to other transfers of property.

The §547(c)(2) exception is designed to limit the trustee's avoiding powers under the preference section to actions that, at least presumptively, are the result of conscious opt-out behavior. Section 547(c)(2) replaces the reason-to-know-of-the-insolvency test under the 1898 Act, and it may work better because it uses an objective standard and does not require an inquiry into the transferee's state of mind. Whether debts were incurred in the ordinary course and whether payments were made in the ordinary course are necessarily questions involving a number of facts, and it is easy to find cases that fall on either side of the line. Our previous example involving a telephone bill paid at the same time in the same way as the debtor and others in the same business usually pay such bills does fall within §547(c)(2). A late payment by certified check after several dunning phone calls is not made in ordinary course.

Determining whether a loan is made in the ordinary course of business, however, is not always so simple. Consider a corporation with a large, long-term operating loan. Was this loan incurred in the ordinary course of business? We know that we cannot exclude the loan from the reach of §547(c)(2) simply because it is long term.[7] Nevertheless, one can argue that when the corporation incurs such a loan only once in its life, the loan is not incurred in the ordinary course. This interpretation of "ordinary course"—focusing on whether obtaining such a loan is an everyday event for this debtor—is consistent with the way the term is understood in §364. That section requires court approval of a postpetition loan that is not made in ordinary course, and no one thinks that the trustee could enter into such a loan without first obtaining court approval. But there is a completely different way of interpreting §547(c)(2). One can argue that "ordinary course" in the context of §547 (as opposed to §364) requires us to identify particular features of the transaction that make it suspect. So long as similar companies typically have such a loan, §547(c)(2) should apply.

Once it is established that the debt itself was incurred in the ordinary course of business, the creditor must show either that the payment was made in the ordinary course or according to ordinary business terms. Fitting into the second category may often be easier than the first. When a business is in trouble, few decisions may be made in the ordinary course. For example, a decision to make timely payments to a business's largest and most important creditor may cease to be ordinary if an implicit decision is made at the same time not to pay others, especially if the debtor's president guarantees the loan and must pay it out of pocket if the debtor defaults.

The Contemporaneous Exchange for New Value. The Bankruptcy Code introduces another grace period in §547(c)(1). Suppose you buy supplies from a supplier and pay by check. You take the supplies back to your store, and the supplier deposits the check the same day. The check clears the next day. Two months later you file a bankruptcy petition. Can the trustee recapture the payment you made to the supplier? Under §547(b), the supplier did not make a transfer to you until its bank honored your check.[8] Only at this point are assets removed from the reach of the other creditors. This transfer was on account of the debt incurred when the supplier gave you the goods several days before. At that time, you already had been using the supplies for a day. For the interval between the time you took the goods and the time the check cleared, the supplier was your creditor. The supplier, however,

---

[7] See Union Bank v. Wolas, 502 U.S. 151 (1991).
[8] Barnhill v. Johnson, 503 U.S. 393 (1992).

was not engaged in opt-out behavior. There was a gap between the time the debt was incurred and the time the transfer was made, but it was too short to be opt-out behavior. We exempt an exchange that is substantially contemporaneous from voidable preference attack.

Secured creditors who make a loan to enable the debtor to acquire collateral enjoy their own safe harbor under §547(c)(3). They may also be able to take advantage of the contemporaneous exchange exception in §547(c)(1). Consider a case where it might matter. At a time when Jones is solvent, you lend Jones money and take a security interest in Jones's machine. Later, when Jones is insolvent and trying to turn the business around, Jones asks for your permission to trade in the machine in which you have a security interest for a new machine. You agree to give up your security interest in Jones's old machine in exchange for a security interest in the new one. Is that a substantially contemporaneous exchange for new value? You are giving new value because you are giving up something that is yours. Your security interest in the old machine is valuable. It would survive the sale, and if you did not give up the interest, you could still seize the old machine even though it was in the hands of the new buyer. Think of it this way: if Jones repaid the loan in full, you would not be receiving a preference. Assume that Jones sold the machine and gave you the proceeds. Jones then asked for a new loan for a new machine. You make the loan on the condition that you get a security interest in this machine as well and Jones agrees. Even if Jones is insolvent and a few weeks away from filing, the transfer of the security interest in the new machine in this case would not be preferential. Because this transaction is not a voidable preference, why should we not allow the substitution of collateral? You are giving up a security interest instead of cash, but the economic effect is the same. The case law on this point is not clear. The less the secured creditor is involved in the details of the replacement of one machine with the other, the less likely a court is to find that the exception applies.

The Floating Lien. A creditor will commonly take a security interest in a debtor's inventory or accounts. These turn over constantly. The supplies the debtor has this month in its store are not the same supplies the debtor will have next month. When is the security interest in the debtor's new inventory transferred to the secured creditor for purposes of §547? You could make an argument that a security interest is like a Heraclitean river. There are no new transfers. The secured creditor has a continuous interest in the inventory, even though the inventory itself is constantly changing. But there is a potential for manipulation. A debtor could favor a secured creditor who was undersecured by acquiring new inventory just before going under. The Bankruptcy Code confronts this problem in §547(c)(5) and §547(e)(3). Section 547(e)(3) provides that transfers cannot take place until the debtor acquires the property, but §547(c)(5) goes on to protect the secured creditor to the extent that it did not improve its position during the preference period. We take two snapshots, one at the start of the 90-day period (or the time of the loan if the loan was made during the 90-day period) and one at the time of the petition. The secured creditor is protected to the extent that it has not improved its position in inventory or accounts between the first snapshot and the second.

Consider the following problem. A florist buys flowers every day from many different vendors in a wholesale market. It gives a bank a security interest in all its inventory, existing and thereafter acquired, to cover a $12,000 loan. On January 1, the loan is made, the florist signs a security agreement, and the bank files its financing statement. On February 1, the inventory is worth $5,000. Exactly 90 days later, the florist files a petition in bankruptcy. During those 90 days, the inventory has completely turned over and the amount of the inventory has increased. When the petition is filed, the inventory is worth $15,000 and the florist still owes the bank $12,000. To what extent does the bank have a security interest that will survive the attack of the trustee?

If §547 did not exist, the bank would have a perfected security interest in the flowers that the florist has when the petition is filed. Article 9 of the Uniform Commercial Code warmly embraces the idea of the *floating lien*. The bank can take a security interest in a pool of assets and date priority back to the time it files its financing statement, even though the things in this pool are constantly changing. So long as the bank's filing is proper, the world is on notice that the bank may be claiming a security interest in the flowers. But what happens under §547? We need to determine if there has been a transfer on account of an antecedent debt, and we have to go through §547(b) before looking to §547(c). When was the debt incurred? The debt was incurred on January 1. When did the transfer of the security interest from the florist to the bank take place? We have to look at the language of §547(e)(3). It tells us that the transfer did not take place until the florist had rights in the collateral. When did this happen? We do not know when the florist acquired any particular flower, but we know that the inventory changed over completely between February 1 and the date on which the petition was filed. It follows necessarily that the florist did not acquire any rights in the inventory it now has until *after* February 1.

Therefore, we have a transfer that took place *after* the debt was incurred (on January 1) and within 90 days of the filing of the petition. Providing that the other conditions of §547(b) are met and providing that nothing in §547(c) calls it off, we have a voidable preference. Has the bank engaged in opt-out behavior here? It may well have. The bank's position improved during the relevant time period. At the start of the 90-day period, the flowers were worth only $5,000. The bank was undersecured to the extent of $7,000. At the time of the filing of the petition, however, the bank was comfortably oversecured. It is possible that there was some kind of side deal. It may not have been mere coincidence that the inventory increased in value. The florist could have been filling its shop with flowers because the bank threatened to pull the rug out from under it even sooner if it did not. Or the florist might have had more flowers on hand for some innocent reason. Perhaps flower shops typically have more stock on hand in May than in February. Without knowing more facts, we cannot determine whether the bank has engaged in opt-out behavior.

The Bankruptcy Code does not engage in such a case-by-case inquiry, however. Instead, it provides for a limited exception to floating liens in inventory or accounts and the proceeds of either. Section 547(b) starts by striking down all new acquisitions of inventory within the preference period, but then §547(c)(5) provides a partial safe harbor. A creditor's security interest is recognized in bankruptcy, but only to the extent that the creditor does not improve its position during the 90 days before the filing of the bankruptcy petition. In our case, the bank was undersecured to the extent of $7,000 at the start of the preference period. Section 547(c)(5) tells us that the bank is going to be an unsecured creditor to that extent, even if the value of the inventory happens to increase during the 90-day period. The bank will therefore have a secured claim in bankruptcy for only $5,000. The bank should be no better off than it would have been before it knew that bankruptcy was on the horizon, and this date is arbitrarily set at 90 days before the filing of the petition (or the time of the loan itself if later). Section 547(c)(5) embraces what is called the *two-point net improvement test*.

To apply the two-point net improvement test, we look at the extent to which the bank is undersecured 90 days before the filing of the petition or on the date that the loan was made, whichever is later. (The language focuses on the extent to which the creditor is undersecured rather than on the amount the creditor is owed because the debtor could opt out by increasing the amount of inventory or decreasing the amount of the debt.) If the bank is no better off on the date of bankruptcy than it was 90 days before, §547(c)(5) will protect the bank with a floating lien on inventory or accounts. The section even allows for the bank to improve its position, if the improvement is not "to the prejudice of other creditors holding unsecured claims." This language is typically interpreted narrowly, however, and applies only when the increase in inventory is attributable to changes, such as harvest cycles, that affect the whole industry and not just the debtor.

Working through the basics is essential to solving any §547 problem. Consider the following case. An automobile dealership has fifty foreign cars. On January 1, the bank lends the dealer $500,000 and simultaneously takes a security interest in the cars. The bank makes a proper Article 9 filing. The dealer sells only five cars and acquires no new ones. Exactly 90 days before bankruptcy, the dealer's inventory of foreign cars is worth $450,000. Thereafter the dealer acquires no new cars, but those the dealer already carries happen to be in short supply, and their value rises unexpectedly. As a result, the inventory is worth $500,000 on the date the bankruptcy petition is filed. The bank's position has improved by $50,000 during the 90 days before bankruptcy. Is there a voidable preference to this extent?

We should begin with the two basic questions of any preference analysis. When was the debt incurred? On January 1. When did the transfer occur? All the inventory that is at issue was in the dealer's hands on January 1. The bank's security interest was both attached and perfected on that date. Therefore, under §547(e)(2), the transfer took place on January 1. There is a transfer on account of a debt, but not a transfer on account of an *antecedent* debt. Under normal definitions of *transfer*, increases in the value of an item attributable solely to market forces are not transfers. Such a definition also fits well with the purpose behind voidable preferences—after all, no opt-out behavior is at issue if the increases are due solely to market forces. The trustee therefore lacks the power to set aside the bank's security interest under §547(b). Whether the bank could assert an exception under §547(c) is therefore irrelevant. Section 547(c)(5) applies only when inventory has turned over.

As the following example illustrates, §547(c)(5) is straightforward in its application, but at the cost of glossing over some activity that might be opt-out behavior. Suppose a bank lends a debtor $20,000 on January 1 and takes and perfects a security interest in the debtor's inventory. At that time, the inventory is worth $15,000. The value of the inventory remains at that level through January, although the inventory turns over several times, but by the middle of February, the value of the inventory plummets to $8,000. The debtor files for bankruptcy on April 1, 90 days after taking out the loan. At that time, the inventory has regained value and is worth $14,000. Because of the turnover in inventory, the bank's interest in the inventory on April 1 was "transferred" to it within 90 days of the filing of the petition. Section 547(e)(3) compels this conclusion. We turn next to the two-point test to determine whether the bank falls within the §547(c)(5) exception. That section requires us to focus on whether the transfers to the bank improved its position. Did they reduce the unsecured portion of its claim against the debtor, the portion that would not be paid in full? In this case, $5,000 of the bank's claim was unsecured 90 days before the filing of the petition. The bank, however, was in even worse shape at the time of the petition. Its loan was undercollateralized by $6,000 on the date of bankruptcy. The bank's position improved dramatically between the middle of February 10 and the filing of the petition on April 1, as the bank went from being undersecured to the extent of $12,000 to being undersecured by only $6,000. But the value of the inventory in February is irrelevant. Under the two-point test we look only at the two end points, not at what happens in the meantime. We sacrifice actual inquiries into preference-type behavior for a rule that establishes rough but cheap justice.

The floating lien is no longer litigated as much as it was under earlier law. Section 547(c)(5) eliminated some of the provisions that had generated litigation under the 1898 Act. Careful inventory financers can avoid preference attacks by ensuring that the debtor's inventory and the proceeds from the sale of inventory are always worth more than what they are owed. Moreover, inventory and accounts financing is not as large a part of the secured credit picture as it once was.

The limitations that §547 places on security interests in after-acquired property matter largely with those who claim interests in types of collateral, such as equipment, that fall outside the ambit of §547(c)(5). A secured creditor faces a preference attack with respect to any equipment the debtor acquires during the 90 days before the filing of the petition, unless the secured creditor gives new value or falls within the exceptions in §547(c)(1) or §547(c)(3) for substantially contemporaneous exchanges and purchase money security interests.

The Scope of §547

As in the case of fraudulent conveyances, the knottiest preference problems arise when there are three parties in the picture. Consider the following situation. A debtor has a long-standing relationship with a bank, and it has a credit line that it can draw on. Any obligations that the debtor owes the bank are secured by interest in all the debtor's assets. The debtor obtains most of its raw materials from one supplier. On January 1, the debtor owes the supplier $100,000. The supplier, sensing that the debtor will likely file for bankruptcy, wants to extricate itself. Rather than demanding payment, something that would subject it to a preference attack, the supplier persuades the debtor to go to the bank and have the bank issue a standby letter of credit, naming the supplier as the beneficiary. The supplier can draw on the letter of credit on March 1 to the extent of any obligations the debtor owes it. The bank knows nothing of the supplier's relationship with the debtor. It is willing to issue the standby letter of credit, however, because, under letter-of-credit doctrine, the debtor is obliged to reimburse it in the event the letter is drawn on, and this obligation, like all the debtor's other obligations to the bank, is fully secured. When March 1 arrives, the supplier draws on the letter of credit. On March 2, the debtor files a bankruptcy petition. The trustee discovers the transaction and seeks either to recover $100,000 from the supplier or reduce the bank's security interest by the same amount.

The trustee's task here is not easy. The supplier will argue that the letter-of-credit relationship between it and the bank is independent of its relationship with the debtor. The transfer of $100,000 of the bank's money under the draw on the letter of credit did not affect any of the debtor's general creditors. When the letter of credit was issued, there was the transfer of a security interest from the debtor to the bank supporting the bank's contingent obligation under the letter of credit, but this transfer took place because of the relationship between the debtor and the bank. It was independent of the relationship between the supplier and the bank.

The bank, for its part, will argue that the transfer of the security interest supporting its contingent obligation under the letter of credit was in return for issuing the letter of credit, not on account of the antecedent debt owed the supplier. In short, the supplier argues it never received anything from the debtor, while the bank argues that it never received a transfer on account of an antecedent debt.

Our instincts, however, should tell us that something is amiss here. We should not allow the bank and the supplier to fragment this transaction into its separate pieces and find that no preference took place when, if we step the various transactions together, there has been a transfer on account of the antecedent debt owed the supplier that left the general creditors worse off.

Courts have allowed preference actions against the supplier in such cases.[9] These courts reason that the transfer of the security interest to the bank was a transfer on account of the antecedent debt owed the supplier. It was not a transfer directly to the supplier, but the language in §547(b) allows preference actions when a transfer is made either to or for the benefit of a creditor on account of an antecedent debt. Section 550 allows the trustee to recover from the supplier the value of the transfer made for the supplier's benefit.

Another type of indirect preference case arises when a payment to a senior, fully secured creditor, benefits indirectly a junior creditor who is undersecured. Assume Bank and Lender each lend Debtor $100 and each takes a security interest in a machine worth $150. Bank enjoys priority over Lender. If Debtor pays Bank $50 within 90 days of the petition, there is no preference as to Bank. The payment does not make Bank better off. The value of the collateral is always more than the $100 it is owed. But there is an indirect preference to Lender. Before the transfer, it was undersecured to the extent of $50. After the payment to Bank, it is fully secured. The machine can be sold for $150, $50 will go to Bank, and the balance is now sufficient to pay it in full.[10]

These cases, however, lead us to additional inquiries. Can the trustee recover from a transferee even if the transfer is not a preference as to it? In the example with the bank and the supplier, the bank did not itself receive a transfer on account of an antecedent debt owed it, but it was the initial transferee, and §550 allows the trustee to recover from transferees even if they were not themselves creditors who were preferred.[11] Sections 547(i) and 550(c) limit the trustee's power to recover from initial transferees, but only in one kind of three-party case. Sup-

[9] See Kellogg v. Blue Quail Energy, Inc. (In re Compton), 831 F.2d 586 (1987), rehearing granted, 835 F.2d 584 (5th Cir. 1988); American Bank v. Leasing Services Corp. (In re Air Conditioning, Inc. of Stuart), 845 F.2d 293 (11th Cir. 1988).

[10] See Gladstone v. Bank of America (In re Vassau), 499 Bankr. 864 (Bankr. S.D. Cal. 2013).

[11] See Levit v. Ingersoll Rand Financial Corp. (In re DePrizio), 874 F.2d 1186 (7th Cir. 1989).

pose a corporate debtor repays a general creditor that has a guarantee from an insider, such as the debtor's principal shareholder. The debtor files for bankruptcy more than 90 days after but within a year of the transfer. The transfer is a preference because it relieved the insider of her liability on the guarantee within a year of the bankruptcy petition. In this three-party case, the trustee's only recourse is against the insider. Given the unequivocal language of §550(a), however, the trustee has unfettered rights to pursue initial transferees that were not themselves preferred in other kinds of transactions.

The example shows how preference law ensures substance prevails over form by stepping discrete transactions together to allow a preference recovery. Our second inquiry asks whether the converse is also true. Can we step transactions together to *prevent* a preference attack when the transaction as a whole is not preferential? On occasion, the proceeds of a new loan are paid directly to an existing creditor. Sometimes the debtor has discretion over the use of the proceeds and asks the new lender to direct them to the existing creditor. Other times it is the new lender who insists that the new loan be used to repay an earlier obligation. The lender's reasons vary. The new lender may, for example, want to ensure the earlier creditor's release of collateral that the debtor has pledged to the new lender. In any case, when a new lender directly pays an antecedent debt, or the debtor is obligated to use the proceeds of a new loan to repay such debt, the new loan is called an *earmarked loan.* The transaction is one in which one lender leaves the picture and another stands in its place. It is the same as if the old lender had traded its claim against the debtor to the new lender.

The trustee would like to argue that nothing requires the two transactions to be stepped together. The new lender's decision to extend credit is one transaction. The repayment to the old lender is a separate one. It should not matter that the new loan was intended or earmarked for the old lender. Although there is no explicit statutory basis for an earmarked loan exception to the voidable preference rules, courts have established such an exception, known as the *earmarking doctrine.* The doctrine applies when the amount of the new loan is no greater, and of no higher priority, than the loan to be repaid. First, one can argue that the proceeds of an earmarked loan do not constitute an interest of the debtor in property and thus are not subject to §547(b) preference rules. Second, one can argue that an earmarked loan does not injure unpaid creditors. When one creditor replaces another, the whole of the transaction does not look like the last-minute grab that preference law is designed to prevent. Thus, courts conclude, no purpose would be served by requiring reimbursement from the recipient of an earmarked loan's proceeds. Nevertheless, even if the first creditor is secured, the second creditor is itself subject to a preference attack with respect to its security interest if it fails to perfect it in a timely fashion.[12]

The way in which transactions are linked together, however, is not always clear. Consider the following case. A retailer engages a supplier to buy clothes for it from abroad. To ensure that it is paid, the supplier requires the retailer to have its bank issue a letter of credit in the supplier's favor. The supplier is entitled to draw upon the letter up to $1 million whenever it has reasonable grounds for insecurity. First Bank issues the letter, and the retailer promises First Bank that it will cover the total amount of the draw on the letter of credit on the same day it is made. The retailer can make such a promise, because it enjoys a $1 million credit line with Second Bank.

The supplier, reasonably fearing that the retailer is in trouble, draws on the letter of credit on August 1. At this point, the supplier has not purchased any goods on the retailer's behalf and it has no claim against retailer. First Bank honors the letter of credit on August 1 and gives the supplier $1 million. Within a few minutes, the retailer transfers $1 million from Second Bank to First Bank. Two months later, before the supplier has given the retailer any goods, the retailer files a Chapter 11 petition. The retailer continues to stay in business. During the next two months, the supplier delivers $1 million worth of goods. The supplier charges the cost of each shipment against the $1 million it received as a result of the draw on the letter of credit.

In March, the case is converted to Chapter 7 and a trustee is appointed. The trustee brings a preference action against First Bank to recover the $1 million it was paid on August 1. The trustee argues that this payment was on account of the retailer's obligation to reimburse First Bank if First Bank was forced to pay on the letter of credit. First Bank will argue that the transfer of $1 million it received should be linked to the $1 million it had given the supplier a few minutes before. If the two transactions are linked, there is no preference. Before the draw on the letter of credit, the retailer had a $1 million credit line with Second Bank. Five minutes later, the retailer had a right to receive $1 million in goods from the supplier. The retailer has converted

---

[12] See Shapiro v. Homecomings Financial Network (In re Davis), 319 Bankr. 532 (Bankr. E.D. Mich. 2005).

a credit line from a bank into an obligation from a third party to ship goods of equal value. Such a transaction does not make the creditors worse off.

If the retailer had simply transferred the money from Second Bank to the supplier directly, there would have been no preference. This transaction is arguably no different. A preference exists only if a transfer diminished the estate.[13] Finding in First Bank's favor, however, depends on the court's willingness to step the transactions together. Letter-of-credit doctrine insists on the independence of the supplier's right to draw on its letter of creditor from whatever rights First Bank might have against the retailer.[14] But whether multiple transactions should be joined together to establish whether a preference has taken place is a question of bankruptcy law, not of the law governing letters of credit.[15]

---

[13] See Kapela v. Newman, 649 F.2d 887 (1st Cir. 1981) (Breyer, J.).

[14] See Sabratek Corp. v. LaSalle Bank, 257 Bankr. 732 (Bankr. D. Del. 2000).

[15] For a case in which the court declined to step the transactions together under these facts, see P.A. Bergner & Co. v. Bank One, 140 F.3d 1111 (7th Cir. 1998).

CHAPTER NINE

The Automatic Stay

The Scope of the Automatic Stay

In a perfect world, a corporate bankruptcy proceeding would be over in an instant (assuming that in a perfect world you would still have bankruptcy). The world we live in, however, is not so simple. Even a straight sale of the business for cash takes time. We need a mechanism to preserve the status quo while we sort out the affairs of the debtor. This is the purpose of §362 and the automatic stay. Section 362 stops individual creditors from taking actions that would thwart the reorganization and, at the same time, allows the debtor to continue doing business with the rest of the world on ordinary terms.

The general creditors of an insolvent debtor must wait until the entire proceeding is over. They will receive only a fraction of what they are owed, and we will not know until the bankruptcy proceeding is over how large that fraction will be. Allowing creditors to take action during the bankruptcy proceeding would undermine bankruptcy's pro rata sharing rule. The justification for continuing the automatic stay against a secured party is, however, different from the one for general creditors. Someone with a property interest that prevails against both the debtor and the trustee will be paid in full at the end of the day. We still need to stay the secured creditor's hand, however. Even though we know how much the secured creditor will be paid, allowing the secured creditor to exercise its rights before the end of the case is likely to interfere with the debtor's attempt to reorganize. But if a secured creditor will receive the property in any event and if the property is not needed for the reorganization, the court will grant a motion to lift the stay.

The automatic stay extends beyond actions of creditors to ensure that the bankruptcy court retains control over the assets of the estate. Bailors, for example, cannot retrieve property from the debtor, but in these cases, the stay is short-lived. Return to the case we considered in chapter 5, in which a dry cleaner files a Chapter 7 petition after you have given it your clothes to clean. In such a case, the automatic stay should preserve the status quo, but only for as long as it takes to sort out whether there is a true bailment. We need to be sure that, consistent with §541(a), the clothes are yours and not the dry cleaner's. In addition, we must be sure that, consistent with §544(a), the general creditors have no ability to levy on them outside of bankruptcy. Once we confirm these conditions, you should be able to recover your clothes.

Judges, however, sometimes resist the notion that a bailor should be entirely free to retrieve its property. In *Plastech Engineered Products*,[1] the debtor was a tier 1 automotive supplier that made plastic parts for cars. It had annual sales of over $1.2 billion and supplied components to major carmakers. It made many of its products with custom tooling that the carmakers owned. Under their contracts, the carmakers had the right to terminate the contract and take possession of their tooling. One, after making a number of accommodations, decided it was better off removing its tooling and finding someone else to supply the components. It terminated the agreement, but before it could take possession of its tooling, the supplier filed a bankruptcy petition. The carmaker asked the bankruptcy judge to lift the automatic stay on the second day of the case.

The carmaker was not trying to collect a debt, and it had terminated the contract before the petition was filed. In theory, the carmaker's property in the debtor's possession was no different than your clothes at the dry cleaner. The debtor had a possessory interest, but no more. In practice, however, the two situations are different. The tooling was part of the warp and woof of the debtor's business in a way that the suit at the drycleaner is not. If the debtor could retain possession of the tooling, the carmaker would be forced to continue to do business with it. And only if the carmaker continued with it could it survive as a going concern.

A debtor has no right to demand that third parties come to its rescue, but it was not as if the debtor had fallen into possession of the tooling casually or by accident. One suspects it would be an entirely different case if the carmaker had been shipping the tooling from one plant to another and the truck carrying it had happened to be at the debtor's factory delivering other supplies at the moment the bankruptcy petition was filed. In both cases, the debtor has a possessory interest in the tooling and no more, but being connected with the prepetition

---

[1] In re Plastech Engineered Products, Inc., 382 Bankr. 90 (Bankr. E.D. Mich. 2008).

life of the debtor seems to make a difference. Bankruptcy judges are reluctant to stick hard and fast to principle at the very outset of a case when taking a firm stand will blow up the business. Hence, they may try to put off a decision for a time in the hope that negotiation and compromise will settle the matter.

A somewhat more complicated issue arises when a third party seeks to terminate an ongoing relationship after the debtor files for bankruptcy. If the right to terminate exists only because the debtor has filed a bankruptcy petition or has become insolvent, then the termination violates the automatic stay. Section 363(*l*) parallels other provisions of the Bankruptcy Code, such as those in §541, §545, and §365, that refuse to give effect to ipso facto clauses. Bankruptcy does not respect rights that are effective in bankruptcy but not outside.

A harder case arises when the third party has a general right to terminate, but exercises it only because of the bankruptcy petition. Consider whether an insurance company can cancel a prepaid fire insurance policy that is cancellable at will once it finds that its debtor has filed a bankruptcy petition.[2] The termination and the bankruptcy filing may not be independent events. The insurance company may have canceled the policy only because the bankruptcy petition alerted it to the poor condition of the debtor and the heightened risk of fire.

Courts are sometimes reluctant to allow third parties to take advantage of the informational signal that bankruptcy conveys. While the debtor has no right to have a contract renewed, a third-party may be unable to terminate if it acts only because of the bankruptcy petition.[3] Courts, however, tend to allow parties to terminate when they are able to show that they would exercise the right apart from the bankruptcy filing.[4]

In all cases, of course, parties must first obtain relief from the automatic stay. A third party that terminates is taking an action that "obtains possession . . . of property from the estate" within the meaning of §362(a)(3). The automatic stay needs to last long enough to establish that, given the third party's right to terminate, the debtor has no right to the property. Even when their ability to cancel at will is "cause" that

---

[2] Holland American Insurance Co. v. Sportservice, Inc. (In re Cahokia Downs, Inc.), 5 Bankr. 529 (Bankr. S.D. Ill. 1980).

[3] In re Ernie Haire Ford, Inc., 403 Bankr. 750 (Bankr. M.D. Fla. 2009).

[4] See In re M.J. & K. Co., 161 Bankr. 586 (Bankr. S.D.N.Y. 1993).

justifies relief from the stay under §362(d), third parties act at their peril when they act unilaterally.

Section 362 for the most part does an effective job of ensuring that rights of prepetition creditors remain frozen in place while ongoing relations with others remain unaffected. You will never see a reported decision in which a general creditor asserts the right to levy on its debtor's assets once the bankruptcy begins. Everyone understands that this action is forbidden. So it is with many other easy cases. As we look at the hard cases, do not forget that §362 does most of its work without great controversy.

First and foremost, §362(a) prevents a prepetition general creditor from enforcing a claim. The automatic stay also applies to other actions to further the pursuit of a prepetition claim. Even if one does not touch property of the estate, §362 forbids one from going ahead in another forum on a prepetition claim. The bankruptcy proceeding is designed to give the debtor's assets a safe harbor. The trustee is supposed to have time to take stock of where things stand. Moreover, the trustee (or, more typically, the debtor in possession) is supposed to be able to deal with all the creditors in a single forum. The bankruptcy court is in charge of determining the size and validity of a claim. The stay allows the bankruptcy court to control where the claim is heard—in the nonbankruptcy forum, or in bankruptcy under either a §502(b) notice and hearing action or under a §502(c) estimation hearing. In addition, §362(a)(4) ensures that attempts to perfect or create liens against property also violate the automatic stay.

Section 362 does not stay all debt collection. Pursuit of postpetition claims is not stayed. For example, you can sue a debtor in a nonbankruptcy forum for a postpetition tort. The automatic stay, however, prevents you from actually levying on the debtor's property. The bankruptcy judge has to be in control of the property of the estate to ensure order. This distinction is reflected in the differences between §362(a)(4) and (a)(6). The automatic stay does not prevent prepetition creditors from going against third parties or exercising control over their assets. Prepetition creditors may pursue guarantors or codefendants. Some courts have found that in unusual circumstances, the automatic stay will apply to actions against third parties. Courts take this extraordinary step only when a judgment against the third-party defendant adversely affects the estate, such as when a judgment against a third party will trigger indemnification obligations.[5] A similar problem arises when the same insurance policy covers the debtor and codefendants. Actions against codefendants could reduce the total obligations of the insurer under the policy.[6] Allowing such actions would again impact the estate. Cases also arise in which a court stays actions against officers of the debtor under §105 on the ground that they need to devote their attention to the affairs of the debtor.[7] Cases in which these are the sole grounds for a third-party stay, however, are rare.[8]

There is one more important point about §362(a) that should be remembered. It is only a presumption. Even if the stay unequivocally applies, you can always ask to have it lifted. For example, if it makes sense for the government to litigate an environmental claim against the debtor in another forum because the litigation in that forum is well under way, the government can always go to court to ask to have the stay lifted. The converse is also the case. When a policy embedded in some provision of the Bankruptcy Code requires an action to be stayed, the court has the power to issue a stay under §105 even if the action is not automatically stayed under §362(a). If one finds an action that ought to be stayed that is not within the scope of §362(a), it does not necessarily mean there is anything wrong with the way §362(a) is written. Rather, the stay is designed to cover actions so common and easy to describe that they can be stayed automatically without requiring a court to review the particulars.

Government Regulations and §362(b)(4)

Bankruptcy is not an occasion to give debtors special breaks from the operation of substantive nonbankruptcy law. Consider a debtor that produces silicon chips. Let us assume that the debtor's assets are worth $2 million if they are used to make these chips. In other words, a buyer would pay $2 million for the assets free of prebankruptcy liabilities. The buyer who buys the assets at a certain price is willing to pay that price only after concluding that the net income of the project

---

[5] See, e.g., Calpine Corp. v. Nevada Power Co., 354 Bankr. 45 (Bankr. S.D.N.Y. 2006).

[6] See A.H. Robins Co. v. Piccinin, 788 F.2d 994 (4th Cir. 1986).

[7] See, e.g., Lazarus Burman Associates v. National Westminster Bank, 161 Bankr. 891 (Bankr. E.D.N.Y. 1993).

[8] In re Mid-Atlantic Handling Systems, LLC, 304 Bankr. 111 (Bankr. D. N.J. 2003).

offers a sufficient return on $2 million. In calculating the business's net income, the buyer will take into account, among many other things, the costs that various legal rules impose. A law may require, for example, the installation of environmental equipment at a cost of $500,000. In arriving at a value of $2 million, the buyer has already taken this cost into account.

If the assets could be used to produce silicon chips without complying with this regulation (and assuming that pollution victims otherwise had no legal recourse), a buyer would pay $2.5 million for the assets rather than $2 million. Hence, relieving a party from the duty of complying with such a rule increases the value of the assets. Again, no bankruptcy policy suggests that the debtor in possession be able to obtain such relief. The need to free an individual from the burdens of past debt or the need to give a business a new capital structure provides no justification for allowing the debtor to play by a different set of rules. We find the same idea at work in 28 U.S.C. §959(b):

> [A] trustee . . . appointed in any cause . . . including a debtor in possession, shall manage and operate the property in his possession . . . according to the requirements of the valid laws of the State in which such property is situated, in the same manner that the owner or possessor thereof would be bound to do if in possession thereof.

This principle is embraced in §362(b)(4), which provides that the automatic stay does not apply to "the commencement or continuation of an action or proceeding by a governmental unit . . . to enforce such governmental unit's police or regulatory power." Debtors in bankruptcy have to play by the same rules as everyone else. For example, they cannot pollute. If a debtor is operating in violation of a state or federal statute, the government should be able to tell it to stop regardless of whether it is in bankruptcy. Spending money to comply with governmental orders is not one of the things that a business should be able to avoid simply because it is in a collective proceeding. Section 362(b)(4) ensures that the government retains this power notwithstanding the automatic stay. This power remains even when the action will have irreversible consequences for property of the debtor, such as a city's demolition of a debtor's building after it has been condemned.[9]

Section 362(b)(4) requires that we draw a line between the actions a governmental unit takes in the exercise of its police or regulatory pow-

---

[9] Javens v. City of Hazel Park, 107 F.3d 359 (6th Cir. 1997).

er and those it takes as an ordinary prepetition creditor.[10] An action does not cease to be regulatory simply because it forces the debtor to spend money. But because the government can always assert that it is advancing a police or regulatory purpose with respect to any action it takes, drawing the line is not easy. The government can argue, for example, that a debtor's obligation to clean up property it did not own at the time of the petition serves a regulatory purpose, even though the obligation predated the bankruptcy petition and even though meeting the obligation requires only paying the agency money.[11]

Consider the extreme case in which an agency auctions off a license but lends qualified buyers part of the purchase price. The agency argues that the purpose of the auction was to identify those who value the license most and it can ensure that this happens only by collecting its loans in full. One of the buyers files for bankruptcy at a time when it is current on its payments to the agency. The debtor believes that, for purposes of collecting the money, the agency is a prepetition creditor rather than a regulator. The debtor ceases its payments to the agency while in bankruptcy. Can the agency cancel the license and then seek to sell the license to someone else?[12] The answer is that it should not. Section 362(b)(4) was not intended to allow the government to act when it is merely vindicating its rights as a creditor. Even if the government is not acting as a creditor, §525 prevents the government from taking actions (such as canceling a license) in response to a bankruptcy petition.[13]

When the regulator is the federal government, the power of the bankruptcy court may be limited in another way. The agency can argue that even when its actions violate the automatic stay, the bankruptcy court may still not be able to do anything about it because it has no subject matter jurisdiction over the actions of federal administrative agencies.[14] Review must be conducted through administrative law judges and then the court of appeals.

[10] In re McMullen, 386 F.3d 320 (1st Cir. 2004).

[11] See Torwico Electronics, Inc. v. New Jersey Department of Environmental Protection, 8 F.3d 146 (3d Cir. 1993).

[12] See In re Kansas Personal Communications Services, Ltd., 252 Bankr. 179 (Bankr. D. Kan. 2000).

[13] F.C.C. v. NextWave Personal Communications, Inc., 537 U.S. 293 (2003).

[14] See In re Federal Communications Commission, 217 F.3d 125 (2d Cir. 2000).

When the government acts as a postpetition regulator, it is not en-gaging in any of the acts prohibited by the automatic stay in §362(a), at least so long as it does not assert control over the debtor's assets. One can argue that the exceptions carved out for actions of the gov-ernment in §362(b) go beyond simply those actions that the govern-ment takes as a postpetition regulator. Under this view, the purpose that §362(b) serves is largely jurisdictional. The government is not obliged to resolve its prepetition disputes against the debtor in the bankruptcy forum when the dispute arises by virtue of the govern-ment's exercise of its police or regulatory power. The government, act-ing in this capacity, is presumptively entitled to pursue the debtor in the forum of its own choosing. In the absence of any order issued un-der §105, the government can pursue its claim in the nonbankruptcy forum.[15]

The Supreme Court confronted a similar problem in *Board of Gov-ernors v. MCorp Financial*.[16] Before filing for bankruptcy, MCorp caused two of its subsidiary banks to extend credit to an affiliate and engaged in other transactions that may have violated federal banking law. The Board of the Federal Reserve commenced one administrative proceeding before the bankruptcy began and then another after MCorp entered bankruptcy. The Supreme Court rejected MCorp's argument that the board was trying to enforce a prepetition claim and therefore violated the automatic stay. In the Court's view, the board's actions fell under §362(b)(4). The proceedings might culminate in a final order that would interfere with the bankruptcy court's exclusive jurisdiction over property of the estate under 28 U.S.C. §1334(d), but until that time, the board's actions did not violate the automatic stay. The Court was not persuaded that "the automatic stay provisions of the Bankruptcy Code have any application to ongoing, nonfinal ad-ministrative proceedings."[17]

MCorp and similar cases suggest that in the case of government regulations, some policies conflict with bankruptcy's goal of resolving all claims against a debtor in a single forum. One might also take the view that both §362 and nonbankruptcy federal law give the govern-

---

[15] See United States v. Nicolet, Inc., 857 F.2d 202 (3d Cir. 1988). The argument in text is set out in Robert K. Rasmussen, Bankruptcy and the Ad-ministrative State, 42 Hastings L.J. 1567 (1991).

[16] 502 U.S. 32 (1991).

[17] Id. at 41.

ment a privileged place among those to whom the debtor owes obligations. One provision of §362(b), for example, exempts Housing and Urban Development foreclosure actions from the automatic stay.

The Automatic Stay and the Secured Creditor

Bankruptcy provides the secured creditor with the value of its secured claim, but it does not allow the secured creditor to exercise the default rights it has under nonbankruptcy law. It cannot physically seize its collateral. To take such an action, the secured creditor must ask for relief from the stay. When is such relief granted? And when it is not granted, what must the trustee do to protect the secured creditor's collateral? As elsewhere in bankruptcy, there are a few basic guideposts that resolve many of the cases we are likely to encounter.

The secured creditor is entitled to have the stay lifted if its collateral is at risk. Section 362(d) provides that the stay can be lifted for cause. If the debtor is damaging the collateral or has stopped insuring it, a creditor will be able to lift the stay. If the collateral is not at risk, the secured creditor has no right to have the stay lifted when the collateral is worth more than the amount the secured creditor is owed. The debtor is the one who stands to gain or lose when the property is sold. The secured creditor is the wrong person to conduct the sale. The secured creditor has nothing to gain from getting more than the amount it is owed. Hence, it will be unlikely to sell it in a way that maximizes its value. We do have rules that require the secured creditor to act reasonably, but we are going to be better off if the person conducting the sale has the incentive to get the best price. The Bankruptcy Code recognizes this idea in §362(d)(2).

In the absence of cause, the secured creditor cannot lift the stay if the debtor has any equity in the property. Sometimes a secured creditor's collateral is worth more than it is owed, but other creditors also have security interests in the property, and all these interests together exceed the value of the property. One needs to ask whether the debtor lacks equity in the property within the meaning of §362(d)(2). Most courts have concluded that the debtor has no equity in the property in such a case.[18] This seems a defensible interpretation of the language of the Bankruptcy Code, but it may not make sense as a matter of first

---

[18] Nantucket Investors II v. California Federal Bank (In re Indian Palms Associates, Ltd.), 61 F.3d 197 (3d Cir. 1995); Viper Mining Co. v. Diversified Energy Venture, 311 Bankr. 712 (Bankr. W.D. Pa. 2004).

principle. If the property is worth more than the secured creditor is owed, the secured creditor may not have the right incentives to obtain the best price for it.

When the debtor lacks equity in the property, it can keep the collateral only if the collateral is necessary for an effective reorganization. A secured creditor has the right to lift the stay where there is no "reasonable possibility of a successful reorganization within a reasonable time."[19] The lift-stay motion forces the debtor to set up a timetable. To persuade a court to deny a lift-stay motion, the debtor has to show how it will reorganize itself and why the amount of time it will take is reasonable. The court can then use the debtor's own timetable to hold it to account at the next juncture in the case, which might be another lift-stay motion, a request to extend the exclusivity period, or a motion to convert the case to Chapter 7. Lift-stay motions, like these others, are the discrete points in a case when the court must decide whether to continue the business or shut it down. Just as the venture capitalist tells the entrepreneur that a new round of funding is assured only if the prototype works by a certain date, the bankruptcy judge will demand that the debtor present objective indicia of the business's prospects.

While the automatic stay is in force, the secured creditor is protected in a number of ways. Often the secured creditor asserts an interest not only in an asset such as a piece of real property but also in the revenue stream that the property generates. Section 552 relieves the secured creditor of the burden of showing that its interest in rents is perfected under nonbankruptcy law. Unlike a security interest in after-acquired personal property, state law sometimes does not allow for automatic perfection of rents (and analogous income streams from hotels). Section 552 reflects the judgment that the notice the bankruptcy process provides obviates the need to demand simultaneous compliance with perfection requirements under state law.

More generally, we require the trustee to ensure that the value of the secured creditor's rights is adequately protected throughout the bankruptcy process. Failure to offer adequate protection is itself cause that requires lifting the automatic stay under §362(d)(1). The meaning of *adequate protection* is illustrated (although not quite defined) in §361. First, the debtor may periodically make cash payments to the

---

[19] United Savings Association v. Timbers of Inwood Forest Associates, 484 U.S. 365, 376 (1988).

creditor, to the extent that the stay decreases the value of the secured creditor's interest in the property. Second, the debtor may provide an additional or replacement lien under the same circumstances. Finally, the debtor may give some other kind of protection (other than giving administrative expense priority) that will result in the indubitable equivalent of the right that the secured creditor is asserting.[20]

Even though adequate protection cannot be in the form of an administrative priority, the secured creditor is entitled to an administrative expense claim that trumps others if what is offered as adequate protection turns out to be inadequate. Assume that the secured creditor is entitled to $100 at the end of the bankruptcy proceeding but is given a lien on an asset that proves to be worth only $80 at that time. The secured creditor is entitled to be paid the $20 shortfall before any other administrative expenses are paid, including fees for the trustee and the debtor's lawyers. §507(b). The value of this super-administrative priority lies largely in the incentives it gives those who run the case. They will ensure that the secured creditor's protection is adequate, because they will not be paid until after the secured creditor's right to adequate protection is vindicated.

Secured creditors enjoy more protection in single-asset real estate cases. These are cases (other than residential property with fewer than four units) in which a single piece of real property generates substantially all the income of the debtor and on which the debtor conducts no substantial business other than operating the property. Even large office buildings fall within these expedited procedures. Section 362(d)(3) requires that in such cases the debtor file within 90 days a reorganization plan that has a reasonable possibility of being confirmed within a reasonable time. If it does not do so, it must make monthly interest payments at the nondefault contract rate to secured creditors equal to the value of its interest in the real estate. Even if a bank is undersecured (its mortgage on Blackacre secures a $100 loan, but Blackacre is worth only $60), the debtor must make payments that protect the time value of the bank's secured claim (that is, to the extent of $60). Imposing this requirement on the debtor in the single-asset real estate case is reasonable. There are no jobs at risk and there is no going-concern value to be protected.

---

[20] The idea of the indubitable equivalent is repeated in §1129 and comes from Learned Hand's opinion in In re Murel Holding Corp., 75 F.2d 941 (2d Cir. 1935).

Other secured creditors are not entitled to adequate protection for the time value of their claims.[21] Assume a bank has lent $100 and has a security interest in a machine that is worth $60 at the time the bankruptcy petition is filed. The bankruptcy will take several years. The bank is entitled to insist only on receiving protection on account of its $60 secured claim sufficient to ensure that, two years hence, it will receive $60 in nominal dollars. Receiving $60 in two years is not the same as receiving $60 today. The effect of interpreting adequate protection in this fashion is to require the bank to make a forced, interest-free loan for the duration of the bankruptcy.

This rule creates a number of inconsistencies. As noted, a single-asset real estate lender does enjoy protection for the time value of its secured claim. The rule also treats different secured creditors differently depending on how their collateral is used. If a debtor owns a machine with an extremely long useful life and leases it out, the secured creditor gets the rental payments under §552 as long as it would have received them under applicable law or under its contract. If the debtor owns a machine and uses it in its business, the secured creditor receives nothing on account of the debtor's use of the property. The streams of income a capital asset produces are economically identical.

Sometimes, the secured creditor repossesses before the bankruptcy petition is filed. Suppose a solvent debtor takes out a loan to buy a drill press, but falls behind on its payments to the bank. The bank repossesses the press and sells it before the debtor files for bankruptcy. In this case, the debtor is simply out of luck. It cannot bring a voidable preference action against the bank because a preference action does not lie against a fully secured creditor who repossesses or is paid off. (Recall that the transfer does not make the bank better off within the meaning of §547(b)(5), another anomaly given the treatment of time value in the bankruptcy case.) Nor can the debtor recover the property from a third-party buyer. Because the buyer is a bona fide purchaser for value, the trustee cannot retrieve the machine. The debtor no longer has any cognizable interest in the drill press, nor do any of the creditors. The person who now owns the drill press is a stranger to the process.

What if the bank repossesses but does not sell the drill press before the debtor files the petition? In this case, we do not have a bona fide

[21] United Savings Association v. Timbers of Inwood Forest Association, 484 U.S. 365 (1988).

purchaser for value in the picture. Let us look first at how this situation is handled outside of bankruptcy. Normally the debtor could recover the machine provided it pays the entire amount of the debt, not simply the value of the machine. The debtor continues to have a property interest in the machine, but its only interest is its right to redeem the property upon payment of the debt, not a right to the machine itself. Now let us examine how the situation is handled inside bankruptcy. Section 542 requires those holding property that the trustee can use, sell, or lease to turn it over. Under §363 the trustee can sell, use, or lease property of the estate, which is defined in §541 as the debtor's interest in the property. It might seem that §542 does not apply to the case in which a secured creditor has repossessed before the petition, because after the repossession the debtor's interest in the machine is only its right to redeem the property by forking over the full amount that the bank is owed. The trustee can use, sell, or lease that right of redemption, but not the collateral itself. The Supreme Court, however, interpreted this problem more broadly in *United States v. Whiting Pools, Inc.*:

> Although these statutes could be read to limit the estate to those "interests of the debtor in property" at the time of the filing of the petition, we view them as a definition of what is included in the estate, rather than as a limitation.[22]

Although this interpretation has an ipse dixit quality, it makes sense as a matter of first principle. The trustee can keep the machine after it is turned over only if the bank is not entitled to have the automatic stay lifted under §362(d). Hence, the only cases in which the issue is important are those in which the repossessed property is essential for an effective reorganization. If the bank were allowed to keep the collateral, the debtor would be forced to pay the bank all of what it is owed, even if the bank were undersecured. The bank, however, should not be entitled to have the unsecured portion of its claim paid in full. So long as the trustee ensures that the value of the bank's rights is adequately protected, the bank is not made worse off if the debtor gets the property back and the general creditors are made better off. Allowing the debtor to take the property back is not much different from curing a default on an executory contract.

---

[22] 462 U.S. 198, 203 (1983).

The Automatic Stay and Special Purpose Entities

The protections offered the secured creditor fall short of making the secured creditor indifferent to the commencement of a bankruptcy case. For this reason, investors have developed a number of devices that insulate them from the bankruptcy process. These often involve a special purpose entity ("SPE"). Investors put cash into a specially created entity, such as a limited liability company, and take a security interest in its assets. The entity then uses this money to "buy" assets, such as accounts receivable, from the debtor. So long as the transfer of assets to the SPE is treated as a "true sale," the debtor's bankruptcy has no effect on the SPE's investors. The SPE merely bought assets from the debtor. The debtor's Chapter 11 filing affects it no more than the Chapter 11 of a toaster-maker affects the consumers who buy their toasters before the filing of the petition.

In the simple cases, the SPE structure ensures that investors will have rights similar to those of secured creditors, but do not have the burdens associated with participating in the bankruptcy process. There is a true sale in which the debtor sells an account receivable outright, and the entity that buys it has no obligation to remit money to the debtor even if the amount collected proves unexpectedly large and no right of recourse even if it proves unexpectedly small. The debtor's bankruptcy leaves the entity and its creditors utterly unaffected.

The easier it is to argue that the transaction falls short of being a fully consummated transfer between two distinct entities, the easier it is to raise doubts about whether the investors are insulated from bankruptcy process. In *LTV Steel*, for example, the court denied emergency relief from the automatic stay for investors in a special purpose entity whose assets included, among other things, molten steel still being processed on the debtor's factory floor.[23]

Nonbankruptcy law ultimately decides whether a true sale has taken place,[24] and some state laws attempt to make such sales easier.[25] In principle, bankruptcy should defer to state law. Several words of caution are in order, however. First, bankruptcy courts will apply the principle of *Chicago Board of Trade v. Johnson* and will look to the attrib-

---

[23] See In re LTV Steel Co., 274 Bankr. 278 (Bankr. N.D. Ohio 2001).

[24] See Duke Energy Royal, LLC v. Pillowtex Corp. (In re Pillowtex, Inc.), 349 F.3d 711, 716 (3d Cir. 2003).

[25] See, e.g., Delaware Asset-Backed Securities Facilitation Act, 6 Del. C. §§2701A–2703A.

utes of the transaction, not the label that a state court has applied. Moreover, as discussed in chapter 7, such transactions must still survive scrutiny of fraudulent conveyance law. A true sale statute can trump only the fraudulent conveyance law in that jurisdiction. Such a law cannot trump the fraudulent conveyance principles embedded in the Bankruptcy Code, nor those of other jurisdictions.

SPEs are typically designed in a way that they do not end up in bankruptcy themselves. This is easier said than done, as it will often be in the interest of the debtor (and its creditors) to pull the SPEs into the case. As a general matter, a debtor cannot waive the right to file for bankruptcy. This rule has been applied not only to individual debtors, for whom such a waiver would eliminate the fresh start, but also to corporate debtors.[26] Courts are sympathetic to more narrow limitations on the ability of a debtor to file, especially when they are part of a nonbankruptcy workout.[27] During a workout, for example, the debtor may accede to a drop-dead clause, in which it promises not to contest a creditor's motion to lift the automatic stay in the event of a bankruptcy filing. Outside the context of workouts, however, courts are apt to view efforts to limit the ability of a debtor to file a bankruptcy petition (such as requiring consent of independent directors whose sympathies lie with the creditors) with considerable suspicion.[28]

One can try to make the SPE an entity that is not eligible for bankruptcy, but courts can recharacterize something denominated as an ordinary trust that is not bankruptcy eligible as a "business trust" that falls within the definition of a corporation and thus is eligible. While one can put people in place who are not likely to file a petition, the debtor may be able to replace them.[29]

Rather than having a single magic bullet that has the effect of keeping a particular entity outside of bankruptcy, investors can take a number of steps, each one of which makes the filing of a bankruptcy petition less likely. For example, the principal who would most likely control any decision to file for bankruptcy can be asked to sign a personal guarantee that is triggered only if the entity were to file for bankrupt-

[26] See United States v. Royal Business Funds Corp., 724 F.2d 12 (2d Cir. 1983).

[27] See In re Colonial Ford, 24 Bankr. 1014 (Bankr. D. Utah 1982).

[28] See, e.g., In re Kingston Square Associates, 214 Bankr. 713 (Bankr. S.D.N.Y. 1997).

[29] In re General Growth Properties, Inc., 409 Bankr. 43 (Bankr. S.D.N.Y. 2009).

cy. The guarantee is valued not because the bank ever expects to call upon it, but rather because the potential liability on the guarantee will keep the principal from ever putting the entity into bankruptcy. The dynamic is captured in the name commonly used to describe it: the "bad boy" guarantee. The principal is liable on the guarantee only if he is a "bad boy."

CHAPTER TEN

The Dynamics of Chapter 11

Before we turn to the mechanics of corporate reorganization in the next chapter, we look first in this chapter at the types of corporations that file for Chapter 11 and the problems that await them. Hundreds of thousands of businesses shut their doors each year in the United States and many more encounter financial distress, but fewer than 5 percent of these file for Chapter 11. For much of this book, we have discussed the principles of bankruptcy more or less removed from the circumstances and characteristics of the typical debtor. To understand how Chapter 11 works in practice, it is useful to have a sense of which businesses end up there and why.

As it happens, Chapter 11 consists of two strikingly different worlds. The vast majority of Chapter 11 petitions are filed by small businesses. These cases comprise the entire docket of most bankruptcy judges. A very small number of Chapter 11 cases concern large corporations. These tend to be filed in Delaware, the Southern District of New York, and a handful of other jurisdictions. Most bankruptcy judges never see them. Because of their complexity and the size of their assets, these cases generate the vast majority of the legal work, and many bankruptcy lawyers see no other kind. We look at each type of case in turn.

Small Business Corporations in Chapter 11

The typical Chapter 11 case involves a small business corporation.[1] The assets are often worth less than $100,000. The business employs only one or two people full-time other than the owner-manager. A computer consultant happens to do business in corporate form. She employs no one besides herself, and she runs the business out of her home. The business assets consist of a telephone and a personal computer. In this case, the business has little connection with the corpo-

---

[1] See Edward R. Morrison, Bankruptcy Decisionmaking: An Empirical Study of Continuation Bias in Small Business Bankruptcies, 50 J.L. & Econ. 381 (2007).

rate entity; the relationships belong to the individual. If as a customer you were happy with the consultant's work last year and wanted to use her services again, you would be indifferent to the existence of the corporation. You might reengage the consultant without ever knowing that she was doing business in corporate form or that the corporate form she is using this year was different from the one she used last year. The business's intangible assets reside in the consultant's expertise. Creditors have no way of reaching it.

Travel and insurance agents, lawyers, chiropractors, undertakers, livery drivers, and other self-employed individuals run a substantial number of the businesses in Chapter 11. These businesses require little more than a car, a desk, and a cell phone. Another sizable group are building contractors. The dry wall contractor, the plumber, the painter, and the electrician often work out of their home. Beyond a small office staff, they have no permanent employees. The people they hire are taken on only for particular jobs. The assets they need to do their work cost just a few thousand dollars.

In these cases, Chapter 11 is not so much about saving businesses as it is about allowing those who run their own businesses to sort out their finances. The owner-manager may have guaranteed a loan from an institutional lender or become personally liable for unpaid taxes. Both these obligations prevent the owner-manager from walking away from the old business before starting a new one. Chapter 11 buys time, even if the case is ultimately dismissed. The owner-manager gains two or three months during which she can preserve the status quo while identifying other options. More important, Chapter 11 creates an environment in which creditors—particularly the IRS and other tax authorities—are willing to stay their collection efforts.

The cost of providing this benefit falls largely upon trade creditors and small-time landlords. The filing of the petition cuts off trade creditors from the business's income stream, and the automatic stay prevents landlords from reentering the premises. And unlike tax authorities and institutional lenders, they lack personal recourse against the owner-manager, so their negotiating positions are weak. In the typical Chapter 11 case, general creditors are left empty-handed, as there is nothing left after the secured creditor and the tax collector are paid.

When we look at small business Chapter 11 cases, we see little that fits the conventional stereotype of a process that allows viable businesses to survive as stand-alone entities. The overwhelming majority are corporations that self-employed individuals create as a vehicle to run a business. Such individuals are, by nature, serial entrepreneurs.

The longer you are in business for yourself, the less likely you will take an ordinary job. Indeed, after you have been in business for yourself for more than 10 years, you are unlikely to work for anyone else again—ever. Starting a business, then closing it, and beginning another is part of your life in the same way that accepting one job, leaving, and going to another is for everyone else.

Serial entrepreneurship is the most persistent and most telling characteristic of small business bankruptcies. The benefits of Chapter 11 in these cases may seem modest, but the costs may be modest as well. Within a few months, bankruptcy judges sort out the debtors who will reorganize successfully and those who will not. Empirical evidence suggests that more than half the debtors who cannot reorganize successfully are identified and dismissed within three months of the filing of the petition; more than three-quarters are dismissed or converted within five months. Owners of small businesses in hopeless condition cannot use Chapter 11 to drag out the inevitable for very long. The Bankruptcy Code requires the debtor to propose a plan within 300 days of the filing of the petition unless the debtor can show that, more likely than not, the court will confirm a plan within a reasonable time period. §1121(e). These deadlines, however, have little effect on able judges. Most of the cases around after 300 days are the ones in which the debtor is likely to reorganize successfully.

These bankruptcy judges seem to rely on several rules of thumb:

1. *The 13 O'Clock Rule.* When a clock strikes 13, you know both that the clock is broken and that you have to doubt anything it has told you before. Judges are likely to dismiss or convert if the debtor has misrepresented anything to the court or has violated a court order, particularly with respect to cash collateral. The court is responding both to the violation itself and the possibility that other misdeeds lie undiscovered.

2. *The Cash-Flow Rule.* The judge receives regular statements that show how much cash has come into the business and how much has gone out. A business that remains cash-flow negative for more than a few months is not likely to make it.

3. *The Two-Strikes-and-You're-Out Rule.* A debtor in bankruptcy must cut square corners. If it fails to file a schedule, misses a §341 meeting, or fails to pay a fee, the United States Trustee will move for conversion or dismissal. The judge will forgive a single misstep if the debtor's owner-

manager quickly appears in court and is sufficiently repent-
ant. But a second failure to follow the rules triggers a dismissal.

4. *The Meet-Your-Own-Goals Rule.* At the status conference
   and in its §308 reports, the debtor asserts it will meet certain goals (such as increasing earnings or finding a new investor) by a particular date. If the goals are not met and
   major players oppose the debtor's effort to extend the deadline, the bankruptcy judge sees a red flag, a sign that the
   company is not on the path to reorganizing effectively.

5. *The Company-You-Keep Rule.* Bankruptcy judges may take
   their cue from the identity of the debtor's lawyer. When
   lawyers appear frequently before the same court, they develop reputations. Some may be more inclined to take on
   cases that have little merit.

Modern bankruptcy judges are triage officers. They have no desire
to help debtors who are merely delaying the inevitable. Those who
cannot successfully reorganize will remain under the radar screen for
only a short period of time. A debtor can file a frivolous Chapter 11
petition, but the case will remain in the system only as long as it takes
a creditor or the United States Trustee to find out about it, file a motion, properly notify the parties, and appear in court. In the absence of
some emergency, this process takes several weeks, but it can take longer if the United States Trustee or the various creditors do nothing.
Bankruptcy judges, like other judges, generally do not act sua sponte,
but only when advocates call matters to their attention.

Large Corporate Reorganizations

Most of the assets (and most of the lawyers) are found in the very
largest cases. We now turn to describing this world. Many of the day-
to-day practices in large Chapter 11 cases are known to insiders, but
inaccessible to anyone else. Much of the action lies in bargaining that
takes place away from the courtroom, and it rarely gives rise to reported decisions. To give one quotidian example, experienced lawyers
know not to expend any energy fighting the fees of the indenture trustee, even though §503(b)(5) allows them only in the event they make a
"substantial contribution" to the case. These fees are routinely included in the plan, without inquiry into whether the indenture trustee's
contribution was in fact "substantial." Junior associates once found out
about this feature of modern bankruptcy practice in a hazing ritual

akin to the one in which the newest apprentice in a French restaurant is sent to retrieve soufflé weights lent to a rival.[2] Aspiring bankruptcy lawyers were instructed to go to plan negotiations and to be unyielding on the question of allowing fees for the indenture trustee, only to be surprised when they were not taken seriously.

Compounding the problem of so much being hidden from view, the dynamics of large Chapter 11 cases today are different from what they were only a few years ago. Managers no longer enjoy the control they once did. When a large business encounters financial distress, the lenders often bring about the appointment of a chief restructuring officer (CRO). With a sophisticated board of directors, the lenders may need only make it clear that they will look more kindly on future waivers of loan covenants if a CRO with whom they have worked is brought in. (By being oblique, they minimize the risk of lender-liability actions outside of bankruptcy and equitable subordination inside. For boards sensitive to Sarbanes-Oxley and potential shortfalls in directors and officers liability insurance, hints are usually sufficient.) Boards, of course, are nominally the ones who appoint the CRO, and creditors stop short of insisting on a particular individual. But only just short. Before WorldCom filed for bankruptcy, its creditors conditioned further financing in the bankruptcy case on the appointment of a CRO and gave the board freedom to choose anyone it pleased—so long as the person was one of three on a list the creditors provided.

The arrival of a CRO alters the terrain of corporate governance. The CRO is not a typical member of the management team. Unlike other corporate officers, the CRO reports directly to the board. The CRO is often expected to identify which members of the management team add value and which ones need to be replaced, including the CEO. Indeed, the Chapter 11 process may go forward only after the CRO has had a chance to investigate the operational problems and settle on a plan of action. The plan often consists of cleaning up the business and selling it. An immediate sale is often not possible. Among other things, no one wants to buy a business if its books are a mess.

In addition, the stakeholders are different from what they were a decade or so ago. Dozens of constantly changing investors occupy every tranche of the capital structure, each pursuing its own agenda. Some

---

[2] See, e.g., Jacques Pepin, The Apprentice: My Life in the Kitchen (2003). There is, of course, no such thing as a soufflé weight.

seek long-term control of the business, while some are passive and short-term. Others may hold a basket of both long and short positions in multiple tranches and complicated hedges involving other businesses.

In the past, the bargains that parties reached among themselves followed a few familiar patterns. While there were many possible deals, the players naturally gravitated towards only a few. In the new environment, with different players holding different stakes, the old patterns no longer apply and new ones have yet to take shape. There are no longer organized groups (like agented lenders or even creditors' committees), but instead investors have "one-off" relationships with the debtor entity (for example, counterparties with individual repos or swaps). The types of institutions vary—from banks and broker-dealers to hedge funds and private equity firms. The current environment is one in which there are no natural leaders (or followers) among the creditors to perform the shuttle diplomacy required to build a consensus. Without familiar benchmarks, there is no shared understanding of what form a plan should take. Coalition formation is harder.

Consider the reorganization of Adelphia. Adelphia was the fifth largest operator of cable systems in the United States. As is common in large reorganizations, the debtor decided to sell its assets under §363 as a going concern. In April 2005, it found a buyer willing to pay $17.6 billion, a substantial premium above its stand-alone value. The purchase agreement required that the transaction close within 15 months, but no creditor group raised serious objections either to the amount or the form of the sale.

By the traditional account, there would seem to be few impediments to wrapping up the case quickly. The only creditors were institutional investors who were owed fixed amounts of money. The only assets were either cash or stock in the buyer (Time Warner Cable). But things were not so simple. Adelphia was not a single corporation, but rather a group of 230 related entities. Each creditor group could contest the valuation of its claim. Even though there were only a few large creditor groups, there was no easy way of putting a value on each one and there was no obvious focal point around which agreement might form. As a result, there was no way to "assuage the concerns of one creditor faction without further alienating another. . . . This effectively froze progress on the confirmation of a reorganization plan, with the deadlock increasingly threatening the . . . sale."[3]

Claims Trading

The rise in claims trading has significantly altered the dynamics of large Chapter 11 reorganizations over the last two decades. The ability to trade in claims against a Chapter 11 debtor began to take hold in the 1980s. At that time, however, some courts interpreted the Bankruptcy Rules to allow them to review claim trades and ensure that those selling them received full disclosure. In 1991, however, the Rules Committee decided to deregulate claims trading, as existing judicial oversight was perceived to impair the liquidity of claims. The effect was to create a market in claims of large debtors.

The basic rationale for claims trading is simple. It allows easy exit from a reorganization proceeding for those who are ill-equipped to navigate it. Claims trading flourishes because it is attractive to buyers as well as sellers. Distressed debt players can profit from their ability to understand the bankruptcy process. They may be better able to assess how much the debtor will ultimately be able to pay on its claims. A hedge fund that examines a company in full is more likely to have a good sense of the entire value of the enterprise than is a trade creditor or small bondholder. Moreover, the investor may be able to find overlooked value in the instruments that the debtor has issued. Either way, the new investor may be able to use its knowledge of the reorganization process to generate a higher return than could the party that owned the claim when the debtor filed for bankruptcy.

In addition, in some instances the ability to buy claims allows strategic investors to gain control of the business. Claims trading plays the same role as a conventional take-over contest outside of bankruptcy, differing only in that the outsider buys debt rather than equity. Indeed, it is easy to identify bankruptcy cases where the fight for control was front and center.

The law governing the trading of claims remains remarkably undeveloped. Many basic questions, including whether claims are "securi-

---

[3] In re Adelphia Communications Corp., 368 Bankr. 140, 159 (Bankr. S.D.N.Y. 2007).

ties" within the meaning of the securities laws, remain unresolved.[4] Moreover, it has brought to the surface fundamental tensions that have yet to be resolved.

Consider the problem raised in *Washington Mutual*.[5] Some distressed debt investors acquired a significant position and entered into negotiations with the debtor. They agreed to cease trading for a time, but only with the understanding that they would not become permanently restricted. If the negotiations failed, the debtor would release to the world whatever confidential information was disclosed during the negotiations. Bargaining proved unsuccessful and, as promised, the debtor disclosed the information that it turned over during the negotiations. The investors began to trade again. Some bought additional claims, while others sold.

Months passed, and eventually the principal players reached a deal. But a group of disgruntled investors—the old equityholders—argued that the claims of the hedge funds that continued to trade should be "equitably disallowed." Those who participated in the negotiations came into information that the market as whole did not have, and the debtor's subsequent release of the information was insufficient to put public investors on an equal footing. The negotiations themselves revealed much about the debtor's prospects for reorganization—in particular the potential willingness of others to settle litigation. This information was not public and never became public. When the hedge funds returned to the market to trade, they knew something about the prospects of reorganization that outside investors did not. It was of no moment that some hedge funds bought and others sold. What mattered is that they did so while possessing inside information.

The logic of their argument seems at first blush to be compelling. The use of private information by insiders was the kind of activity that goes to the heart of what the reforms of the 1930s were about. As Justice Douglas observed in *Pepper v. Litton*:

> [An investor] cannot utilize his inside information and his strategic position for his own preferment. . . . He cannot use his power for his personal advantage and to the detriment of

---

[4] See Robert D. Drain & Elizabeth J. Schwartz, Are Bankruptcy Claims Subject to the Federal Securities Laws?, 10 Am. Bank. Inst. L. Rev. 569 (2002).

[5] See In re Washington Mutual, Inc., 461 Bankr. 200 (Bankr. D. Del. 2011), *vacated in part*, 2012 WL 1563880 (Bankr. D. Del. 2012).

> the stockholders and creditors no matter how absolute in
> terms that power may be and no matter how meticulous he
> is to satisfy technical requirements.[6]

The Bankruptcy Code has no formal prohibitions against trading by investors who gain access to information about the debtor and insiders, but none are necessary. The equitable powers of the bankruptcy judge suffice.

The bankruptcy judge possesses the power to subordinate and even disallow claims by those who violate the norms that govern the reorganization process. Some facts underlying the cause of action, such as whether the information is material, may be in doubt, but the equityholders persuaded the court that the claim was colorable. A few months later, as part of a settlement of the case, the judge agreed to vacate this portion of the opinion, but the opinion remains in the *Bankruptcy Reporter* and its underlying logic survives.

The logic of *Washington Mutual* seems to suggest that claims trading and negotiations on the part of all the players cannot co-exist, but modern large reorganization practice assumes the contrary. Whenever you negotiate with someone, the negotiations themselves give you information that the rest of the world does not know. If such information constitutes material nonpublic information that trips up the prohibitions against insider trading, then anyone who agrees to negotiate forfeits her ability to trade. One might think that, now that *Washington Mutual* has been vacated, all can be forgotten, but things in fact are not so easy. The reasoning that powers the decision remains, and the tension that led to it has not been resolved.

Several devices have emerged to facilitate trading when those involved are likely to be exposed to information that the market as a whole does not possess. None is likely to be both effective and widely available.

Those who possess inside information can try to create a barrier between themselves and others in their firms. Such barriers, once properly in place, allow those inside the firm not involved in negotiations to continue to trade even while others are restricted from trading by virtue of the private information they possess. These barriers, however, are no panacea. First, their physical cost is nontrivial. One needs such things as separate computers, separate locked files, and soundproof rooms. A protocol needs to be in place that establishes that

---

[6] 308 U.S. 295, 311 (1939).

those who trade will not come across confidential information. Someone needs to be charged with compliance.[7]

For a large financial institution with a well-established bureaucracy, setting up such compliance is not hard, but the typical hedge fund is a small affair. Notwithstanding its control of billions in assets, its physical presence consists only of a few trading desks. Imposing the procedures of large bureaucracies on them is no simple matter. If one did not care whether such traders existed (or affirmatively wished that they did not), it might not seem a problem, but if one believes that claims trading is and should be a fundamental part of reorganization practice, one cannot pretend that information barriers solve all problems.

Reforms that push too much in this direction may have the effect of entrenching the status quo. The old-line banks do not mind and hedge funds do. We should be suspicious of any regulatory fix that favors those who have been around for a century at the expense of those who just arrived on the scene.

In all events, the major problem with information barriers for the typical hedge fund is not the physical cost, but rather the problem of having sufficient size so that one can staff both the negotiation side and the trading side. One needs to have both a trader and an analyst on both sides of the wall. If one needs active investors to monitor the debtor and savvy traders to provide a well-functioning market, expertise is needed in both places. For a large institution, this again is often not a problem, but the typical hedge fund does not have this depth of expertise.

Hedge funds sometimes navigate around this problem by dispatching lawyers to negotiate on their behalf. When the question concerns the settlement of a disputed piece of litigation, lawyers may possess the necessary skills, but if the question concerns competing business plans, they are likely out of their depth. It is possible that somewhere there are lawyers who excel when it comes to weighing two different business deals and making a quick decision on which hundreds of millions depends, but if such lawyers exist, they have picked the wrong line of work. Other emissaries present problems as well. One can sometimes employ and dispatch another trader, but this again presents problems if the negotiations are to persist over long periods. An im-

---

[7] See In re Van D. Greenfield & Blue River Capital LLC, Release No. 34-52744, 86 S.E.C. Docket 1623, 2005 WL 2978438 (2005).

portant virtue of the successful trader is the ability to adapt strategies as fluid situations change.

In addition to information barriers, claims traders in the past relied on Big Boy letters.[8] The gravamen of Rule 10b-5 liability is deception. The essence of the complaint is that the seller failed to disclose information that was relevant to the buyer. Claims traders can ask each other to sign a letter acknowledging that the other may be in possession of material nonpublic information and is not disclosing it. Once a buyer acknowledges that he is a "Big Boy," he cannot complain about not receiving information he insisted he did not need. By signing a Big Boy letter, the trader shows that he is not relying on the other side's silence. One cannot waive causes of action under the securities law, but by signing a Big Boy letter one abandons one of the essential elements—reliance—that is part of the cause of action.

The SEC, however, has the independent power to enforce the securities laws, and it is not bound by the representations that traders make with one another. It might seem that the SEC is wrong to get involved here. Trades in which claims traders both sign Big Boy letters do not have the vice at which the securities laws are aimed. Everyone involved is a grown-up. There is no harm to the innocent investor, the dentist in Peoria, who deserves a level playing field.

The problem is not so simple, however. First, there is the worry about trading that is further down the chain. The SEC may worry not about the person who buys after signing a Big Boy letter, but rather the person to whom this buyer sells. The person who signs a Big Boy letter knows that the security she has may not be what it appears to be, but her buyer does not.

Second, the reach of Rule 10b-5 liability has expanded over time. It reaches those who trade on information that has been disclosed to them on the understanding that they not trade upon it.[9] You may be free to trade on information not known to others, but not someone to whom you told the information in confidence, such as the lawyers who were helping you plan a hostile takeover. They are committing wrongs

---

[8] *See* Edwin D. Eshmoili, Big Boy Letters: Trading on Inside Information, 94 Cornell L. Rev. 133 (2008).

[9] United States v. O'Hagan, 521 U.S. 642, 652 (1997).

against you by trading. Those injured are not those trading with the lawyers and hence their waiver is irrelevant.[10]

This rationale, one upon which the SEC has relied to bring actions against those who traded with Big Boy letters, is not easy to square with the facts of *Washington Mutual*.[11] The hedge funds that traded after negotiating with the debtor were not misappropriating information. The debtor itself blessed their trading. Any information they possessed was information that, at least from the debtor's perspective, was information they were entitled to use. They stood in a completely different position from, let us say, a member of the creditors' committee who trades on information she has been told in confidence.

But this argument is quite beside the point. The absence of reliance on the part of the buyer does not prevent the SEC from bringing an enforcement action, and there is no guarantee that it will restrain itself merely because the logic of the action is conceptually flawed. If an investor who possesses material nonpublic information sells without disclosing the information, she is vulnerable to an SEC action even if all the buyers signed Big Boy letters.

The costs of being charged by the SEC with insider trading are high for hedge funds. They need new investors, and prudent investors do not want to be associated with a fund that is being investigated by the SEC for insider trading. Hedge funds desire safe harbors, and Big Boy letters are no longer thought good enough if securities are involved. Big Boy letters might be useful for other reasons. If the debt is not a security, then one does not need to worry about an SEC action. A Big Boy letter both ensures that there will not be a private cause of

---

[10] Ted Kamman & Rory T. Hood, With the Spotlight on the Financial Crisis, Regulatory Loopholes, and Hedge Funds, How should Hedge Funds Comply with the Insider Trading Laws?, 2009 Colum. Bus. L. Rev. 357, 435–38 (2009).

[11] This is not to say the equityholders in *Washington Mutual* did not try. They argued that some of the information the debtor revealed was held in confidence by it. The hedge funds, they alleged, knew that the debtor held this information in confidence. This is enough. Someone who receives a tip from someone she knows to have misappropriated information is liable under Rule 10b-5. In other words, the debtor is in the same position as a lawyer who betrays a client who is about to do a hostile takeover and the hedge fund is in the position of a friend who receives a tip from her. Among other things, it seems odd to tag hedge funds with "tippee" liability, given their arm's length and typically adverse relationship with the debtor.

action and, more importantly, puts pressure on buyers who are repeat players not to complain when things do not turn out well for them.

One relatively new device that is more likely to work, if it can be obtained, is an order from the bankruptcy court finding that the content of settlement negotiations is not material nonpublic information. At least one such order has been entered.[12] It might seem strange that parties would insist upon the court's explicit blessing before trying to negotiate with one another, something that comes to bankruptcy professionals as naturally as breathing. But this is the path that *Washington Mutual* may have set us upon.

And judicial orders are far from a cure-all. A court's determination that settlement proposals do not constitute material nonpublic information does not necessarily bind those who are not parties to the negotiations, including the SEC. Moreover, many negotiations take place before the debtor is in bankruptcy. Finally, the problem is broader than merely settlement negotiations. The bankruptcy process, by its nature, involves extensive contact among the participants and astute traders can infer information from these interactions. They inevitably possess information that others do not even when they are not brought into the confidence of the debtor and are given confidential information with the understanding that they will not trade on the basis of it.

New Creditors and New Capital Structures

Even apart from claims trading, the identity of those who hold debt in distressed businesses has changed. Banks have long syndicated their loans, but the composition of lending syndicates has changed. Membership is no longer limited to bank and pension funds. Hedge funds can participate in the syndication stage. Moreover, there is a rapidly developing secondary market in syndicated loans.

A hedge fund that holds a position identical to the one held by a bank at an earlier time does not look at the world the same way. Though they own the same instrument, they have drastically different business models. Banks are repeat players. A bank can have a relationship with a business that lasts for decades. The bank provides a large

---

[12] See, e.g., In re Vitro, S.A.B. de C.V., Case No. 11-33335-hdh-15, Order in Aid of Settlement Discussions (Jan. 26, 2012) (providing, among other things, that "Settlement Proposals shall not constitute material nonpublic information").

suite of services beyond simply making the loan. In addition, commercial norms and its reputation constrain its conduct in any particular relationship. While it might, for example, have the legal right to call a loan in default, its concern about its reputation with other borrowers may lead it to waive the covenant. A hedge fund, by contrast, has a limited life, provides no services, and acts under no reputational constraints.

In addition, those who work for banks and those who work for hedge funds bring different skill sets. Those who work for banks excel at monitoring the debtor and ensuring their collateral is safe. Hedge funds hire entrepreneurs with industry expertise who have the skills needed to take a much more active role in the affairs of the company. When a loan covenant is violated, a bank might insist on additional collateral, while a hedge fund might insist on a new CEO. Finally, there are regulatory differences. A hedge fund can buy into a troubled debtor with a view to holding equity in the business for a number of years in the event it is reorganized. By contrast, a bank is limited in its ability to hold stock.

Capital structures have also changed. The first layer of secured debt often does not exhaust the borrowing capacity of the business. Borrowers in need of additional funds borrow from lenders who will take a junior position (in return for a higher interest rate). In years past, the debtor would access this additional value through mezzanine financing on an unsecured basis. In the 1980s, this financing was provided by savings-and-loan associations and insurance companies. These were relatively passive investors who had little ability to affect the operation of the company. To the extent that any investor was monitoring the debtor, it was the lead bank in the lending syndicate.

Today, the debtor often accesses the difference between the senior loan and full enterprise value through a second-lien loan. The second-lien lender takes a security interest in the same assets as the first lender. Its right to payment, by and large, is not subordinated to the senior debt. Maturity schedules are set so that the borrower is required to make payments on both loans. The second-lien lender can seek to be repaid at the same time as the senior lender is being repaid. Moreover, unlike subordinated debt, it does not have to pay any monies that it collects to the senior debt. Rather, it is second only in terms of its claim on the collateral package. Only when collateral is sold for cash does the senior lender have first dibs. The second-lien market has exploded over the last several years. As with syndicated first-lien loans, there is a robust secondary market for second-lien loans. Hedge funds are primary purchasers of second-lien debt.

The first- and second-lien holders sort out their respective rights in an intercreditor agreement. This agreement specifies the relationship between the two lenders. It addresses in detail their respective rights should the borrower file for bankruptcy. For example, the intercreditor agreement often grants the senior lender the right to sell the collateral without the consent of the second-lien lender. The intercreditor agreement also typically gives the senior lender the right to finance the debtor postpetition and provides that this financing will have priority over the loan of the second-lien lender.

The Code has proven sufficiently flexible (and the judges and the lawyers sufficiently creative) to overcome the problems that have arisen so far. Doubt exists about features of these new capital structures, especially the enforceability of provisions of the intercreditor agreement that tie the second-lien holders' hands during the bankruptcy process. Courts insist that any waiver of rights be spelled out clearly, especially when the second-lien holders are in the money or close to being in the money.[13] They have shown a willingness to enforce agreements to refrain from demanding an examiner, objecting to the use of cash collateral, or opposing a plan of reorganization.[14] At the same time, however, courts tend to confront the merits even as they recognize the obligation of junior investors to be silent. In the typical case, the court finds both that the party lacks the ability to object and that the objection lacks merit.

Courts seem less inclined to recognize agreements that undermine the plan reorganization process itself. When parties stand passively by and allow others to act in their stead, one may fear that more is going on than sorting out the rights between two parties to the same share of the debtor's assets. When one party can cast the votes of another, the

[13] In re Boston Generating, LLC, 440 Bankr. 302, 320 (Bankr. S.D.N.Y. 2010).

[14] See In re Erickson Retirement Communities, LLC, 425 Bankr. 309, 316 (Bankr. N.D. Tex. 2010) (bound to refrain from seeking examiner); Aurelius Capital Master, Ltd. v. TOUSA Inc., 2009 WL 6453077 (S.D. Fla. 2009) (bound not to object to use of cash collateral); Ion Media Networks, Inc. v. Cyrus Select Opportunities Master Fund, Ltd., 419 Bankr. 585, 597 (Bankr. S.D.N.Y. 2009) (agreement not to object to plan).

integrity of the plan process itself may be compromised and affect the rights of third parties as well.[15]

Credit default swaps have further complicated restructuring large businesses, especially in advance of bankruptcy. A credit default swap is a two-party contract under which one party (the protection seller) acquires the credit risk of a loan from a counterparty (the protection buyer) in exchange for a fee. If there is a default or some other "credit event" (such as bankruptcy) on the loan, the protection buyer receives cash equal to the face value of the loan.

Credit default swaps are created without the input of the debtor. Some are even created by investors with no current interest in the company at all. They are often side bets in which parties care only about "credit events," events that trigger settlement obligations under the swap. In such a case, the seller of a credit default swap will fight vigorously to prevent a bankruptcy filing from taking place (at least until the expiration of the swap) and the buyer will affirmatively encourage it, regardless of whether filing makes any sense for the company. This failure to attend to the interaction between these new investments and the bankruptcy process threatens to put unprecedented strain on the current system of addressing financial distress.

Buying a credit default swap differs from syndication in terms of control rights. When a lead bank sells part of the loan, it bundles with that loan any applicable control rights. The syndicate needs to agree to any waiver of an event of default. The agent may be able to cajole syndicate members to follow its recommendation, but it is still the case that those who own the loan have to make the decision. If a hedge fund sells its piece of the loan in the secondary market, it loses its ability to have an input on any decisions that the syndicate has to make. The economic exposure and the attendant control rights remain bundled, even if the package changes hands multiple times.

When a lender purchases a credit default swap, however, it retains the control rights that accompany the loan. The protection seller now bears the economic risks of the loan, but rights under the credit agreement remain lodged in the protection buyer. If a waiver of an

---

[15] In re 203 N. LaSalle Street Partnership, 246 Bankr. 325 (Bankr. N.D. Ill. 2000); In re SW Boston Hotel Venture, LLC, 460 Bankr. 38 (Bankr. D. Mass. 2011), vacated on other grounds, 2012 WL 4513869 (B.A.P. 1st Cir. 2012). Not all courts share this view. See, e.g., Rosenfeld v. Coastal Broadcasting System, 2013 WL 3285936 (D.N.J. 2013).

event of default is needed, the holder of the loan is free to vote as it sees fit. But now its economic interest has changed.

Credit default swaps shift the focus of negotiations outside of bankruptcy in a fundamental way. The holders of the swaps, who may have a seat at the table by virtue of holding the underlying asset, may care more about whether any course of action is a "credit event" than whether it increases the value of the company. In the extreme case, if the lender has purchased more in credit default swaps than it has at risk in terms of the loan itself, it may be to its financial advantage if the loan goes into default. Blowing up the company may generate a higher return than saving it.

Lyondell, a transnational corporation with assets in both the United States and the Netherlands, put its American operations into Chapter 11. The operations in the Netherlands, however, remained outside of any insolvency proceeding. This situation sparked a fight over whether the American bankruptcy court would enjoin the holders of bonds issued by the Dutch entity from declaring a default. Were the bondholders to declare a default, the Dutch company would be forced into Dutch bankruptcy proceedings, where the outcome would most likely be a value-destroying liquidation that would leave everyone worse off. Why would the bondholders need to be enjoined from an action that seems so contrary to their own self-interest? Some suggested that it arose from their simultaneously holding a large amount of credit default swaps that would pay handsomely upon default by the Dutch company.

Credit default swaps create a moral hazard problem before the Chapter 11 begins and then in its immediate aftermath. A Chapter 11 case is a "credit event" that terminates the swap. The accounts are settled up and the control of the claim against the debtor soon is again placed in the hands of the person who holds the economic interest in it. Credit default swaps may seriously complicate (and potentially even distort) workouts that take place before bankruptcy, and they also matter at the start of the case, where much of the action takes place. Many issues—from the approval of the debtor-in-possession ("dip") financing to the composition of the creditors' committee—are resolved in the first month.

Total return swaps create problems that extend far into the life of the bankruptcy case as they are not necessarily settled in the wake of a credit event. In a total return swap, the owner of a loan (total return payer) exchanges the income from the loan and any appreciation for a guaranteed income stream plus protection against capital depreciation.

While the owner thus off-loads the economic risks associated with the loan, it retains the loan and all associated control rights. The total return swap allows an investor (total return receiver) to enjoy the economic rights in a loan without the associated control rights and hence there is a danger that it will make decisions that are not value-maximizing.

Over time, the difficulties these new financial instruments introduce should be self-correcting. The potential purchasers are likely to be the distressed debt professionals who will have both the expertise and the incentive to be active in the case. They too, of course, must rely on the willingness of the record owner to act as they wish, but in the typical case the record owner follows their wishes. To the extent that a tension exists, parties will try to recombine the control and formal ownership to overcome the agency problem that exists whenever ownership and control are separated. Solving the problem, however, will likely take time, and winners and losers may appear while this is being sorted out.

Continuing the Business in Chapter 11

The trustee (and by inference the debtor in possession) must maximize the value of the estate rather than promote the interests of any particular group.[16] Chapter 11 does not rely entirely on the debtor in possession to ensure this outcome. Creditors are given their own representative in reorganization proceedings through the creditors' committee. Moreover, courts may measure the performance of professionals in connection with fee requests by asking whether they have advanced the interests of the estate as a whole.

The Bankruptcy Code puts in place oversight mechanisms to ensure that the managers are looking out for everyone's interests, not just their own. These procedures, embodied in §363, begin with the idea that many day-to-day business decisions are not controversial. The trustee (and hence the debtor in possession) has the general authority to use, sell, or lease property of the estate.[17] It would be crazy to require a retailer to go to court every time a customer came into the store

---

[16] In re Central Ice Cream, 836 F.2d 1068 (7th Cir. 1987). This is consistent with nonbankruptcy law. See, e.g., Production Resources Group, LLC v. NCT Group, Inc., 863 A.2d 772, 790–92 (Chancery Del. 2004).

[17] The trustee has this power only if the trustee has the authority to run the business, but such authority is presumed in Chapter 11 cases.

to buy something. The debtor in possession has to be able to buy raw materials and sell finished products. If the existing managers cannot be relied on to do at least that, a trustee should be appointed. If a transaction falls outside the ordinary course of business, it is subject to judicial scrutiny. The debtor can act only after there has been notice and a hearing.[18]

In bankruptcy, courts must take care to ensure the absence of self-dealing and a process that is likely to "obtain the highest price or greatest overall benefit possible for the estate."[19] The diverse interests that require the bankruptcy proceeding in the first place also require the court to ensure that they have not colored the decision at hand. At the same time, the bankruptcy judge must take advantage of market mechanisms when available.[20] Hence, it should come as no surprise that bankruptcy courts are less likely to accept doctrines such as the business judgment rule when the debtor's actions have circumvented the marketplace.[21]

If the players are to pursue any option other than a piecemeal liquidation of the business, a way must be found to keep the business operating if only for a time. Postpetition obligations must be paid before the general creditors receive anything. These are "administrative expenses," the "actual, necessary costs and expenses of preserving the estate." They are given priority over the unsecured claims of the debtor under §507(a)(1). Moreover, the plan of reorganization must pay administrative expenses in cash.

The rationale behind this rule is straightforward. Money spent to increase the value of the estate should be borne by the estate. The rule is necessary to pay the fees of the professionals who orchestrate the reorganization, as well as ensure that people do business with the debtor, but its reach is broader. It ensures, for example, that those whose tort claims arise after the petition is filed are paid before the prepetition general creditors.[22] The risk of incurring tort liability is

[18] Requiring notice and a hearing within the meaning of the Bankruptcy Code is not the same, of course, as requiring a hearing. See §102.

[19] Cello Bag Co. v. Champion International Corp., 99 Bankr. 124, 130 (Bankr. N.D. Ga. 1988).

[20] See Bank of America v. 203 North LaSalle Street Partnership, 526 U.S. 434 (1999).

[21] See, e.g., In re Bidermann Industries U.S.A., 203 Bankr. 547 (Bankr. S.D.N.Y. 1997).

[22] Reading Co. v. Brown, 391 U.S. 471 (1968).

one of the necessary costs incident to taking time to sort out the debtor's affairs. We can ensure that those who benefit from the bankruptcy proceeding internalize this cost by giving postpetition tort claims priority over unsecured claims.

Although not an "administrative expense" proper, §503(b)(9) gives an administrative expense priority to sellers of goods received by the debtor within 20 days of filing the case. Even if there were some reason for offering them priority among prepetition creditors, it is hard to see why they are more deserving of priority than unpaid workers (who enjoy a lower priority that is capped) or tort victims (who enjoy no priority at all, in bankruptcy or out). The need for cash to pay these suppliers in full can become a major obstacle when there is an absence of liquidity in the credit markets.

Even when the debtor in possession has no need for new funds to continue operating, it may need a credit line that reassures suppliers that they will be paid, and it may be hard to find someone other than the existing senior lender to provide it unless the debtor possesses unencumbered assets. And changes in capital structure, particularly the rise of second liens, now leads to many cases in which there are no unencumbered assets.

The rights of the secured creditors in large cases today narrowly limit the options of the bankruptcy judge. A third-party lender will have no interest in taking behind the secured creditor, and the judge cannot give that party a "priming lien" over the secured party, as it will not be possible to give the secured party adequate protection.

Problems exist even when the debtor does not need to borrow if its cash, bank accounts, and other cash equivalents are themselves subject to a security interest. Keeping the business running requires the use of this "cash collateral." The trustee (and hence the debtor in possession) must go to court before the business can draw on cash collateral and prove that it is giving "adequate protection" to the party with the security interest in it. Making such a showing at the start of the case with everything else that is going on is hard. Debtors have the best chance of success if they can strike a deal with its senior lender before the petition.

In many large Chapter 11 cases today, the secured creditor is the 800-pound gorilla in the room. The debtor's inability to obtain financing elsewhere may give the secured creditor an effective veto over the filing of the petition. Indeed, in many instances the Chapter 11 petition is filed only because the secured creditor wants to use the bankruptcy forum to sell its collateral rather than exercise its foreclosure rights under state law—often an impossible task if assets consist of real and personal property scattered across many different jurisdictions.

Even though the Bankruptcy Code is built around the premise that general creditors are the residual claimants, there is nothing in the Bankruptcy Code that prevents a bankruptcy from going forward that benefits only secured creditors. Indeed, the nineteenth century equity receiverships from which Chapter 11 evolved typically involved firms with chiefly secured debt in their capital structure.

In recent cases, conflicts are often not between secured and unsecured creditors, but among secured creditors at the same priority level. They may disagree about such questions as whether to bid at a sale of the firm as a going concern. Bankruptcy judges in these situations look to whatever agreements the secured creditors entered among themselves and enforce them according to their terms.[23]

When the secured creditor is the beneficiary of the Chapter 11, it must be prepared to pay the toll. The trustee has the power under §506(c) to charge against the collateral the reasonable and necessary costs and expenses of preserving the property, but in practice this power is often waived. Instead, there are negotiations at the outset of the case in which the secured creditor agrees, within limits, to fund the case. In these "carve out" agreements, the secured creditor gives up a part of its claim on the collateral to ensure that postpetition expenses are paid. Moreover, the secured lender will consent to the use of its cash collateral and, if necessary, provide debtor-in-possession financing to keep the business running. At the same time, however, the secured creditor will likely insist on a number of conditions. Among other things, the secured creditor will want to limit the extent to which its own money can be used to challenge the liens it holds on the collateral.

The debtor-in-possession loan may grant the lender virtually complete control over the reorganization process. The typical dip financing agreement has many financial covenants, and the violation of any of them gives the dip lender the ability to terminate the financing. The dip loan also limits the reach of bankruptcy's automatic stay. The dip lender in the Winn-Dixie bankruptcy insisted that it could seize any of its collateral upon default so long as it provided the debtor with five days' notice. The dip lender provides only limited degrees of freedom for the business while it remains in Chapter 11. One typical provision

---

[23] In re Metaldyne Corp., 409 Bankr. 671 (Bankr. S.D.N.Y. 2009).

waives the debtor's right to seek to use the lender's cash collateral over the lender's objection, and another waives the debtor's right to seek a priming lien on the secured creditor's collateral. Moreover, the dip financing agreement may provide that the loan terminates if the debtor fails to arrange for a sale of its assets by a specific date.

The dip lender can control both how long the debtor takes to formulate a plan and the shape the plan ultimately takes. The dip financing agreement sometimes provides that it is an event of default if a plan is not filed within a certain time period. Such a provision effectively puts the decision about the length of the exclusivity period in the hands of the dip lender rather than the court. The debtor's freedom to shape a plan of reorganization is limited as well. The financing agreement may include a promise not to file a plan or even make a motion in the bankruptcy case without the lender's prior written consent.

As part of the negotiations over the cash collateral order and the secured creditor's right to adequate protection, the secured creditor will sometimes demand a "roll-up." As old accounts are paid off and new accounts come into being, secured creditors demand that their old, prepetition loans be converted into secured postpetition loans entitled to administrative priority. Provisions such as these effectively remove the debtor's power to cram down a plan over creditor dissent, as administrative expense claims have to be paid off in cash at the time the plan is confirmed. Debtors try to push back against such demands, but their ability to do so may be limited if there are not others willing to finance the business in Chapter 11.

Appellate courts have cast a skeptical eye on efforts of lenders to link prepetition with postpetition loans, particularly at the outset of the case.[24] As with so much else in bankruptcy practice, however, there is something of a disconnect between what happens in the courts of appeal and what happens on the ground. Many questions become moot long before they can be heard on appeal. Separate practices develop in each district—and sometimes with each judge in a given district. By cobbling together provisions that pass judicial muster in the chosen venue (a choice over which the secured lender has considerable influence), the senior creditor as dip lender can hold enough levers to

---

[24] See, e.g., Otte v. Manufacturers Hanover Commercial Corp. (In re Texlon), 596 F.2d 1092 (2d Cir. 1979); Shapiro v. Saybrook Manufacturing Co., 963 F.2d 1490 (11th Cir. 1992).

ensure that no major decision is made in a way that it finds objectionable. Cash collateral orders often contain similar provisions.

Creditors once had to demand the appointment of a trustee if they wanted to displace the management. Under modern Chapter 11 practice, however, they have no reason to ask the court to order the appointment of the trustee, as they can often bring about a change in management on their own. Indeed, they do not want a trustee appointed, as it will cede control to someone else. Appointment of a trustee has become an event of default in the dip financing agreement.

The dip financing and the carve-out order are only two of the many major decisions made at the outset of the case. Chapter 11s are rarely successful unless careful planning is done in advance. Among other things, to plan effectively, lawyers need to know in advance what sorts of challenges they will face.

One common problem is the need to make payments immediately to some prepetition unsecured creditors. If the Chapter 11 petition is filed on Thursday, the workers owed paychecks on Friday are merely general creditors to the extent of their unpaid wages. To be sure, they are entitled to priority under §507, but nothing entitles them to be paid before the end of the case and often the firm is worth far less than what the secured creditor is owed in any event. But paying the workers is essential to keep the business running.

In many instances, the logic of honoring some prepetition claims is so compelling that no one gives it much thought. In the Chapter 11 of Marvel Entertainment Group, for example, the largest group of general creditors consisted of the business's comic book subscribers. The business's obligation to send them comics in return for their prepaid subscriptions was a "claim" within the meaning of the Bankruptcy Code. The automatic stay should have applied to them as to everyone else, but the sheer silliness of bringing thousands of 12-year-olds into a Chapter 11 reorganization and the disastrous effect suspending their subscriptions would have on the business kept anyone from objecting. Frequent flyer miles are typically honored without dissent either.

The debtor sometimes needs to pay a vendor whose goods are crucial to its continuing operations and who threatens to cut the debtor off if prepetition debt is not paid. Paying prepetition creditors who can complicate the life of the debtor postpetition may make everyone better off. Bankruptcy judges approve these "critical vendor orders" under §363(b), but they are vigilant. They typically refuse to approve payments merely because it makes things easier for the debtor. Those asking for it need to show that the payments are in the interests of the estate as a whole.[25]

Courts are also likely to distinguish between payments that need to be made at the very outset of the case (such a pay checks or money for carriers who will refuse to give up crucial raw materials in their possession) from those that can await the formation of the creditors' committee. The former are approved on the first day; the latter only after the creditors' committee has had a chance to object. Here, as elsewhere, prebankruptcy planning makes life much easier. If a debtor's business depends on shipments from a particular vendor, the debtor ought to have a contractual right to those shipments. By entering into such a contract and then assuming it in bankruptcy, the debtor can ensure continued access to the goods.

As businesses depend increasingly on human capital, they become more vulnerable to departures of key employees. When a business finds itself in financial distress and wants to continue as a going concern, its most valuable managers need to remain and new managers often need to be recruited. Moreover, when the business is to be sold or wound down, it is often necessary to keep current managers in place for a time even though they have no future with the business and every incentive to jump ship. Bringing this about without rewarding incompetent managers who put the debtor in its dismissal state presents judges with another challenge.

The Bankruptcy Code contains several provisions aimed at this problem. Section 548(a)(1) makes voidable a transfer to an insider under an employment contract if the transfer was made outside the ordinary course of business for less than reasonably equivalent value. Section 503(c) prohibits retention payments to insiders to induce them to remain with the business unless a number of conditions are satisfied. Conditions include a showing that the person has a bona fide job offer from another employer and that the person provides services essential to the business.

Encouraging a business's most valuable employees to fish for offers elsewhere makes little sense and making such a showing is virtually impossible in any event. Instead of trying to satisfy these unworkable provisions for "retention" payments, the practice has emerged of providing "incentive" compensation for key employees. How these are

---

[25] In re Kmart, 359 F.3d 866 (7th Cir. 2004).

structured is again a matter that is subject to both negotiation and judicial scrutiny.[26]

Going-Concern Sales

Section 363 authorizes the trustee or the debtor in possession to engage in transactions outside the ordinary course of business, provided creditors are given notice and a hearing. The nonbankruptcy principles likely to provide the best guidance here are those that operate when a corporation is "in play" outside of bankruptcy. Under the *Revlon* doctrine, once a takeover becomes inevitable, the board of directors "has a duty to maximize the company's value at a sale." The board members become "auctioneers" with a duty to get the best price.[27] In *Committee of Equity Security Holders v. Lionel Corporation*, the Second Circuit established the idea that going-concern sales can go forward in bankruptcy, as long as there is a good business reason.[28]

Among the issues that remain unclear is the degree to which a buyer can in fact purchase a going concern free and clear. The Third Circuit has interpreted broadly the language in §363(f) allowing for sales free and clear of "any interest," including claims that might arise out of successor liability actions under state law.[29] This approach makes sense as a matter of first principle. To allow some creditors to pursue the assets in the hands of the new buyer would both diminish the price at which assets could be sold and shift assets from one group of creditors to another. Whether this interpretation becomes generally accepted remains to be seen.

The issue going forward has become not so much the appropriateness of going-concern sales, but rather how they are conducted. In cases in which the secured creditor has control over the case, it will establish the dynamics of the sale process as well. Under §363(k), the secured creditor is entitled to bid and offset its claim against the purchase price.[30] The ability to "credit bid" is conceptually sound. The

---

[26] In re Global Home Products, LLC, 369 Bankr. 778 (Bankr. Del. 2007); In re Dana Corp., 358 Bankr. 567 (Bankr. S.D.N.Y. 2006).

[27] Revlon, Inc. v. MacAndrews & Forbes Holdings, 506 A.2d 173, 182 (Del. 1986).

[28] 722 F.2d 1063 (2d Cir. 1983).

[29] In re Trans World Airlines, 322 F.3d 283 (3d Cir. 2003).

[30] Cohen v. KB Mezzanine Fund II (In re SubMicron Systems Corp.), 432 F.3d 448 (3d Cir. 2006).

secured creditor is entitled to the proceeds of the sale up to the amount that it is owed. Every dollar the secured creditor turns over to the auctioneer as a buyer is a dollar to which it is entitled as the person with first dibs on what is being sold. Credit bidding merely saves the secured creditor from the costs and risks of obtaining a loan for the short time the money is out of its hands.

Because they do not gain from postponing a sale and face all the downside if things go worse than expected, the secured creditors have an incentive to force through a speedy sale. If the firm is worth less than what the secured creditor is owed, there is no problem with a sale being conducted under its aegis. We need to worry, however, that the secured creditor is pushing through a sale even when the assets are worth more than what it is owed. A fire sale for an amount equal to what it is owed costs it nothing and hurts everyone else.

When the secured creditors want either to sell the firm or acquire it outright with a credit bid, the bankruptcy judge can be put in an awkward position. The secured creditor appears and asserts that it is willing to authorize the use of cash collateral only if the judge approves an expedited sale. Most of the junior creditors will have had little time to organize any opposition, and the secured creditor obtains the cooperation of those who do appear by cutting a deal with them. The short timetable ensures that only the secured creditor itself or a buyer it has recruited before the fact will appear at any auction.

Courts must approve sale procedures, and they are entitled to limit credit bidding for cause under §363(k). Courts should not limit credit bidding merely to ensure that an auction with competing bids develops. They may well limit the right to credit bid, however, when an intransigent secured creditor pushes for a quick sale and the validity of its liens is still in doubt.[31]

Bankruptcy judges are most comfortable approving quick sales when those pushing for the sale can show that the business has been thoroughly shopped before the bankruptcy petition and that all the administrative fees will be paid. Bankruptcy judges are likely to balk if the debtor has conducted its search for potential buyers narrowly and proposes bidding procedures that require buyers to assume exactly the same obligations as its chosen stalking horse. If buyers are forced to accept particular obligations, one needs to worry that bids that take

---

[31] In re Fisker Automotive Holdings, Inc., 2014 WL 210593 (Bankr. D. Del. 2014).

other forms (and are perhaps less favorable to insiders) are being sti-fled. In *Chrysler*, the bankruptcy judge approved a going-concern sale only after uncontested testimony that a liquidating sale would yield less. In the *Sun Times* bankruptcy, the judge insisted on broadening sale procedures to allow for liquidating bids.

No buyer wants to expend substantial resources investigating the debtor and committing itself to buy the business only to watch some-one else enjoy the fruits of its research, make a slightly higher bid, and walk away with the company. Outside of bankruptcy, the first bidder commonly insists on being paid a fixed amount if the corporation is ultimately sold to someone else. It constitutes both a payment for its work in preparing the bid and a payment for a "put," the right to sell an asset for a fixed price. This breakup fee can have a chilling effect on the bidding, but it can also entice someone to make a solid bid that generates additional bids. Some bankruptcy judges have not been as deferential to breakup fees as judges outside of bankruptcy.[32] Never-theless, judges have been willing to approve them when their purpose and effect was to increase the sale price.[33]

Bankruptcy judges should not be in the business of second-guessing market mechanisms, but they must be vigilant in ensuring that the mechanisms are working. In small markets, it is often not easy to tell the difference. Potential buyers may be insiders. Potential buyers may acquire major positions in a corporation's debt or equity to ensure themselves a place at the bargaining table. The mechanism that ignites bidding in one case can smother it in another. Here, as elsewhere, the court is charged with a high-wire act.

As sales become more frequent, bidding procedures become more complicated. Nothing requires interested third parties to make cash bids, and indeed bankruptcy judges have conducted sales in which there were competing noncash bids. The more going-concern sales take such form and include assumption of some liabilities and not oth-ers, however, the more one has to worry that what we have is not a sale at all, but a plan of reorganization for which all the protections of

---

[32] See, e.g., Calpine Corp. v. O'Brien Environmental Energy, 181 F.3d 527, 535 (3d Cir. 1999); AgriProcessors, Inc. v. Fokkena (In re Tama Beef Packing, Inc.), 321 Bankr. 496, 498 (B.A.P. 8th Cir. 2005) (noting breakup fees in bankruptcy usually limited to 1 to 4 percent of purchase price).

[33] Official Committee of Subordinated Bondholders v. Integrated Re-sources, 147 Bankr. 650 (S.D.N.Y. 1992).

the plan confirmation process are required. These procedures are the focus of the next chapter.

CHAPTER ELEVEN

Forming the Plan of Reorganization

Overview of the Reorganization Process

We now turn to the plan of reorganization and the reorganization process. The ideal sequence as envisioned by the drafters is as follows. A corporation that is unable to make its loan payments, but is worth keeping intact, files a Chapter 11 petition. The old managers continue to run the business. They can make nonordinary course decisions only after notice and a hearing, but for the most part, they can run things as before. The rest of the world continues to do business with the corporation the same way as before. Shortly after the petition is filed, the United States Trustee appoints a committee of creditors. This committee usually consists of the creditors with the seven largest unsecured claims who are willing to serve or the creditors who formed the committee that tried to do a nonbankruptcy workout. This committee may hire professionals to look into the debtor's affairs, and it provides a vehicle for negotiations between the debtor and the creditors.

Outside of the official creditors' committee, creditors can form their own "ad hoc" committees in order to advance a common interest. These committees allow creditors to have more credibility and sway in negotiations, and even in some instances have their attorneys' fees paid for as part of the administrative expenses. But unlike official creditors' committees, ad hoc committees do not owe a fiduciary duty to all of the creditors. Until recently, there was little oversight over these committees. Now, under §2019, any ad hoc committee must disclose its members, as well as any economic interests that are "affected by the value, acquisition or disposition of a claim or interest." This rule ensures that the bankruptcy judge and other actors in the reorganization know with whom they are dealing.

While the debtor's business continues, the debtor tries to come up with a reorganization plan. Even when one or more groups of claimholders oppose a plan, the debtor may still be able to confirm it if the plan meets, in addition to all the usual tests, the special ones set out in §1129(b). The process of obtaining confirmation of a plan over the objection of a class is called *cramdown*. But cramdown requires outside valuations, and these are expensive and unreliable. Ideally you want a plan each class of claimholders can live with. Even if you could cram down a plan on each class of creditors, you would prefer not to have to do so. Those who are even plausibly in the money typically will insist on something.

The Bankruptcy Code initially gives the debtor 120 days to file a plan of reorganization. The judge can extend the plan, but is likely to do so only if the debtor can show things are on track and that those in control are meeting the goals they set for themselves. For most small business corporations in Chapter 11, 120 days is enough time to see whether the business can survive. Large corporations need more time. Nevertheless, if the debtor does not propose a plan of reorganization within 18 months of the filing of the petition, other parties in interest have a chance to propose their own plan. See §1121(d)(2).

The plan divides the claims of the creditors into various classes and proposes a treatment for each class. After the debtor files the plan, the debtor must try to get the plan accepted. The debtor must write a *disclosure statement* and persuade the court to approve it. The purpose of the disclosure statement is to explain the plan to those who must vote on it. Once the disclosure statement is approved, the debtor may begin seeking acceptance of the plan from the various classes.

The debtor may obtain approval in one of two ways. First, those whose claims are in a given class can approve the plan. A majority of the creditors holding claims in the class who vote must vote in favor of the plan, and their claims must have a value equal to at least two-thirds of the value of the claims of those who are voting. In the case of equity interests, the debtor simply needs two-thirds of the shares being voted. This is consistent with state corporate law in that the number of shareholders does not matter, just the number of shares. Second, the debtor can receive constructive approval from a class if that class is *unimpaired* within the meaning of §1124. Generally speaking, a class is unimpaired if it consists only of claims that the plan does not restructure. A creditor's claim, for example, is unimpaired if the original terms of the loan are reinstated (and all defaults are cured).

After the votes are received, the debtor can ask the court to approve the reorganization plan. The court must satisfy itself that the plan meets all the requirements of Chapter 11. Many are spelled out in §1129(a). The plan must, for example, pay off administrative expense claims in cash. §1129(a)(9)(a). This requirement may be burdensome for businesses that lack ready access to capital markets. Among other things, the debtor must find the cash to pay all vendors who shipped goods within 20 days of the filing of the petition as these are classified as "administrative expenses" even though they are incurred before the petition. §503(b)(9). Practices have emerged that make this requirement less rigid than it might first appear. Administrative creditors are free to scale back or modify their claims in a side deal. Their willingness to do so depends on their past and future relationship with the debtor. For example, among the largest administrative claims may be payments owed to debtor's counsel, and these are often structured initially with a schedule over time.

This need for cash sometimes makes the success of a Chapter 11 reorganization turn on the debtor's ability to bring a preference or fraudulent conveyance action. Failing that, the only source of new cash may be the old equityholder. For such small businesses, a reorganization may be possible only if the old equityholder has at least enough cash to pay administrative expenses. The longer the reorganization lasts, the greater this amount will be and the harder it will be for the debtor to confirm a reorganization plan, at least without extraordinarily patient accountants and lawyers.

Similarly, §1129(a)(9)(b) requires that a plan provide cash for specified prebankruptcy claims afforded high priority by §507(a)(3)–(7). These include, for example, specified obligations to employees and employee benefit plans. Immediate full payment is required for such claims if the class of claims has not accepted the plan. If the class has accepted the plan, an individual creditor cannot demand immediate payment, but may insist on full payment over time, including appropriate interest. This is the case even if the claim is not of a high enough priority to have warranted payment in full under Chapter 7.

Perhaps the most important of these requirements is the condition stated in §1129(a)(9)(c) that a plan provide for the deferred cash payment of those taxes afforded priority by §507(a)(8), including income, excise, and withholding taxes. These cash payments must be made within a six-year period and must have a value, as of the date of the plan, equal to the amount of taxes owing, whether or not the claim would have been paid in full under Chapter 7.

This provision governing the priority of tax claims is clear and gives rise to few reported decisions. Nor does it loom large in large cases. Nevertheless, tax claims may dominate the landscape of many debtor corporations. A debtor in bankruptcy may not have been earning enough before bankruptcy to become liable for significant corporate income tax, but even an unprofitable business owes or must withhold taxes related to the business's role as an employer. Small businesses often fail to meet these obligations when they encounter trouble, notwithstanding the risk of criminal liability to the businesses' managers.

(Tax laws treat the failure to turn over taxes withheld from employees' paychecks much more seriously than a failure to pay the business's own taxes.) Negotiations over how these tax obligations will be paid are often the primary focus of Chapter 11 when the debtor is a small, family-run business.

Another requirement that is not often litigated but can affect the plan is in §1129(a)(10). Even if a plan meets the absolute priority rule, a court cannot confirm it unless at least one class of impaired claims approves the plan. A Chapter 11 plan is supposed to be a product of negotiations among the interested parties. To show that there were negotiations and at least some give and take, you must gain the approval of one class that has the right to reject. Although there is rarely a dispute about whether a class has accepted, there has been a great deal of litigation over whether the initial classification of claims was manipulated to create one class that would accept the plan. The greater the debtor's ability to divide claims into many separate classes, the more likely it is that one class will vote in favor of the plan.

A number of requirements in §1129(a) become focal points of plan negotiations. For example, §1129(a)(13) requires that the plan provide for the continued full payment of retiree benefits as modified under §1114. These obligations, as well as shortfalls in a corporation's pension plan, are sometimes the dominant issue in the Chapter 11 cases of large industrial corporations. At the time it entered Chapter 11, Bethlehem Steel had 120,000 retirees entitled to benefits, but only 11,500 active employees. Its pension plan was underfunded to the tune of $2.9 billion. Promised health and insurance benefits totaled $3.1 billion, and these were not funded at all. A plan of reorganization could not be confirmed without confronting these obligations, and they alone rendered the company insolvent. Put differently, these obligations could not be paid in full even if the obligations owed everyone else disappeared. As with so many other modern Chapter 11 reorganizations of large corporations, Bethlehem Steel's bankruptcy ended with a going-concern sale.

Section 1129(b) embodies the substantive component of the absolute priority rule. When a class (as opposed to a minority within a class) dissents and a class junior to it is receiving something under the plan, the court must ask whether the dissenting class is being paid in full. As reviewed below, determining whether a plan satisfies §1129(b) requires a valuation that uses marketplace benchmarks. By contrast, courts tend to use a less rigorous method when an objection is brought by an individual creditor. Under §1129(a)(7), the court must be satisfied that each individual creditor either consents to the plan or is getting as much as it would have received in a Chapter 7 liquidation. This is commonly called the *best-interests-of-creditors test*. When a business can be sold as a going concern, the value that might be realizable in Chapter 7 may be the same as the value of the business reorganized in Chapter 11. The less rigorous valuation methods, however, make §1129(a)(7) much easier to meet than §1129(b). There are times, however, when the different rules of Chapter 7 entitle a stakeholder to receive more than she would receive in Chapter 11. In such cases, the best-interests test improves her bargaining position.[1]

There is one other important requirement. The court must be satisfied that the corporation will not end up in a reorganization again. §1129(a)(11). This is commonly called the *feasibility test*. It is subjective, but the court can give it some hard edges by comparing the capital structure of the reorganized corporation with other corporations in the same industry. A reorganization plan that leaves a corporation too highly leveraged relative to other corporations in the same industry may not be feasible within the meaning of the Bankruptcy Code. The judge, however, must rely on the record before her. Like any other legal rule in a system committed to an adversary process, this requirement has bite only to the extent that those objecting to plan confirmation present the necessary evidence.

If the court confirms the plan, the plan is carried out according to its terms. Under §1141, confirmation of the plan discharges *all* debts (that arose prior to confirmation) except for (and insofar as) those debts that are dealt with in the plan. On its face, Chapter 11 permits the discharge of all corporate debts. Due process, however, mandates a minimum level of notice, and this ultimately places a check on the scope of the bankruptcy discharge in Chapter 11.

The discharge does not abrogate any obligations that arise after the plan is confirmed. Recall, for example, the debtor that owns property on which it (or someone else) had dumped toxic wastes before the filing of the bankruptcy petition. The environmental claims that arose before confirmation are discharged (provided they are indeed "claims"[2]), but the discharge of these claims is not sufficient to insulate

---

[1] See In re Washington Mutual, Inc., 461 Bankr. 200 (Bankr. D. Del. 2011), vacated in part, 2012 WL 1563880 (Bankr. D. Del. 2012) (shareholders of solvent corporation better off in Chapter 7 where creditors are entitled only to legal rate of interest, rather than the contract rate).

[2] See United States v. Apex Oil Co., Inc., 579 F.3d 734 (7th Cir. 2009).

the debtor from cleanup obligations if it remains the owner of the property and incurs obligations in that capacity. Such a debtor remains liable for environmental cleanup obligations that arise by virtue of postbankruptcy ownership in the same way that someone to whom the debtor sold the property would be liable.[3] Similarly, a tort committed prepetition may generate ongoing disclosure obligations on the part of the reorganized entity that the discharge does not remove.

A number of rules in Chapter 11 treat small businesses in a way that is quicker and more streamlined. The court is required to confirm a plan that complies with the dictates of Chapter 11 within 45 days of the filing of the plan. §1129(e). The disclosure statement itself can be submitted on standard forms, and the court may conditionally approve it. The disclosure statement is subject to close scrutiny only after the voting takes place at the same hearing in which the court decides whether to confirm the plan. §1125(f).

Chapter 11 is also available to individual debtors. The individual might be a lawyer or a doctor. She does not do business in corporate form, and her personal finances have become intertwined with those of her practice. If no trustee is appointed, it is the individual debtor, rather than the debtor in possession, who runs the business and proposes a plan. The rules for confirmation are the same. Unlike the corporate debtor, however, the individual maintains an identity separate from the productive assets she owns. Thus, an individual debtor under Chapter 11 commits only that future income promised by the plan. There are exceptions to discharge for certain obligations, such as child support.

When a creditor insists, the debtor must commit her disposable income (as measured by §1325(b)(2)) to paying back creditors for five years. See §1129(a)(15). Creditors, however, will not necessarily insist on such plans, as the debtor can often convert to Chapter 7 and obtain an outright discharge. Individual debtors are not subject to means testing under §707(b) as long as most of their obligations are business rather than consumer debts, and many professionals who file for Chapter 11 fall into this category.

Friendly Persuasion

Coalition building lies at the heart of the corporate reorganization. A financially distressed business needs a new capital structure, and

---

[3] See In re CMC Heartland Partners, 966 F.2d 1143 (7th Cir. 1992).

many different allocations of cashflow rights and control pass muster. The parties must form a coalition around one of many possible agreements. Parties must reason, cajole, and somehow forge consensus even though their interests conflict diametrically with all those around them. They must persuade those reluctant to join a coalition, but they cannot go too far or they will risk sanctions. They cannot strong-arm or bribe anyone. Nor can they deny a creditor the right to participate in the process. The trick, of course, is distinguishing friendly persuasion from sharp practice. What one player views as a sensible agreement that puts the case on a path to a confirmable plan might be what another player views as a side-deal that freezes her out and denies her a voice in the bargaining process.

In many instances, the creditors who negotiate a plan of reorganization will be comfortable using the Chapter 11 process to put the elements of their deal in place only if they can be reasonably confident that the debtor will support it. To this end, they seek the debtor's commitment to support in bankruptcy the deal they have reached. The Bankruptcy Code encourages parties to negotiate outside of bankruptcy. As a general matter, the agreements parties reach there are enforceable. Nevertheless, there are limits on the ability of the debtor to enter such "plan support agreements" or "reorganization support agreements."[4] Courts will be reluctant to enforce such agreements if, instead of reflecting an effort to enter a workout on terms that are fair to all, they favor those who are party to the agreement at the expense of those who are not.

The particular doctrines being invoked are explicitly based in bankruptcy law, such as the requirement that a plan be proposed in good faith. Yet, the underlying principles are firmly rooted in nonbankruptcy law. A corporation's directors cannot relieve themselves of their obligation to exercise their fiduciary duties.

Plan support agreements commonly contain a "fiduciary out." The board reserves the right to withdraw from the plan support agreement if remaining with it would be insistent with its fiduciary duties. Because lenders want the debtor's commitment to be strong, they draft clauses with fiduciary outs drawn as narrowly as possible without undermining the director's duty of care and duty of loyalty—duties that

---

[4] For an overview of plan support agreements, see Kurt A. Mayr, Unlocking the Lockup: The Revival of Plan Support Agreements under §1125(g) of the Bankruptcy Code, 15 Norton J. Bankr. L. & Prac. 729 (2006).

require them to take into account the interests of all investors and not just shareholders.[5]

In re Bush Industries, Inc. illustrates the dynamic.[6] Bush was a manufacturer of ready-to-assemble furniture. It expanded aggressively and then faced severe financial problems when the economy turned. As a group, the secured creditors entered into negotiations with the debtor. The debtor agreed to propose, and the secured creditors agreed to accept, a plan of reorganization in which the secured creditors would have their notes substantially scaled back and would receive the equity in the reorganized corporation in their place. All other creditors would be paid in full, but the interests of the old equityholders would be cancelled. The old equity objected to the plan.

The court was satisfied that the value of the business was less than the $160 million owed the senior creditors. The plan support agreement, however, contained features that troubled the court. First, the plan released the officers of the debtor from any liabilities they owed the corporation. The liabilities were for $2.5 million in loans made to the officers and directors. Releasing the officers and directors from liability was not much different from giving them cash in return for supporting a particular plan.

Moreover, the agreement also required the senior lenders to continue to pay the CEO of the company, even though there was no expectation that he would do any work. Indeed, he had already left the company and moved to Florida. The court was not objecting to the "golden parachute" per se. As the court explained, "So long as allowed claims exceed the value of a reorganized debtor, the class of prepetition interest holders has no inherent right to object to an employment contract whose cost is effectively paid by new owners of the reorganized debtor."[7] But the golden parachute along with the release showed that the officers and directors had advanced their own interests in negotiating the plan support agreement, not the interests of the shareholders.

The secured lenders and the directors ultimately agreed on a plan in which the releases and the golden parachute were eliminated, but this

[5] See In re Innkeepers USA Trust, 442 Bankr. 227 (Bankr. S.D.N.Y. 2010) (declaring "it is 'Bankruptcy 101' that a debtor and its board of directors owe fiduciary duties to the debtor's creditors to maximize the value of the estate").

[6] 315 Bankr. 292 (Bankr. W.D.N.Y. 2004).

[7] 315 Bankr. at 305.

"cure" was not enough. The existence of the agreement itself showed that the debtor did not put forward a plan in good faith. The objection was not to the releases or the golden parachute in their own right, but to the way in which they distorted the plan process. If the process is not fair to the nonparticipating investors, then the plan that arises from it cannot be confirmed, regardless of whether it has been modified along the way to comply with any substantive rules that apply.

The agreement in *Bush Industries* stands in contrast to the agreement in *Residential Capital*.[8] A postpetition plan support agreement emerged in that case after many months of negotiation, aided in part by court-supervised mediation conducted by another bankruptcy judge. A CRO who was not beholden to the debtor's parent represented the debtor, and the plan support agreement put the debtor on the path to settling billions of disputed claims. The court approved the debtor's entering the plan support agreement and also found that each of the parties to the agreement acted reasonably and in good faith.

Residential Capital involves a plan support agreement that was negotiated after the bankruptcy had started. It illustrates how modern practice evolves in ways that are different from what the Bankruptcy Code on its face seems to require. Because Residential Capital's plan support agreement was forged after the petition was filed, it would appear to run up against §1125. By its terms, §1125 seems to limit the ability of parties to commit to a plan of reorganization once bankruptcy starts until the court has approved a disclosure statement.

Section 1125 is aimed at protecting ordinary trade creditors, and public investors are in no position to know the debtor's true financial condition. By requiring that they be provided with a disclosure statement before being asked to vote on a plan, the Bankruptcy Code helps them make sensible decisions. Investors need to have, in the words of the Bankruptcy Code, "information of a kind, and in sufficient detail, as far as is reasonably practical . . . to make an informed judgment about the plan," taking into account the ability of the typical holder of a particular class of claim or interest to acquire information from other sources.[9]

While the policy underlying §1125 is sound, the section puts an obstacle in front of sophisticated parties who need to negotiate with

---

[8] In re Residential Capital, LLC, 2013 WL 3286198 (Bankr. S.D.N.Y. 2013).

[9] See 11 U.S.C. §1125(a).

one another before the contours of a confirmable plan can take shape. It is often not enough for parties to bargain with each other in advance of the formal voting process until they find themselves on the same page. Each wants some assurance that the others—and those to whom they subsequently trade their claims—will continue to support the same compromises and will not change their positions.

Notwithstanding the blanket rule that §1125 appears to lay down, a number of courts, like the court in *Residential Capital*, have found that postpetition agreements in which parties commit to support a particular plan are permissible and do not constitute improper solicitations under §1125.[10] These courts point to clauses that give fiduciary outs to the parties, the existence of various termination events, and the fact that they cast their actual votes only after the disclosure statement is approved.

Because of the tension between this practice and the unqualified language in §1125, it is not surprising that the parties in cases such as *Residential Capital* seek the formal blessing of the court for their postpetition plan support agreement. Among other things, the court's approval of the agreement eliminates the possibility that those who are a party to it will later be found by the court to have acted in bad faith and should on that account have their votes designated or their role in the Chapter 11 process limited.

Some courts lament the difficulty of determining what communications are permissible. As the court put it in *Century Glove*, "[w]e find no principled, predictable difference between negotiation and solicitation of future acceptances."[11] Such line-drawing problems, however, are easy to overstate, as courts tend to rely here, as elsewhere, on the ability of sophisticated parties to watch out for their own interests.

A sensible interpretation of §1125 looks at whether the communication effectively preempts an unbiased reading of an approved disclo-

---

[10] In re Heritage Organization, LLC, 376 Bankr. 783 (Bankr. N.D. Tex. 2007); In re Indianapolis Downs, LLC, 486 Bankr. 286, 296 (Bankr. D. Del. 2013) (All the parties were "sophisticated financial players and have been represented by able and experienced professionals throughout these proceedings. It would grossly elevate form over substance to contend that §1125(b) requires designation of their votes because they should have been afforded the chance to review a court-approved disclosure statement prior to making or supporting a deal with the Debtor.").

[11] See Century Glove v. First American Bank, 860 F.2d 94, 101 (3d Cir. 1988).

sure statement. Distributing a draft plan and disclosure statement to lawyers who by training and inclination are attuned to the smallest changes in fine print is radically different from distributing a draft to tens of thousands of tort victims whose opinions, once formed, may be unlikely to change.

The hearing on the disclosure statement is an important event and provides an opportunity to resolve many issues. These include whether exclusivity should be lifted to allow a creditor to propose its own plan. The information in the disclosure statement itself, however, may not be as useful as one might expect. Section 1125(b) explicitly states that "[t]he court may approve a disclosure statement without a valuation of the debtor or an appraisal of the debtor's assets." A creditor that has to vote on a plan should want to know at least whether it is being treated better than it would be under a liquidation. That seems to require some sort of valuation. In addition, if one is receiving stock, it may not be possible to know the value of what one is receiving under a plan without taking account of how much the debtor's assets are worth.

Classification

The Bankruptcy Code does not set out in detail how much freedom the debtor or any other plan proponent enjoys in the way in which claims are sorted into different classes. Section 1122(a) provides that only substantially similar claims or interests can occupy a single class. Each secured claim is typically in a class by itself. Two claims are not substantially similar if they are secured by different collateral, for example, nor are they substantially similar when they are secured by the same collateral if one claim enjoys priority over the other.

Other determinations are harder to make. Consider, on one hand, a deficiency claim held by a secured creditor for the difference between the amount it is owed and the value of its collateral and, on the other, the claim of a trade creditor who looks forward to continuing business with the reorganized debtor. When these two claims are put in one class, the ability of one of them to invoke the absolute priority rule may turn on whether the other wants to invoke it as well.

The bankruptcy judge must decide whether a plan proponent can put different claims in the same class, must put them in separate classes, or can enjoy the freedom to do either. Section 1122(a) tells us that we can put together substantially similar claims "except as provided by subsection (b)." The latter subsection allows a plan to designate a separate class of unsecured claims below a plan-specified threshold if necessary for administrative convenience.[12] The "except as provided by subsection (b)" language in §1122(a), therefore, suggests that except for administrative-convenience claims, substantially similar claims *must* be put into the same class. Arguably, unsecured claims are, by their nature, substantially similar because their legal attributes under nonbankruptcy law are identical.

Another way to read §1122(a) starts with the observation that substantially similar claims *may* be put in the same class but are not *required* to be.[13] Yet this interpretation does not obviate the need to decide whether the claims are indeed substantially similar. Returning to our example of creditors with trade and deficiency claims, one could argue that the claims are substantially similar because both are unsecured claims and neither enjoys priority over the other. But there is another view.

If those whose claims are in the same class have differing interests, one cannot be sure that the majority will make a decision that is in the best interests of the group as a whole. The possibility of manipulation if unsecured claims could be placed in a class with secured claims is obvious. Secured creditors should be paid in full and general creditors only a few cents on the dollar. It makes no sense for those holding one kind of claim to be able to speak on behalf of those holding another.

Tensions can arise even when deciding whether to put unsecured creditors in the same class. Consider the question whether the claims of trade creditors can be put in the same class as the claim of a bank that has made an unsecured loan to a debtor. The bank may be anxious to cut its losses and may intend to have no future dealings with the debtor. By contrast, the trade creditors may look forward to future dealings. They have much more to gain from a successful reorganization and may be more inclined to vote in favor of a plan that gives creditors less and leaves the company better capitalized. The bank and the trade creditors have interests that differ radically, even though their legal rights—those of unsecured creditors—are the same.

There are, however, no ready benchmarks by which to judge whether a creditor is *sufficiently* different to justify its claim being put in a separate class. It may be that the bank is not different enough

[12] See §1122(b).

[13] For a useful summary of the case law, see In re Dow Corning Corp., 244 Bankr. 634, 644–51 (Bankr. E.D. Mich. 1999).

from the trade creditors. Moreover, in a world in which claims trading is commonplace, focusing narrowly on the legal characteristics of the claims may make sense. The holders of claims are likely to be distressed debt investors who are interested only in the legal rights associated with the claims and not with the circumstances under which they arose. The usual presumption is that creditors holding claims that have the same legal status should be placed in the same class. The claims of the trade creditors and the bank would ordinarily be grouped together.

Creating two or more classes makes confirmation harder. Cramdown can be avoided if all the classes consent. When all the classes agree, the plan may contain "gifts" to out-of-the-money investors to help move matters forward. The smaller each class, the larger the role each dissenting creditor has. Requiring the debtor to put creditors into separate classes increases the odds that dissenters will be able to keep their class from approving a plan. In the face of the rejection by this class of creditors, the debtor has to show that, as to them, the absolute priority rule is satisfied. This consequence leads the debtor to want to put claims of unhappy creditors in a class dominated by others. But there are times when the debtor wants the claims of dissidents to be in their own class. A court can confirm a plan only if one class of impaired claims approves the plan and by putting the claims dissidents in their own class, the debtor's allies can control another.

Many of the classification cases arise when the debtor's only asset is a single parcel of real estate. The secured creditor holds a large deficiency claim, and there are a variety of small trade claims. The question is whether the deficiency claim may be classified separately.[14] Most courts ask whether the separate classification has been undertaken solely for the purpose of creating an impaired class that will vote in favor of the plan.[15] As the court put it in *In re Greystone III Joint Venture*, there is "one clear rule that emerges from otherwise muddled caselaw on §1122 claims classification: thou shalt not classify similar

[14] The Seventh Circuit has held that when the secured claim is nonrecourse outside of bankruptcy and the deficiency claim exists only by virtue of §1111, it *must* be classified separately, as the legal rights are different. The trade claims have different rights in Chapter 7 and these in turn affect their rights under the best interests-of-the-creditors test under §1129(a)(7). See In re Woodbrook Associates, 19 F.3d 312 (7th Cir. 1994).

[15] See In re Save Our Springs Alliance, Inc., 388 Bankr. 202, 234 (Bankr. W.D. Tex. 2008) (only limitation on the creation of classes is that a plan proponent may not do so to gerrymander a vote).

claims differently in order to gerrymander an affirmative vote on a re-organization plan."[16] Separate classification is easier to justify outside of the single-asset real estate case.[17] As the Second Circuit has observed, however, "separate classification of unsecured claims solely to create an impaired assenting class will not be permitted; the debtor must adduce some credible proof of a legitimate reason for separate classification of similar claims."[18]

In assessing the boundaries of what is and is not possible outside the real estate context, one can expect that bankruptcy judges will pay attention not only to the black letter rules governing classification, but also to the larger principle of whether the classification scheme evidences a tainted negotiation process. Technical questions of whether claims are substantially similar or even whether the plan has been gerrymandered are relevant, but may not be decisive. Courts remain divided on the extent to which claims may be put in separate classes.[19] Formal attributes do not matter as much as whether those objecting can make the "gerrymandering" label stick.

In re Charter Communications illustrates.[20] In that case, the plan was challenged on the ground that noteholders were put in a class separate from other general creditors. The court rejected that argument and held that noteholders could be classified separately. They had "disparate legal rights and payment expectations" from those holding claims

---

[16] 995 F.2d 1274, 1279 (5th Cir. 1991).

[17] See, e.g., In re Jersey City Med. Ctr., 817 F.2d 1055 (3d Cir. 1987) (separating claims of physicians, medical malpractice victims, employee benefit plan participants, and trade creditors); In re U.S. Truck Co., 800 F.2d 581 (6th Cir. 1986) (separating claims of collective bargaining unit members). For a summary of the classification controversy and extended analysis of *U.S. Truck*, see Scott F. Norberg, Classification of Claims under Chapter 11 of the Bankruptcy Code: The Fallacy of Interest Based Classification, 69 Am. Bankr. L.J. 119 (1995).

[18] In re Boston Post Road Limited Partnership, 21 F.3d 477, 483 (2d Cir. 1994).

[19] Compare In re 18 RVC, LLC, 485 Bankr. 492 (Bankr. E.D.N.Y. 2012) (separate classification of deficiency claim guaranteed by the debtor's principal found to be gerrymandering), with In re Loop 76, LLC, 465 Bankr. 525 (B.A.P. 9th Cir. 2012) (court may consider third-party guarantee in allowing separate classification of deficiency claim).

[20] JP Morgan Chase Bank, N.A. v. Charter Communications. Operating, LLC, 419 Bankr. 221 (Bankr. S.D.N.Y. 2009).

that arise from "litigation, employment, or operational relation-ships."[21] There were multiple material distinctions, including rights of recovery against third parties. Although not all of these distinctions gave the creditors different rights against the debtor, what mattered was that, taken together, the noteholders had a set of incentives that made their separate classification appropriate. The court went through the traditional analysis, but the engine that drove the analysis was simply that the plan proponent was putting together a reasonable coalition.

In large Chapter 11 reorganizations, the business consists of many corporations in a corporate group. The corporate structure itself affects the dynamics of plan confirmation. Consider the following two cases. In the first, there is a single debtor and three creditors. Bank, Lender, and Bondholder have each lent $100. Corporation has a single asset. It will be worth $225 in a year's time, but it is generating no cash and cannot meet any interest payments today. Bank has a first lien and Lender a second. Bondholder's claim is unsecured. A plan is put forward in which NewCo emerges as the reorganized entity. Bank and Lender are given notes due in a year's time, secured by first and second liens, respectively, and Bondholder receives the equity. Bank and Bondholder vote in favor of the plan, but Lender does not. The existence of consenting impaired classes allows the court to confirm this plan over Lender's objection.

Consider alternatively the case in which there is ParentCo, HoldingCo, and OperatingCo. OperatingCo holds the exact same $225 asset as above. Bank has lent OperatingCo $100. Lender has lent HoldingCo $100, and Bondholder has lent $100 to ParentCo. Instead of security interests, there is structural priority among the lenders, but again Bank is first, followed by Lender, and then Bondholder. (The structural priority is easy to see by imagining that the asset were sold and there was $225 available for distribution. Bank, as a creditor of OperatingCo, is entitled to $100. The remaining $125 would belong to OperatingCo's only shareholder (HoldingCo). As HoldingCo's only creditor, Lender would be entitled to $100 of this amount. The remaining $25 would go to ParentCo as the shareholder of HoldingCo. Bondholder would lay claim to it as ParentCo's creditor.)

A plan is proposed that restructures the obligations to Bank, Lender, and Bondholder in exactly the same way as the hypothetical in

[21] Id. at 264.

which a single legal entity did the borrowing. Bank and Bondholder vote in favor of the plan and Lender objects. It is not obvious that this plan can be confirmed. Lender can make the argument that the plan in the case of this corporate group cannot be confirmed. Technically, there are three different plans—one each for OperatingCo, HoldingCo, and ParentCo, respectively. Under §1129(a)(10), it would seem that *each plan* must garner the support of an impaired class of creditors.[22] Because Lender is the only creditor of HoldingCo, it can veto this reorganization. There is no other class to approve *HoldCo's* plan.

The logic of this argument is impeccable. But the case is not substantively any different from the case with the same hierarchy of investors involving a single corporate entity. The treatment offered to Lender offends none of the principles of Chapter 11. The plan is not playing any games with the absolute priority rule. Lender is not the victim of a side-deal. No one has thrown it under the bus. One court has gone so far as to find that the question of whether a plan was favored by one consenting class of impaired creditors was to be assessed on a plan-wide basis, not on the basis of individual debtors within a corporate group.[23]

Impairment

Sections 1124 and 1126(f) take the right to vote away from classes of claims or interests when they are not being compromised in the reorganization. To use the language of the Bankruptcy Code, such claims are not "impaired." If a class of claims receives the same set of rights in the reorganization that it had before the reorganization, those who hold such claims have nothing to complain about. §1124(1). A loan is unimpaired if the debtor is willing to continue to make the same payments and accept the same terms. A loan may also be deemed unimpaired under §1124 even if the loan is in default.

Section 1124 confronts a problem we encountered before in the context of executory contracts. Just as a debtor may breach an executory contract on the eve of bankruptcy only because it has too little incentive to watch out for the interests of others, a debtor may also allow

---

[22] See §1129(a)(10).

[23] JP Morgan Chase Bank v. Charter Communications Operating, LLC, 419 Bankr. 221, 250 (Bankr. S.D.N.Y. 2009). Not all courts agree. See In re Tribune Co., 464 Bankr. 126 (Bankr. Del. 2011).

a favorable loan to go into default. Like §365, §1124 overcomes this problem by allowing past defaults to be cured and the original loan reinstated. Just as the trustee can keep an executory contract in place by curing defaults and assuming its obligations, the trustee can reinstate a loan. Disputes can arise over whether some kinds of defaults are capable of being cured, as well as whether some provisions are in the nature of unenforceable ipso facto clauses.[24]

Making a creditor unimpaired is one way of avoiding a cramdown. The trustee (or, more likely, the debtor in possession) will favor reinstatement when it allows the corporation to enjoy the benefits of a below-market loan from a fully secured creditor. Assume a bank has lent $1 million on a long-term basis at an interest rate that is now substantially below the market rate. The debtor, however, is now in default. Unless the debtor takes advantage of §1124, the default accelerates the loan and makes the entire $1 million in principal due and owing. Under §502, the bank has a claim for $1 million. In the absence of any special rule, the best-interests-of-creditors test would entitle the bank to a bundle of rights with a present value of $1 million.

Section 1124(2), however, allows the bank's claim to be "de-accelerated." The terms of its contract are reinstated, and the bank is deemed unimpaired. The bank is deemed to have accepted the plan, and hence the bank cannot invoke the best-interests-of-creditors test, let alone the absolute priority rule, even though the present value of the stream of payments the bank will now get is significantly less than $1 million. As in this example, continuing a below-market loan makes the most sense when the loan is oversecured. The oversecured creditor is entitled to interest under §506(b) and therefore will be paid in full in any event. There is no cost associated with taking advantage of the loan's favorable terms.

Creditors with unimpaired claims are deemed to have accepted the plan, and no solicitation of them is required. §1126(f). The reorganization plan is not affecting these creditors, thus their approval of the plan is irrelevant. By similar reasoning, a class that receives nothing under the plan is deemed to have rejected it. §1126(g). There is no reason to ask whether the plan gives them enough. (Rejection, of course, brings the absolute priority rule into play.)

---

[24] See JPMorgan Chase Bank v. Charter Communications Operating, LLC, 419 Bankr. 221 (Bankr. S.D.N.Y. 2009).

When the debtor is in search of one impaired class to accept its plan, it may take a class (such as a fully secured bank lender that has worked with the debtor to form the plan) that it might otherwise treat as unimpaired and alter that class's rights in a trivial fashion. The class continues to support the plan, but because it is technically impaired, it provides the one impaired accepting class that §1129(a)(10) requires. Some courts have found such artificial impairments a form of forbidden gerrymandering.[25] Others have focused on the language of the statute itself, which seems to render an alteration, no matter how trivial, a form of impairment.[26] For these courts, those objecting to the plan cannot rely on §1129(a)(10) and must instead show that the plan was not filed in good faith. These courts believe that §1129(a)(3)'s good faith inquiry "fully empower[s] the bankruptcy courts to deal with chicanery."[27]

Like other provisions of the Bankruptcy Code, §1124 does not recognize ipso facto clauses. The debtor is entitled to reinstate a loan even if the bankruptcy filing triggered a default under an ipso facto clause. Even though this default is not curable, the Bankruptcy Code ignores it for the same reason it ignores ipso facto clauses as a general matter.

The effect of this prohibition on ipso facto clauses is not always clear when a corporate group enters bankruptcy. Consider the following hypothetical. Bank makes loans to each of the subsidiaries of a common parent. Each loan may provide for the termination of the loan if one of the other subsidiaries files for bankruptcy. If the plan calls for reinstating Bank's loan, Bank will argue that the default of each subsidiary is not curable and that the prohibition of ipso facto clauses does not apply. In the case of each subsidiary, it is the bankruptcy *of the other subsidiary* that triggers the default. The more a court looks at the corporate group as a single entity, the more likely it is to reject this argument.[28] The court can also point to the relevant statutory language that bans clauses that are geared to "the commencement of *a case* under this title." This language does not require the case that

---

[25] See In re Windsor on the River Associates, Ltd., 7 F.3d 127 (8th Cir. 1993).

[26] In re Village at Camp Bowie, 710 F.3d 239 (5th Cir. 2013).

[27] 710 F.3d at 248.

[28] See JP Morgan Chase Bank v. Charter Communications. Operating, LLC, 419 Bankr. 221, 251 (Bankr. S.D.N.Y. 2009)

triggers the default to be the same case as the one involving the debtor that is seeking reinstatement of the loan.[29]

Bargaining in the Shadow of Chapter 11

The dynamics of Chapter 11 elude easy summary. The important question is not whether outsiders can define with precision the distinction between strong-arm tactics and friendly persuasion. Instead, the question is whether insiders understand it. The bright vision of reorganization law is one in which there is a shared understanding of what constitutes aggressive side-deals and manipulation of the rules on the one hand and "fair offers" in a just reorganization on the other. There is a difference between an aggrieved minority that has been frozen out and a small group of dissenters willing to torpedo a plan in order to gain a small advantage for themselves. The dark vision is that a principle based on the idea of "I-know-it-when-I-see-it" creates too much uncertainty and makes the challenge of putting together a plan too uncertain. Regardless whether we embrace the dark or the bright vision, the question itself underscores the largest challenge we presently face: building coalitions in a world in which so many of the players are constantly changing. In doing this, the players must look towards the specific tests that the bankruptcy judge will use in confirming the plan. These are the subject of the next chapter.

---

[29] Lehman Brothers Special Financing, Inc. v. BNY Corporate Trustee Services Limited, 422 Bankr. 407 (Bankr. S.D.N.Y. 2010).

CHAPTER TWELVE

Confirming the Plan of Reorganization

After the vote on the plan, the court must decide whether to confirm it. The court must satisfy itself that a plan meets the requirements of Chapter 11, particularly §1129. Section 1129(a)(1) requires a court to review a plan to make sure it complies with "the applicable provisions of this title." Thus, the court is supposed to review things such as classification sua sponte.

When a plan is confirmed, all accounts are supposed to be squared and the controversies between the contending parties settled once and for all. Bringing about such a global peace, however, is not easy. To settle matters definitively, parties desire resolution of all the outstanding issues. An old equityholder who is contributing new value to the enterprise does not want to wake up after the reorganization only to discover that the old creditors are still pursuing her for alleged misdeeds in the run-up to bankruptcy. Directors and officers do not want to be sued as individuals by disgruntled stakeholders for violating their duties.

As part of the plan, the debtor can abandon whatever rights it has against others. Such a release on the debtor's part is essentially a settlement of litigation that the bankruptcy judge can approve under Rule 9019 as long as she is satisfied it is in the best interests of the estate.[1] Less clear is whether, outside the context of asbestos-related injuries, the court can enjoin parties from pursuing the debtor even when they do not have "claims" within the meaning of the Bankruptcy Code.

It is also hard for the bankruptcy judge to protect third parties from actions others might bring against them. There have been cases that

---

[1] In addressing this issue, courts often rehearse a multi-factor test set out first in In re Master Mortgage Investment Fund, Inc., 168 Bankr. 930, 934–37 (Bankr. W.D. Mo. 1994). See, e.g., In re Zenith Electronics Corp., 241 Bankr. 92 (Bankr. D. Del. 1999). This is a conceptual mistake. Multi-factor tests are rarely illuminating and, in any event, *Master Mortgage* was a case about non-debtor releases, an altogether different subject. The test for binding a consenting party present in the courtroom is altogether different from one for someone who does not consent and may not even be present.

courts have allowed such clauses in a massive global settlement.[2] Courts have also allowed exculpation clauses that protected the reorganized debtors, professionals, and claimholders from liability for acts or omissions in the Chapter 11 case itself.[3] As a general matter, however, courts are extremely reluctant to enter orders that release third parties from liability unless the affected party consents. The fighting issue in recent cases has been the nature of the consent that is required.

Courts have shown a willingness to allow third-party releases that are reasonable under all the facts and circumstances when those affected are given, while voting on the plan, a chance to opt out. By failing to object, they have consented to releasing the third party from liability. The effect is to bind the many who never vote on a plan.[4] In such cases, however, disclosure is essential. Those who fail to do so fully and conspicuously play with fire.[5]

Two of the more important items the court reviews are the substantive standards for confirmation—the best-interests-of-creditors test and the absolute priority rule. As we have noted, §1129(a)(7) requires that for a plan to be confirmed, either every member of every class must have accepted it or each member that voted against it must receive at least the liquidation value of its claim. Given the costs of asserting its rights under §1129(a)(7), a creditor may be better off consenting to a plan, even if the creditor would have done better in Chapter 7. Moreover, as we have already observed, the valuation procedures under §1129(a)(7) are not rigorous. Section 1129(a)(7) requires us to posit the counterfactual world in which a corporation that properly belongs in Chapter 11 finds itself in Chapter 7 under the control of a trustee, and courts tend to assume that any liquidation that takes place in Chapter 7 involves the piecemeal sale of corporate assets. Finally, bankruptcy judges may use different and less careful valuation proce-

---

[2] See, e.g., Securities & Exchange Commissionn v. Drexel Burnham Lambert Group, Inc., 960 F.2d 285 (2d Cir. 1992).

[3] See, e.g., In re National Heritage Foundation, Inc., 478 Bankr. 216, 233 (Bankr. E.D. Va. 2012); In re PWS Holding Corp., 228 F.3d 224, 246 (3d Cir. 2000). Exculpation clauses do not go so far, however, as to protect parties from gross negligence or criminal misconduct.

[4] In re Indianapolis Downs, LLC., 486 Bankr. 286 (Bankr. Del. 2013).

[5] In re Neogenix Oncology, Inc., 2014 WL 954124 (Bankr. D. Md. 2014); In re Lower Bucks Hospital, 2013 U.S. Dist. LEXIS 94 (E.D. Pa. 2013).

dures than under §1129(b). More casual valuations can work against the creditors' interests, especially if the judge believes that finding in favor of a dissenter will undermine the corporation's prospects for a successful reorganization.

When multiple plans on the table satisfy §1129, the Bankruptcy Code charges the bankruptcy judge with choosing a plan after considering "the preferences of creditors and equity security holders." This provision is not helpful, as such preferences will likely go in opposite directions in cases of any moment.

Implementing Absolute Priority

Assume that §1129(a)(7) is satisfied (perhaps because we can avoid rigorous valuations). The plan still has to satisfy the absolute priority rule if a class rejects a plan. Section 1129(a)(8) prevents the plan from being confirmed unless the plan meets the tests set out in §1129(b). Section 1129(b)(2) provides that each class must be paid in full before a class junior to it can get anything. During the era of the equity receiverships, the absolute priority rule was a right that each creditor enjoyed. Under the Bankruptcy Code, however, it applies only to dissenting classes.

Section 1129(b)(2) contains three different glosses on the rule, and the one to be applied depends on the nature of the claim or interest of the class on whom the plan is being crammed down. Section 1129(b)(2)(A) deals with the issue of secured claims, §1129(b)(2)(B) with unsecured claims, and §1129(b)(2)(C) with interests. (As noted, the difference between "claim" and "interest" is the difference between debt and equity.) The basic point is this: either the claimants in the senior class must get the full amount of their claims as of the effective date of the plan—a present value concept—or junior classes must get nothing. Junior classes can receive something on account of their former rights against the corporation only if one of two conditions is met: (1) the senior classes, by class-wide vote, consent to their participation, or (2) the senior classes receive payment in full.

Junior classes, however, have the right to invoke the procedures of Chapter 11 (and particularly the valuation procedures) in every case. This right can dramatically alter the positions of junior parties from what they would be if the business were sold for cash and the cash parceled out according to nonbankruptcy priorities. Senior creditors may prefer a plan that does not fully compensate them if it induces the consent of the junior parties. This course may be preferable to incurring the costs of the procedures to which the junior parties would be entitled if they opposed the plan. So long as a class approves the plan, it no longer matters whether the dictates of the absolute priority rule are being met.

A parallel principal at work in §1129(b)(1) is the requirement that the plan not discriminate unfairly. The "unfair discrimination" test ensures parity across claims at the same priority level, just as the absolute priority rule ensures that the hierarchy between junior and senior claims is respected. Claims at the same priority level must presumptively be given the same pro rata share. If the general creditors are in the same class, each must receive identical treatment. It is possible, however, to put general creditors in two different classes and pay them in different coin when there is sufficient justification.

A plan does not discriminate unfairly merely because it gives cash to one class of general creditors and long-term notes to another. The plan will pass muster if there is a reason for the different treatment and if the cash payments and the notes give claims in each class the same pro rata share of the debtor's assets. A tort victim who needs surgery, for example, might be paid in cash, while an institutional lender might receive a note, as it has no similar need for payment in cash.

Courts have stopped short of insisting that the "unfair discrimination" principle has the same hard edges as the absolute priority rule. Nor have they insisted that the value given to classes at the same priority level must be equal in all cases. Some courts have concluded that they enjoy broad discretion in assessing whether a reasonable basis exist for the differences in treatment and whether the plan can be confirmed without the discrimination.[6] Other courts regard the need to give classes of the same priority equal amounts as a strong presumption that can be overcome only "by showing that a lower recovery for the dissenting class is consistent with the results that would obtain outside of bankruptcy, or that a greater recovery for the other class is offset by contributions from that class to the reorganization."[7] They usually impose a heavy burden if the difference in treatment is particularly large or if the plan could be readily confirmed without it.[8]

[6] See In re Aztec Co., 107 Bankr. 585, 590 (Bankr. M.D. Tenn. 1989).

[7] See In re Tribune Co., 472 Bankr. 223, 241 (Bankr. D. Del. 2012). This test was first put forward by Bruce Markell. See Bruce A. Markell, A New Perspective on Unfair Discrimination in Chapter 11, 72 Am. Bankr. L.J. 227, 228 (1998).

[8] In re Deming Hospitality, LLC, 2013 WL 1397458 (Bankr. D.N.M. 2013).

Understanding the rights of a secured creditor under §1129(b) requires a close examination of the special rights the secured creditor is given under §1111(b). Nonrecourse claims are made recourse, and a secured creditor can waive its unsecured claim and have its entire claim treated as secured. Much is unknown about the consequences of making the §1111(b) election, but identifying what is at stake is not difficult. Consider a bank that lends a debtor $1 million. The loan is secured by Blackacre. The loan is nonrecourse. Outside of bankruptcy, the bank can look only to Blackacre for satisfaction of its claim. If Blackacre sells at a foreclosure sale for only $600,000, the bank is out of luck on the remaining $400,000. What would happen in bankruptcy if §1111(b) did not exist? The bankruptcy judge would put a value on the bank's claim. If the judge valued it at $600,000, the bank could be crammed down with a package of rights having a present value of $600,000. The bank would have no unsecured claim because of the nonrecourse nature of the loan. The $400,000 deficiency would simply disappear. Congress introduced the §1111(b) election because it thought that a bankruptcy judge should not be able to eliminate the bank's deficiency with the stroke of a valuation pen.

The problem that Congress addressed in §1111(b) gained wide attention after *Great National Life Insurance Company v. Pine Gate Associates*, a decision under the old 1898 Act.[9] In that case, a nonrecourse secured creditor unsuccessfully objected to a plan in which its collateral would be appraised and the creditor would be paid the appraised value. The secured creditor wanted either to be paid in full or to have the property surrendered to it.

If the appraisal were done correctly, of course, the secured creditor would have been paid as much as it would have received if it sold the property. The secured creditor, however, feared that the appraisal would not be done correctly. Because its claim was nonrecourse, it had no unsecured claim for any deficiency and hence no vote in the reorganization. Section 1111(b) responds to this situation—known as the *Pine Gate* problem—first by saying that all loans, whether or not they are recourse outside of bankruptcy, are recourse in Chapter 11. Thus, the bank mentioned in our example above will (unless it elects differently) have a $400,000 unsecured deficiency claim. By holding this claim, the bank can vote with the unsecured creditors.

---

[9] 2 B.C.D. 1478, 1976 U.S. Dist. LEXIS 17366 (Bankr. N.D. Ga. 1976).

Section 1111(b) also gives the secured creditor an *election*. If the election is made, the creditor is deemed to have a secured claim for the entire amount of the debt, irrespective of the collateral's value. Thus, in the above example, the bank would have a secured claim of $1 million, not $600,000. The bank does not, however, receive a stream of payments worth $1 million. Under §1129(b)(2)(A)(i)(II), the bank would be given a stream of payments with a *present value* of $600,000. (The section provides that the stream of payments must equal "the value of such holder's interest in the estate's interest in such property." The court has valued the property at $600,000.) In this respect, the bank is treated the same as if it had not made the election. By making the election, the bank seems worse off as it must give up its deficiency claim of $400,000. But the election has consequences that may prove favorable.

To satisfy §1129(b)(2), the stream of payments needs to be worth only $600,000, but the face amount of these payments must total $1 million. Moreover, the stream of payments is secured by a *lien* of $1 million instead of $600,000. Unlike the debtor in *Pine Gate*, a debtor today who receives an artificially low valuation from the bankruptcy judge cannot get rid of the secured creditor by giving it the judicially appraised value in cash. In many cases, the debtor is content to give the secured creditor a long-term note. The term of the loan is long enough that a note can have a present value of $600,000 and still have a stream of payments over $1 million. For this reason, the §1111(b) election typically benefits a secured creditor only if the court undervalued the property *and* there is likely to be either a default in the near future or a sale that would accelerate the $1 million obligation.

It is worth looking at how the different parts of §1129(b)(2)(A) operate. For a plan to be fair and equitable with respect to a secured creditor, the plan must provide the secured creditor with (1) a lien on its collateral and a note equal to the value of its secured claim, (2) a sale subject to credit-bidding, or (3) "for the realization by such holders of the indubitable equivalent of such claims." The language is written in the disjunctive, but each must be read in light of the other. For this reason, the ability of the plan proponent to argue that its plan gives the secured creditor the indubitable equivalent of its claim is quite limited. The debtor, for example, cannot put forward a plan that includes a sale of the assets without credit bidding and argue that it satisfies §1129(b)(2)(A) on the ground that the secured creditor is receiving the indubitable equivalent of its claim. The specific requirement that a sale come with a right to credit bid implicitly limits the general power to propose a plan that provides the secured creditor with the indubitable equivalent of its claim.[10]

The §1111(b) election in conjunction puts another limit on the ability to provide the secured creditor with the indubitable equivalent of its claim. Assume that Debtor owes Bank $100 and owns Blackacre, which the bankruptcy court finds is worth $50. Bank makes the §1111(b) election and demands it be given a lien on Blackacre for $100 and a note that has a discounted present value of $50. Debtor proposes a plan that it claims provides Bank with the indubitable equivalent of its claim. It offers to give Bank a stream of payments backed by a treasury bill that is worth $50.

There is no doubt that the stream of payments that Bank is being offered is in fact worth the value of its secured claim as measured by the bankruptcy judge. Unlike the note secured by Blackacre, the note secured by the treasury bills has a readily ascertainable market value and this value was $50. Hence, the debtor argues, the secured creditor is getting the indubitable equivalent of a $50 claim.

A court that is mindful of *Pine Gate*, however, is likely to resist such a plan. A plan that gives Bank a lien on Blackacre for the amount of its claim gives it a chance to capture upside in the event that the property proves to be worth more than the bankruptcy judge decides it is worth. The ability to enjoy liens provides a cushion against undervaluation—as does the ability to credit bid. When the secured creditor is provided with senior secured debt under a plan, it is more likely to be paid the true value of what she is owed even when the bankruptcy judge misvalues the underlying assets.[11]

Absolute Priority and New Value Plans

The Supreme Court set out the contours of the absolute priority rule in *Bank of America v. 203 North LaSalle Street Partnership*.[12] In that case a group of real estate investors acquired 15 floors of an office building in downtown Chicago and obtained a nonrecourse mortgage from a bank. Real estate values dropped in the early 1990s, and the partners sought to restructure the bank's loan in Chapter 11. The partnership offered a plan that, in its view, left the bank with more

---

[10] RadLAX Gateway Hotel, LLC v. Amalgamated Bank, 132 S. Ct. 2065 (2012).

[11] See In re River East, 669 F.3d 826 (7th Cir. 2012).

[12] 526 U.S. 434 (1999).

than it would receive through a state law foreclosure yet allowed the prebankruptcy investors in the partnership to remain as owners and enjoy significant tax benefits. When the bank turned down the partnership's plan, the bankruptcy court had to decide whether the plan could be confirmed over the bank's objection.

New value cases arise when the old equityholders cannot reach a deal with their most senior creditors. The senior creditor cannot object to a new value plan wearing its hat as the holder of a secured claim. If the plan passes muster under §1129(b)(2)(A), then the secured claim is being paid in full. As a holder of that claim, the senior creditor has nothing to complain about. It can object, however, as the holder of its unsecured deficiency claim.

The precise legal issue can be set out simply. To the extent that it was owed more than its collateral was worth, the bank held an unsecured deficiency claim in addition to its secured claim. The Seventh Circuit had already decided that the bank's §1111(b) deficiency had to be put in a class by itself.[13] Hence, when the bank voted against the plan, a class of unsecured claims necessarily voted against it as well. Section 1129(b)(2) of the Bankruptcy Code provides that when a class of unsecured claims dissents from a reorganization plan and is not being paid in full, a plan is fair and equitable only if, among other things, "the holder of any [junior] interest . . . will not receive or retain under the plan on account of such junior . . . interest any property."

In writing for the Court, Justice Souter found that this language required adherence to "absolute priority." Under a regime of absolute priority, old equity cannot receive any "property" if a dissenting class was not being paid in full. A plan that gives old equity the exclusive right to acquire the new equity gives them property within the meaning of §1129(b). The plan, in substance, gave the old equityholders the exclusive right to the equity of the reorganized entity. Such an exclusive right was a stock option, something ordinarily regarded as property and thus property within the meaning of the statute. Hence, equity could not participate without the process being opened up.

As the Court explained, "If the price to be paid for the equity interest is the best obtainable, old equity does not need the protection of exclusiveness . . . [I]f it is not the best, there is no apparent reason for giving old equity a bargain."[14] The Court noted that a judicial evalua-

[13] See In re Woodbrook Associates, 19 F.3d 312 (7th Cir 1994).
[14] 526 U.S. at 456.

tion did not ensure that "top dollar" was realized and "the best way to determine value is exposure to a market." The Court, however, did not set out exactly what path a debtor that wanted to buy into the equity of the new firm had to follow: "Whether a market test would require an opportunity to offer competing plans or would be satisfied by a right to bid for the same interest sought by the old equity, is a question we do not decide here."[15]

In the decade that followed *203 North LaSalle*, a number of bankruptcy courts found that that lifting exclusivity was enough. These courts reasoned that the key objection to the plan in *203 N. LaSalle* was that the old shareholders possessed an exclusive right. But as long as others had a right to propose a plan, the exclusive right old equityholders enjoyed under their own plan was not objectionable. When exclusivity has been lifted, the right to buy equity under a plan no longer has option value. Any party in interest can acquire the same right by proposing her own plan. Hence, the equityholder is no longer receiving "property."[16]

Other courts have rejected this view. For them, the expiration of the exclusivity is not enough: "An impaired lender who objects to *any* plan that leaves insiders holding equity is entitled to the benefit of competition."[17] It does not matter whether exclusivity has expired. A plan of reorganization that includes a new investment must allow other potential investors to bid.

The difficulty of cramming down a new value plan on senior lenders often leads the equity to try to reach a deal with the senior creditor. Such a bargain might seem unobjectionable. If the senior creditor backs a plan that includes old equity and is itself not being paid in full, the general creditors are out of the money. The senior creditor is entitled to the entire firm. Hence, it might seem it should be able to do with the firm what it pleases. As we discussed in chapter 3, however, "gifts" that skip over a class are suspect. The focus in these cases is not on whether equityholders are contributing value, but rather whether the gift itself has corrupted the Chapter 11 process.

---

[15] 526 U.S. at 458.

[16] In re Red Mountain Machinery, 448 Bankr. 1, 18 (Bankr. D. Ariz. 2011).

[17] In re Castleton Plaza, LP, 707 F.3d 821, 824 (7th Cir. 2013) (emphasis in original).

It is not unusual to see token payments being made throughout the capital structure to avoid the expense of a cramdown hearing. The general creditors receive enough so that the complications of the absolute priority rule can be avoided entirely. Payouts to these classes are often structured in such a way to induce consent. For example, plans sometimes contain "death traps." A class is offered a small payment if the class as a whole votes in favor of a plan, but nothing if it votes against. The plan does not violate the prohibition against equal treatment, as everyone in the class receives the same thing (either a small payment or nothing, depending on the class-wide vote). The dynamic is similar to the one we see in plea bargaining, in which criminal defendants may plead guilty, rather than insist on a trial and risk a long sentence.

Good Faith and Vote Designation

The bankruptcy judges continue to have the ability to police creditors for misconduct during the case. One of the principal weapons is §1126(e), which gives the bankruptcy judge the power to "designate" the vote of someone who casts it in bad faith. The court is to scrutinize "the circumstances surrounding the acceptances, the special or ulterior motives which may have induced them, the time of acquiring the claims so voting, and the amount paid therefor, and the like."[18] As Justice Douglas explained:

> Where such investigation discloses the existence of unfair dealing, a breach of fiduciary obligations, profiting from a trust, special benefits for the reorganizers, or the need for protection of investors against an inside few or of one class of investors from the encroachments of another, the court has ample power to adjust the remedy to meet the need.[19]

A long line of cases has tried to identify what types of behavior are permissible and what types are not. They start with Justice Black's opinion in *Young v. Higbee Co.*[20] He found that two preferred shareholders acted improperly when they agreed to drop an appeal from the confirmation of a plan and sell their stake to those controlling the re-

---

[18] American United Mutual Life Ins. Co. v. Avon Park, 311 U.S. 138, 145 (1940).

[19] 311 U.S. at 146.

[20] 324 U.S. 204 (1945).

organization for an amount that was greater than what others in their class would receive under the plan.

Young v. Higbee remains a landmark case and continues to cast a long shadow. The challenge is what to make of it. Under one view, the reorganization process should ensure that everyone in the same class receives the same amount. Someone who wants to purchase claims in a particular class must offer to buy on the same terms to everyone. Someone cannot buy up claims in order to ensure the confirmation of a plan if the amount paid for those claims is higher than what the remaining claimholders will receive under the plan. This is the approach the Second Circuit seems to have taken in *In re P-R Holding Corp.*[21]

The willingness to pay more for a claim than the claim will receive in the reorganization seems a sign that mischief is afoot. Unless the buyer is getting a benefit someplace else, why should she pay more for a claim than what she will receive under the plan? It is like buying a dollar bill for $1.01. But there are more benign explanations. A substantial stakeholder may be willing to buy additional claims in a class to ensure a plan is defeated because she believes that the proposed plan puts the debtor on the wrong path. If the plan contemplates the sale of the business to a competitor who will not be able to run it effectively, someone may buy claims to vote against the plan and ensure that it remains as a going concern, or at least is liquidated at a higher price. He is purchasing claims to protect the value of the firm and his own stake in it.[22]

In many instances, including *P-R Holding Corp.*, the higher price reflects in large part a control premium. Take the simplest case. There is a single class of debt and the plan calls for giving one share of stock in the reorganized entity for each dollar of debt. An investor buys a large enough stake in the debt so that it obtains a controlling interest in the reorganized firm. The selling shareholders are receiving more than the remaining minority shareholder because they are capturing

---

[21] 147 F.2d 895, 897 (2d Cir. 1945) ("certainly there is 'bad faith' when those purchases result in a discrimination in favor of the creditors selling their interests").

[22] See, e.g., In re Pine Hill Collieries Co., 46 F. Supp. 669 (E.D. Pa. 1942). The creditor in this case had previously managed the debtor and was also an equityholder. One could imagine the case going the other way, as it is possible that the record supports the inference that the creditor was not merely protecting its interest as creditor, but also protecting other business interests as well. See id. at 672.

some of the control premium. The same phenomenon occurs in the case of a hostile takeover outside of bankruptcy. Ordinarily, a controlling shareholder can sell at a premium and has no obligation to share it. Doing otherwise dampens the market for corporate control and leaves investors as a group worse off.

It is important to recognize this separate undercurrent of fair treatment. We see it in *In re Allegheny International, Inc.*[23] In response to an outsider who bought a controlling interest in the fulcrum security, the court fashioned a remedy that ensured that the control premium was extended to everyone in the class. There are other cases in which no abuse is found precisely because the claim-buyer was willing to buy out everyone in the class on the same terms. This fact is not always sufficient, but it helps as it removes from the table at least this concern.

Also at work in a case such as *Higbee* is the desire to protect against "greenmail." Outside of bankruptcy, the problem arises when a person buys up a block of votes and threatens the managers with an ugly takeover battle unless his shares are repurchased at a premium. Someone acquires a blocking position in a critical class and threatens to vote against the plan unless he is paid off, saying in effect, in William O. Douglas's words: "For a price you can have our vote."[24] The misbehavior, in other words, is not on the claims buyer, but on the claims seller. The offense is threatening to take an action merely because of the harm it will cause someone else in order to obtain a payoff. With such a rule in place, those in the position of the preferred shareholders will not threaten an expensive appeal in order to exact a payoff because they will gain nothing by it.

We must worry about the integrity of the reorganization process. Aggressive claims trading may unsettle the procedures that are designed to assure that the process is not abusive and strategic players are not able to capture value that rightfully belongs to others. Judge Clark captured this idea succinctly in *In re Applegate, Property, Ltd.*[25]:

---

[23] 118 Bankr. 282 (Bankr. W.D. Pa. 1990).

[24] DISH Network Corp. v. DBSD North America, Inc., 634 F.3d 79, 103 n.10 (2d. Cir. 2011) (citing Revision of the Bankruptcy Act: Hearing on H.R. 6439 Before the House Comm. on the Judiciary, 75th Cong. 182 (1937) (statement of William O. Douglas)).

[25] 133 Bankr. 827 (Bankr. W.D. Tex. 1991).

> Sanctioning claims acquisition for purposes of blocking an opponent's plan would . . . ignite a scramble for votes conducted almost entirely outside the Code's carefully developed structure (plan, disclosure statement, equal treatment, regulated solicitation, court-supervised confirmation), leaving creditors to select not the best plan but the best deal they might be able to individually negotiate. Creditors would be paid, no doubt, but not equally, and not on the basis of accurate information. Such a wild free-for-all may appeal to the entrepreneurial capitalist, but it also issues a gilt-edged invitation to fraudulent and corrupt practices . . .[26]

Purchasing a claim to ensure a plan is approved or rejected is no different than buying a vote in a municipal election. You can try to persuade voters that you are the better candidate, but you cannot pay them to vote for you. Naked vote buying in Chapter 11 is no different.

Courts inclined to such a view can, among other things, cite the Borah Act, which criminalizes knowingly and fraudulently giving, offering, receiving, or attempting to obtain any money or other advantage for acting or forbearing to act in any bankruptcy case.[27] Read broadly, any claim bought for the purpose of casting a vote for or against a plan is forbidden. It is worth noting, however, that, notwithstanding their broad language, the cases that cast general suspicion on strategic claims buying tend to involve insiders.

Because of the fiduciary duties they owe to others, insiders' conduct is necessarily subject to greater scrutiny than that of ordinary outside investors, even those who are acting strategically. An outside buyer who takes control by buying the fulcrum security is not likely to encounter the same trouble as an insider or an outside buyer who buys up a class to derail a plan. It is even less likely when the person buying the fulcrum class is willing to buy on the same terms from anyone who tenders.

The Bankruptcy Code is structured around the idea of classwide voting. This approach—one that relies upon common interests among dispersed creditors—is easiest to justify when investors come in only a few flavors. Holding complicated positions that combine ordinary claims in multiple tranches, however, has become a routine. Courts have not sorted through the complications of how to reconcile class-

[26] Id. at 836.
[27] 18 U.S.C. §152.

wide voting with a new world in which many creditors occupy many different layers of the capital structure. Unfortunately, much of the case law that regulates the behavior of creditors holding positions in multiple classes deals with single-asset real estate cases that have a dynamic entirely different from the one in which a large corporation has the same investors wearing multiple hats.

The owner of a large rental apartment development enters bankruptcy.[28] It has one secured creditor owed many millions and a handful of unsecured creditors. The largest unsecured claim, which amounts to just more than a third of all those outstanding, belongs to a 12-year-old who was not paid $20 for mowing the lawn the Saturday before the bankruptcy petition was filed.

The debtor proposes a plan in which it would gradually convert the rental apartments into condominiums. If the plan succeeds, the equityholders will benefit enormously. If it fails, the secured creditor will bear the entire downside. It will spend years trying to sort out the mess of an unsuccessful property that is half-rental and half-condo. The debtor's plan gives the secured creditor a note that it asserts is worth the value of its secured claim. The plan pays the unsecured creditors a penny less than each is owed in cash.

The secured creditor approaches the 12-year-old and buys the debt at par and casts this vote against the plan. By thus ensuring that there is no impaired class willing to accept the plan, the plan is unconfirmable. There is no need for an expensive valuation hearing. The secured creditor's vote of the 12-year-old's claim, of course, had nothing to do with its interests as an unsecured creditor and everything to do with protecting its position as a secured creditor. Allowing the secured creditor to buy up a third of the unsecured class and use its vote to sink a plan allows it to impose its agenda as a secured creditor on the entire class of unsecured creditors. It is simply silly to think that the secured creditor's vote reflects in any sense its interests *as a holder of an unsecured claim*.

Counting the secured creditor's vote in such cases may be a form of rough justice. Allowing the secured creditor to speak for the unsecured creditors is justified because it makes little sense to give voice to the general creditors in the first place. The case is a battle between a secured creditor owed millions and a real estate developer. We allow the

---

[28] This hypothetical is based loosely on Figter Ltd. v. Teachers Insurance & Annuity Association, 118 F.3d 365 (9th Cir. 1997).

secured creditor's purchase of claims to sink the debtor's reorganization because we are skeptical that the debtor has garnered sufficient support for a plan. Enjoying the confidence of a handful of unsecured creditors owed a trivial amount of money should not be enough.

More important, the lessons of these cases should not apply to the more complicated cases in which strategic investors wear multiple hats. It is a different situation entirely. The current structure of the Bankruptcy Code puts the judge in an awkward position. If the judge allows the creditor with multiple hats to speak for the minority, the minority is disenfranchised. But if the creditor with multiple hats has its votes designated, *it* is disenfranchised. There are no easy solutions. If claims of a conflicted creditor are put in their own separate class to make sure that everyone votes and no one has a conflict, then the creditor with multiple hats is entitled to insist on cramdown in every case. A creditor who wants a cramdown hearing just needs to buy a claim in another class.

Courts seem to be gravitating to one of three approaches. The first approach is Judge Gerber's approach in *In re Adelphia Communications Corp.*[29] The presence of creditors with positions in multiple classes is inevitable in large cases. As long as insiders are not involved and as long as those involved are merely advancing their own position as creditors (even if as a creditor in another class), then the rules are the ones that governed knife fights in the Old West: there are no rules.

The battle is between seasoned professionals. No widows or orphans are involved. The playing field is level. In the end, everyone enjoys the substantive rules of §1129, and any plan that is confirmed must meet the standards of the Bankruptcy Code. There may be brinkmanship, but brinkmanship exists in other environments as well. One hopes that cooler heads will prevail. But if they do not, they have only themselves to blame.

The second approach is the one the court seems to have adopted in *Aladdin Hotel Co. v. Bloom.*[30] It is both an old case and one that took place entirely outside of bankruptcy, but it is discussed in the legislative history of the Bankruptcy Code and still provides a useful illustration. The outstanding bond issue on the Aladdin Hotel allowed a two-thirds majority to extend the date on which the principal was owed. The hotel struggled for a long time. Members of one family ultimately

---

[29] 441 Bankr. 6 (Bankr. S.D.N.Y. 2010).
[30] 200 F.2d 627 (8th Cir. 1953).

gained control of the hotel and began managing it. By this point, interest had not been paid in years, and the hotel was in need of a number of improvements. The family owned a majority of the stock and more than two-thirds of the outstanding bonds. The family invested $300,000 in improvements to the hotel, began paying interest, retired a first mortgage, and nearly tripled the gross income. At the same time, they extended by 10 years the date on which the principal was due. They could impose this modification to the bonds because they controlled the bonds as well as the common stock.

After this modification, Josephine Bloom acquired some of the bonds and sued the hotel on the ground that the family's position as shareholders should have disabled them from voting to extend the date that the principal was due. The Court of Appeals found that the family had acted in good faith and that Bloom (or more precisely, her predecessors) had ratified the changes by failing to make a timely objection.[31]

Aladdin stands for the idea that the behavior of the investor with multiple hats is subject to close scrutiny. They are not prohibited from acting, but when they do act, they have to have the interests of the firm as a whole at heart. Members of the family were controlling shareholders and hence obliged with all sorts of fiduciary duties. But they did not violate them. They were intent on maximizing the value of the debtor as a whole, and they had adhered to the formal requirements of the bond indenture itself.

The situation in *Aladdin* can no longer arise outside of bankruptcy, as the Trust Indenture Act no longer allows such modifications outside of bankruptcy, no matter how sensible.[32] Still, one can argue that the approach of *Aladdin* is the one that §1126(e) adopts. There is no per se prohibition, but there is scrutiny—scrutiny that should be especially searching when the conflict involves insiders or those with their hands on the levers of control.

The third approach is one that prevents those with conflicts from voting altogether. The House version of the Bankruptcy Code had a provision that was designed to overrule *Aladdin*. It expressly authorized the court to designate the vote of an "entity that has, with respect to such class, a conflict of interest that is of such a nature as would justify exclusion of such entity's claim or interest" from the amounts

[31] 200 F.2d at 633.
[32] 15 U.S.C. §77aaa.

and number of claims or interests required for acceptance.[33] On this view, there is an inherent problem with allowing the family to wear two hats. The family's interest as equityholder kept it from being able to represent the interests of the bondholders at the same time.

While there is debate about how creditors should be treated when they wear multiple hats, there is no debate about the basic principle that third parties who act with ulterior motives cannot exploit the levers of the reorganization process to advance their own agendas. When third parties acquire and then vote their claims, the challenge ultimately comes in drawing the line between an ulterior agenda and permissible behavior.

Some cases are easy. For example, disgruntled former employees who have started a competing firm cannot acquire claims and cast their votes to inflict misery on their former employer.[34] A developer who recaptures rights if a debtor goes through foreclosure instead of reorganization cannot buy claims for the purpose of defeating the reorganization.[35]

The origins of this doctrine can be traced to *Texas Hotel Securities Corp. v. Waco Development Co.*[36] That case revolved around a fight over the Roosevelt Hotel in Waco, Texas. A group of local businessmen took over an old hotel and brought in Conrad Hilton to renovate it, build a new tower, and operate it. It was to be Hilton's third hotel in Texas. The transaction began with a sale of the old hotel to Hilton. He took out a significant mortgage on the property and made extensive renovations. Hilton then sold the hotel property back to the businessmen but retained a 99-year lease on the property and remained responsible for paying off the mortgage. Business fell off during the Great Depression. Hilton continued to meet the mortgage payments, but fell behind on lease payments. Litigation followed in state court. The Waco businessmen prevailed. They were able to oust Hilton for his failure to pay the rent and cancel the lease.

---

[33] H.R. 8200, 95th Cong., 1st Sess. (1977), included this provision as §1126(e). For more analysis of the legislative history, see Mark G. Douglas, Disenfranchising Strategic Investors in Chapter 11: "Loan to Own" Acquisition Strategy May Result in Vote Designation, 6 Pratt's J. Bankr. L. 383, 387 n.31 (2010).

[34] See In re MacLeod Co., 63 Bankr. 654 (Bankr. S.D. Ohio 1986).

[35] See In re Dune Deck Owners Corp., 175 Bankr. 839 (Bankr. S.D.N.Y. 1995).

[36] 87 F.2d 395 (5th Cir. 1936).

The local businessmen soon found themselves in much the same position as Hilton. They did not have to pay rent, but they did have to make the mortgage payments, and soon they could not even do this. They filed a bankruptcy petition. Hilton, still mightily irritated that the local businessmen used local courts to take back the hotel and displace him as manager, bought a blocking position in one of the impaired classes and voted against the plan. Hilton did not regain control of the hotel, but the Fifth Circuit upheld Hilton's right to cast his vote as he had.[37] The legislative history of the Bankruptcy Code suggests that giving the bankruptcy judge the power to designate votes was intended to overrule this case.

Putting to one side the question whether Hilton should have been ousted in the first place (and the improvements Hilton made inure to the benefit of the local businessmen), Hilton's motives are suspect. His purpose in voting against the plan was to reacquire the management of the hotel, not to maximize the value of the claim or even the value of the hotel itself. By buying up just more than a third of one class of debt, Hilton acquired this blocking position. Unlike a strategic buyer who thinks he can put the firm to its best use, Hilton was advancing his interest as a prospective manager of the property rather than as a prospective owner.

The case would be different if Hilton wanted to buy the hotel and was acquiring votes as part of that strategy. But we have to view even such actions skeptically. We need to worry that a strategic purchaser could buy a controlling position or a blocking position in a critical class and use it to forestall any plan that did not deliver the debtor's assets to it on favorable terms.[38] An outsider cannot acquire claims merely to control the reorganization process and nudge it in her direction.

A creditor who buys claims during the case who is later charged with possessing an ulterior motive typically responds that, even if it is now attempting to gain control of the debtor, it "purchased claims for the purpose of maximizing its investment and advancing its own economic interest rather than for the purpose of advancing a strategic

---

[37] See 87 F.2d at 399–400.

[38] DISH Network Corp. v. DBSD North America, Inc., 634 F.3d 79 (2d. Cir. 2011).

competitive interest against the Debtor."[39] The difficulty, of course, is that advancing one's economic interest is often consistent with advancing strategic interests that conflict with those of others.

The hard case arises when the buyer makes a major investment in the fulcrum security and then seeks to buy additional claims to secure the approval of a plan. It is wearing both its hat as an investor and as a buyer. Nonbankruptcy law tries to handle such problems by imposing duties on shareholders in such situations. It does not work completely successfully in that environment, but in bankruptcy, where there are generally no duties at all imposed on creditors, there are even fewer benchmarks.

In understanding this problem, as with any other that lacks an easy answer, we must return to first principles. In doing this, we should understand both bankruptcy law and its limits. Legal rules cannot cure nonlegal problems. Legal rules cannot make the imprudent wise and the unlucky fortunate. Nor can they insulate a poorly run business from the realities of the marketplace. The goals of bankruptcy are necessarily modest. Honest but unfortunate individuals should be given a fresh start. Corporations that have value as going concerns should be able to acquire a new capital structure, and those that cannot survive should be able to wrap up their affairs expeditiously. Bankruptcy law cannot work miracles, and more harm than good comes from seeking that which cannot be had. We should, in our efforts to make the bankruptcy system work, recall what my late colleague and mentor Walter Blum often observed: in law, 95 percent is perfection.

---

[39] In re Lichtin/Wade LLC, 2012 WL 6576416 (Bankr. E.D.N.C. 2012).

Table of Cases

Table of Statutes

Index